Studia Fennica
Anthropologica 2

The Finnish Literature Society (SKS) was founded in 1831 and has, from the very beginning, engaged in publishing operations. It nowadays publishes literature in the fields of ethnology and folkloristics, linguistics, literary research and cultural history.

The first volume of the Studia Fennica series appeared in 1933. Since 1992, the series has been divided into three thematic subseries: Ethnologica, Folkloristica and Linguistica. Two additional subseries were formed in 2002, Historica and Litteraria. The subseries Anthropologica was formed in 2007.

In addition to its publishing activities, the Finnish Literature Society maintains research activities and infrastructures, an archive containing folklore and literary collections, a research library and promotes Finnish literature abroad.

OA.FINLIT.FI

Editorial Office
SKS
P.O. Box 259
FI-00171 Helsinki
www.finlit.fi

Beyond the Horizon

Essays on
Myth, History, Travel and Society

Edited by Clifford Sather & Timo Kaartinen

In Honor of Jukka Siikala

Finnish Literature Society • Helsinki

Studia Fennica Anthropologica 2

The publication has undergone a peer review.

VERTAISARVIOITU
KOLLEGIALT GRANSKAD
PEER-REVIEWED
www.tsv.fi/tunnus

© 2008 Clifford Sather, Timo Kaartinen and SKS
License CC-BY-NC-ND 4.0 International

A digital edition of a printed book first published in 2008 by the Finnish Literature Society.

Cover Design: Timo Numminen
EPUB: eLibris Media Oy

ISBN 978-951-858-068-6 (Print)
ISBN 978-951-858-070-9 (PDF)
ISBN 978-951-858-069-3 (EPUB)

ISSN 0085-6835 (Studia Fennica)
ISSN 1796-8208 (Studia Fennica Anthropologica)

DOI: http://dx.doi.org/10.21435/sfa.2

A free open access version of the book is available at http://dx.doi.org/10.21435/sfa.2
or by scanning this QR code with your mobile device.

Contents

MYTHICAL AND TEXTUAL PERSPECTIVES ON THE PAST

Introduction

Timo Kaartinen and Clifford Sather

The constant presence of the world beyond the horizon in the two senses of the word, past and abroad, became my main interest during field work. Travelling from island to island and country to country and telling about the past seem to be two of the main ways the Cook Island culture and society constitutes itself. – Jukka Siikala (1991: 3)

The impulse for writing this book has been the wish, by friends, colleagues and students, to mark the year of Jukka Siikala's 60th birthday. Jukka's theoretical interests, as he tells us in his monograph on the Southern Cook Islands, are concerned with theoretical and methodological topics evoked by the idea of horizon. After focusing on Melanesian cargo cults in his early work (Siikala 1982), he moved on to engage the debate about structural history – the question of how society is informed by its mythical and historical accounts of the past (Siikala 1990b; 1991; 1996). In each case his ethnographic analysis reveals that cultural models of the world are built on associations as well as analogies, continuities as well as breaks, and represent more than a specific interpretation of local events.

Jukka's latest writings have stressed the methodological implications of his view of cultures as inherently global systems. Not only does discourse about society circulate in a structured manner which informs perceptions of social being (Siikala 2000): society, taken as a whole, "distributes itself" in culturally characteristic ways and extends beyond such contexts as can be immediately observed by the anthropologist (Siikala 2001a). By virtue of these structures of distribution, the meaningful potential of ethnographically studied phenomena (texts, artifacts, relationships and practices) exceeds the implications of these phenomena in their immediate social context. Contrary to empiricist views which persist even in the most recent anthropology, the differences which order and constitute society are not merely ones that differentiate behavioral roles and social groups. Awareness of social relationships always extends beyond the local domain of interaction to diverse spheres of social existence, most of which are only accessible through cultural concepts. Attention to society as a conceptual world thus alerts us to its horizons and values, even if we can only study these through their local, empirical manifestations. Therefore it is possible to claim that the field sites in which we carry out our studies are located inside conceptual worlds rather than in geographic places (Siikala 2001b: 41).

Jukka's argument echoes Claude Lévi-Strauss's point that the object of ethnographic research is larger than what can be observed from a single point of view – large enough, in fact, to be of the same order as the observer's own global perspective (Lévi-Strauss 1987: 29). The common objection to this view is that it claims for the anthropologist the ability to look at culture as a totality which no native could grasp. What is easily missed, however, and what many recent writers are careful to point out, is that anthropology does not aim at representing this totality in an empirical sense. We no longer claim to describe ethnographic phenomena in a language of universally valid concepts but qualify our objectifying language as a "prop" (Wagner 1981: 9) or "refraction" (Dresch 1988: 61) which makes it possible to recognize cultural differences and alternative conceptual worlds. What makes it possible to go beyond this point is the fact that people reflect on their world through language. In the Herderian definition Jukka uses here, "reflection" is not merely about intellectual speculation but about the human ability to remember and recall the fullness of symbolic sensations when their external source is no longer present (Siikala 2001b: 30). No external causes or functional motivations need to be present for people to relive and elaborate certain salient experiences and events. This, however, does not mean that culture is reduced to the "imaginary." In order to interpret the conceptual world, the analyst needs to pay attention to "practical activities in a specific location" and the relationship of these activities to the unseen experiences and events accessible through language (Siikala 2001b: 42).

As Greg Urban (1996: 10) points out, linguistic and other publicly occurring signs are simultaneously sensible and intelligible. They are not only used to give symbolic expression to situated meanings but to frame, inscribe and objectify specific kinds of discourse as culture. Instead of actualizing situated meaning, certain genres and performative uses of language foreground its signifying potential and thus expand the interpretive horizon of speakers and audiences. Urban's argument makes it possible to define horizon in a second sense as an expanded perspective on time and place. The past circulation of discourse – repeating and quoting verbal utterances in numerous successive contexts – produces for those engaged in this circulation a "sediment" of accumulated relations of signification, and the association of verbal utterances with genres or types expands their potential to be applied to numerous kinds of contexts in the future (Hanks 1996: 124, 131).

The sedimenting effect is obviously not limited to language use: gift exchange is another example of a social practice which forces people to pay attention to the broader temporal perspectives and social trajectories that follow from what they do in a particular time and place (Hoskins 1993). The human capacity for reflection enables discursive signs and objects to represent more than a template of routinized conditions and actions. In Paul Ricoeur's phrasing they contain a "surplus of meaning," a potential to disclose a world and not just a situation (Ricoeur 1976: 80).

Horizon, by one usage, refers to the limits of an observer's point of view (Jolly 1994: 377). In anthropology it has become customary to emphasize such limits and point out the dangers involved in applying our own culturally-based categories to cross-cultural understanding. The title of this book marks the writers' awareness of such caveats but also their commitment to reach beyond their own culturally grounded perspectives.

In another sense horizons are salient aspects of cultural experience located "elsewhere," "unseen," "past," "coming," or otherwise at a distance from the immediate interactional and perceptual field. In this sense of the word, horizon is not so much about limits of knowing but about potential being projected from a background of familiar experience (Hirsch 1995: 4). This definition of horizon brings up significant anthropological topics, but it also forces us to engage certain methodological issues as well. "Horizon" suggests perception which totalizes or transcends personal being; by the same token, however, it implies a subjective, situated position in the world. In the sense of "mediated perception," horizon seems to presuppose unmediated pre-cultural existence.

In order not to privilege these readings, we emphasize a third definition of horizon as a "conceptual world." It does not simply refer to things that stand in opposition to routine existence in the here-and-now. The most concrete, immediate things in our lives have a horizon – a metaphoric and metonymic potential to stand for something else as soon as they become a part of intentional projects. What we wish to stress, however, is the reflective process of appropriating the power of narratives about travels, origins, and strange events to disclose other dimensions of existence through which their horizons on the world are fused with more limited perceptual horizons (Ricoeur 1976: 93).

The fusion of horizons – a dialogue with no determined addressee – is fundamental for cultural awareness about global processes. Melanesian cargo cults as well as Western ideologies of development and progress conceive of the horizon as the source of new kinds of experience – unfamiliar, awesome things with the power to reconstitute and transform social life. In Roy Wagner's words we "invent" culture by making sense of those unfamiliar things as plausible manifestations of human intention. Through the invention of culture, people's awareness of the conditions of their existence is always projected beyond the here-and-now. Rather than being a system of concrete, phenomenal things and events, culture in this view is a virtual order, a set of meaningful relations between categories. As Marshall Sahlins has argued in formulating this view, cultural awareness of new events may either value them for their similarity to the already constituted system, or else the culture may respond to the shifting conditions of its existence and reproduce itself as a logic of its own change. The latter alternative, which is more interesting for current historical anthropology, implies that the symbolic system is "highly empirical" and "continuously submits the received categories to worldly risks, the inevitable disproportions between signs and things" (Sahlins 1985: xiii).

We might thus characterize horizon as the interface between empirical perceptions and their orienting categories, values and epistemological ideas. An obvious case are the spatial orientations and mental maps in terms of which people define their place in the world and imagine their relationship to things outside their immediate perceptual field. Equally important are the temporal horizons through which the orientation and value of actions are defined by reference to past and future events. At a closer look, none of these horizons is determined by the immediacy of individual perception and action. A basic property of horizon lies in fusing facts which are known with unknown objects, agents and forces. For this reason horizons are never just cognitive frameworks, but inherently symbolic in the sense of collapsing into each other different contexts of signification.

The aim of this book is to explore these theoretical concerns with reference to specific ethnographic issues which are also central in Jukka's writings. The articles in this collection address the significance of outside contact, migration, travel, and the production of cultural texts as elements of cultural worldviews and the diverse ways in which cultures and societies constitute themselves by means of travel and through their use of myth and narrative histories. We present cases from a number of societies of the Pacific and Austronesian-speaking Southeast Asia. Our focus on cultural horizons in these two areas reflects the sense in which their historical perspectives, social reproduction and ideas about value hinge on relations with agents and domains outside society.

The threefold division of articles in this collection follows their emphasis of different aspects of symbolic awareness. The first part of the book offers ethnographic examples of societies living inside a forest in which the immediate, perceptual horizon is usually very near. In order to maintain itself as a valued, moral framework and avoid coalescing with the surrounding bush, society faces the need to constantly transcend, dissolve or obviate its horizons. This may give rise to an eschatological interest in religion and an intense attempt to divine and interpret what is *particular* about afflictions, strangers and unforeseen or catastrophic events. The second part of the book deals with island societies which face a maximally distant physical horizon. These cases bring into focus the technologies and cosmological concepts which people identify with their own ability of reaching beyond the horizon. Such activities as navigation, boat-building and catching fish are ordered by specific orientations towards the cosmos, but, as our examples show, they also involve people reflecting on the transformational possibilities of their ordering categories. In the third part of the book, our attention turns to performances and texts. Recent discussions about cultural performances stress their potential to frame the object of performance as something that exists apart from the particular telling or artistic display. Cultural texts in this sense instantiate a virtually existing tradition with a complex social life of its own. Historical and mythical narratives thus reach beyond the horizon of immanent social relationships and interaction, towards alternative horizons evoked by the practices of narration.

Horizons of experience

As we have suggested, the papers comprising this first section address variously conceived horizons, how they are transcended or dissolved, and the role they play in shaping social practice, cosmologies, and history.

In the first essay, Joel Robbins reminds us of the potential significance of yet another "horizontal outlier" – besides abroad and the past – namely, "the world that lies beyond the present in time," that is to say, the future. Since the late 1970s, the Urapmin of West Sepik, Papua New Guinea, have embraced and now intensely hold to a charismatic form of Christianity that profoundly stamps their cosmological orientation and is mirrored in virtually every aspect of their everyday life. A notable feature of Urapmin Christianity, Robbins tells us, is its markedly millennial character. Thus, the Urapmin fervently await the Second Coming which they believe is imminent. When Jesus returns He will rapture those who believe in Him into heaven, destroy the earth, and consign sinners to hell. Most Urapmin therefore aim to lead lives that demonstrate their belief in God so as to assure themselves a place in heaven and consequently have developed elaborate rituals that serve to absolve sin, restore their moral selves, and prepare them for God's final judgment. With such rituals dominating community life, heaven can justly be described as the group's overwhelming preoccupation.

Heaven for the Urapmin is beyond the horizon in several significant senses. Temporally, it exists in another time; not in the present, but in the future. Spatially, it exists elsewhere; not where the Urapmin now live, but in another place, in this case, in the sky, where, the Urapmin hold, believers will dwell after the earth has been destroyed. In contrast to the Polynesian cosmologies on which Siikala has written with such insight, the world beyond the horizon to which the Urapmin attach greatest value is not the past, conceptualized, as it is by the Cook Islanders, as a place of origin, but rather the future, conceptualized in other-worldly terms as their ultimate destination. The Urapmin, as Robbins says, even in the present, "live for the future." The question he poses is: do the different values that the Urapmin and Cook Islanders assign to places beyond the horizon have different social consequences? Do they, in other words, shape social action, structures, and the making of history in different ways? In partial answer, he notes that the corresponding differences in cosmologies differently hierarchize space. For the Urapmin, the earth is not only less valued than heaven, but on earth the Urapmin themselves occupy a particularly marginal, underdeveloped region, which they identify as "bush." Here, conditions least resemble those of heaven. In the future, by attaining heaven, they will come to live in a decidedly different place, where all of the distinctions that currently define earthly hierarchy to their disadvantage will disappear. By adopting a future-oriented point of view, millennial Christianity thus provides the Urapmin, Robbins argues, with a way of confronting their current situation and of dealing with present-day political, racial, and economic realities that otherwise leave them, in stark actuality, both marginal and powerless.

The next essay by Peter Metcalf moves us from New Guinea to central Borneo and back in time to the 1970s. Here, Metcalf describes his field site, the longhouse at Long Teru, Sarawak, as a small riverbank "island," surrounded, not by vast stretches of sea, but by a virtually horizonless rainforest. As with the Urapmin, here, too, local cosmologies hierarchize space. For the people of Long Teru, their own small "island" is regarded as a "metropolis" bearing the characteristics of everything they consider to be civilized. From here, directions take their bearings from the river that runs along one side of this "island." The main coordinates are thus upriver// downriver, away from//towards the river. While most outsiders reach Long Teru from the coast by coming upriver, the dead, by contrast, after a liminal period spent in the rainforest, leave this world by traveling downriver, journeying almost to the sea, and then turning upriver again, thereby entering the invisible abode of the ancestors. Contrary to the evidence of linguistics and prehistory, the Long Teru people and their upriver neighbors trace their origins, not downriver, and eventually to the sea, but upriver, to an inland plateau above the river watersheds along which they live. From here, their ancestors are said to have descended, moving down and outward along these present-day watersheds. The river, on whose banks the longhouse stands, opens an otherwise rare vista to the sky. Here, within this "window to the heavens," augurs in the past called for the major omen bird, *plake*, who, by his appearance and flight, carried messages from the upperworld Creator Spirit, Bili Ngaputong. Today, all of this is gone. The "island" is no more; the rainforest is largely felled by commercial logging operations and the people who once lived at Long Teru are dispersed, many of them now living in timber camps or in coastal cities and towns.

The next essay by Clifford Sather is also set in Borneo, but among a far more numerous, outwardly mobile and expansive people, the Saribas Iban. The immediate Iban spatial world is also defined by reference to rivers. These, however, together with their connecting watersheds, coastal mouths and tributaries act more as gateways or avenues, facilitating travel and migration, allowing people, particularly men, to move in search of farmland, employment opportunities, profit, and adventure. Today, even more than in the past, travel is a prominent feature of everyday Iban life. It is also a major metaphor in traditional Iban religion. Thus, virtually every important ritual is enacted and verbally structured as a journey. The gods and spirit-heroes are also seen as travelers and became differentiated from the ancestors as a result of past migrations, the gods having moved to the sky, and the spirit-heroes to a raised world intermediate between the sky and what is now the human world. Although now spatially and visually separated, for the Iban, continued life and success in this-worldly affairs depend upon maintaining contacts with these now distanced supernaturals. The task of keeping alive these contacts falls chiefly to the shamans and priest-bards, who, acting as ritual intercessors, call down the gods from the upperworld, enlist their involvement in human affairs through the intermediating agency of the spirit-heroes, and, more generally, insure that their human clients are not forgotten, but remain fixed within the benevolent gaze of these otherworldly supernaturals.

Here the principal horizon that Sather addresses is cosmological, as well as spatial and perceptual, dividing, as it does, the human world from the upperworlds of the gods and spirit-heroes and, at the same time, separating what, in human terms, is visually perceptible from what is not. Sather additionally reminds us that horizons are defined by the perspectives of situated observers and that different vantage points may entail different modes of awareness and knowing and of acting upon whatever falls within their different purviews. In interceding with the gods and spirits, Iban shamans employ a mode of knowing that involves the personification of nonhuman others. Personification implies attributing to others a point of view, and to intercede successfully requires that the shamans apprehend and are able to project and work within these differently conceived vantage points. Taking as his point of departure a major ritual of intercession, the Gawai Betawai, Sather shows how its performance is structured as a horizon-crossing journey through the use of shifting perspectives and the employment of verbal imagery that at times mystifies the ordinary, while at other times, renders mundane what lies beyond the direct apprehension of its human audience.

In the final essay in this section, Roy Wagner explores what it means to fashion a way of life in the absence of apparent horizons. In contrast to the visual remoteness of the Cook Island horizon, for the Daribi people of Mount Karimui, Papua New Guinea, the horizon has seemingly contracted virtually to the point of disappearing altogether. One is tempted to liken the result to an ethnographic analogue of a black hole in space from which nothing that passes within its gravitational field reemerges. Thus, Wagner tells us that here roads, rather than bearing those who use them to some destination, "go into the ground and are never seen or heard from again," "talk turns back on itself as it is spoken," exchange never comes out equal, and perspectives are replaced by introspection.

Travel and models of relationship

The second set of papers deals variously with travel and its social and culturally constitutive effects.

The first essay by Harri Siikala explores a general comparative issue. Taking Polynesian history and society as his subject, Siikala examines two key symbols or "ordering tropes" by which, he argues, Polynesians organize and conceptualize their societies: namely, the house and the canoe. Both, as containers of persons, are constructed as total social bodies or totalizing representations of society to which, in each case, distinctive histories are attached. While both objects thus articulate social groups with their origin, they do so, he argues, in complementary ways. In Polynesian oral traditions, society is often depicted either as fixed by reference to a point of origin or as a mobile whole that becomes internally differentiated as a result of political segmentation and geographic dispersal. Where a fixed point of origin is emphasized, social hierarchy is established by the rootedness of groups to the land. Here the house becomes a central symbol, expressing continuity and wholeness and the legitimization of social groups as land-connected territorial units. By contrast, where mobility determines origins and results in segmentation, authority is characteristically established through the mythic migrations of founding ancestors. Correspondingly, the canoe receives special emphasis. Drawing on the work of Bellwood, Fox, and others, Siikala terms societies in which the spatial fixity of the house is emphasized as "Origin

13

Societies" and those in which the mobility of the canoe is stressed as "Settler Societies." As he argues, these symbolic forms are not mutually exclusive, but, rather, they coexist in complementary relation to one another, and his principal purpose in distinguishing them is to show how, he tells us, in moving across Polynesia in a roughly historical trajectory, from west to east, they interact and transform each other in ways that reflect different structural forms, histories, patterns of hierarchy and chiefly power.

In the next essay, Frederick Damon also looks at some of the ideas that boats embody. The boats that directly concern him are those that sail between the islands comprising the classic Kula Ring. Here, Damon tells us, boats act as moving metaphors. As sailing craft, they synthesize extraordinarily complex relationships both in their construction and in the circumstances of their operation. Within the Kula region they act, for example, as complex "communication technologies." Thus, between the different island societies making up the Kula Ring, boats serve as the principal means for conveying words, products, and people. They are also a moving model of relationships, including those of inter-island exchange, differentiation, and dependency. Finally, and, Damon suggests, most saliently of all, boats "enchant." Like myths, they are the object of aesthetic as well as of technical interest, whose form serves as a model for the appropriateness of other forms and relationships. Boats, in this case by their form and operation, and also by the remarkable body of technical knowledge and experience that goes into their construction, communicate, Damon argues, "the fundamental conditions of existence in the region." Underlying these conditions is an *el niño*-dominated environment that subjects various life processes to a level of unpredictability best characterized, he argues, as "chaotic." Consequently, fit into the design of these boats are both elements of chaos itself and solutions to the unpredictable circumstances that these elements impose. By concentrating on the selection by skilled boat-builders of different tree species of the genus Calophyllum for use in fashioning the vital parts of these boats, and drawing on cybernetics and chaos theory, Damon shows how principles of chaos are reflected in the structure of these parts and in their successful functioning. In this connection, boats, he tells us, operate like mathematical equations. Highly dependent upon initial conditions, they display transformative relations between their various parts. Thus, for example, the keel, as the most operationally sensitive part of a sailing craft, establishes the initial conditions to which the other parts, such as masts and outriggers, must proportionally conform. There are two dominant types of boats that operate within the Kula Ring and each provides for those who build and sail them both a model of reality and a way of coping with its inherent unpredictability.

The next paper by Antony Hooper takes up several topics particularly dear to Jukka, among them, fishing, the sea, manhood, and the wisdom of the elders. Hooper's paper describes an epic 16 days of community skipjack fishing that occurred more than thirty years ago on the Tokelau atoll of Fakaofo. Events of those days, which, he tells us, have never been repeated since, dramatically brought to the fore a number of vital, but otherwise largely unarticulated features of Tokelau society, namely, the continuing authority of the elders over community life, the value accorded to technical knowledge, male proficiency and skill, and the importance of cooperation, generosity, and of working together with others under the direction of the elders in a spirit of humility. Although most of the principal actors who took part in these events are no longer alive, the knowledge and underlying values that were revealed during those eventful days continue to live on among the people of Fakaofo, both at home and abroad, in the more dispersed modern world, either as ideals or increasingly today as consciously compiled "heritage."

James J. Fox, in the last paper in this section, turns to a topic central to much of Jukka Siikala's writings – cosmogonic myths and their social significance. The myths he deals with in this case concern the coming into being of natural periodicities: notably, the rhythms of night and day, the apparent movements across the sky of the sun and moon, and the ebbing and flowing of the tides. For the Rotinese of eastern Indonesia, all important cultural goods and processes derive, according to origin narratives, from exchanges between the Sun and Moon and the Sea and Ocean. Thus, the Sea and Ocean exchanged knowledge, women, and wealth with the Sun and Moon, and, in the past, the ancestors of the Rotinese benefited from these exchanges through mythic encounters with various sea creatures. As Fox argues, these ritual narratives reveal a distinctive cultural conceptualization of these natural periodicities, linking them at once to both ordinary Rotinese routines, such as tree planting, farming and fishing, and to an idealized conception of perfection represented by a heavenly order that, in the human world, can be only imperfectly realized.

Narrative horizons on culture, history and myth

The third set of papers deals with the cultural horizons invoked by text and performance. For some time, these words were used to stand for two contrasting methodological orientations as anthropologists and folklorists stressed the production of meaning in the actual contexts of interaction and discarded the idea of culture as a more lasting, objective phenomenon. More recent theoretical debates show a resurgent interest in people's awareness of their own culture and the various objects and modalities of such awareness. In her contribution to this volume Judith Huntsman discusses a written, autobiographic text which, she argues, should not be seen as part of the repertoire of the oral tradition of the writer's community, but nevertheless makes a commentary on its structure and values. The author of this text, a spokesman for the Catholic minority of Tokelau, reflects on a long history of interaction between outside powers and the inhabitants of Tokelau, consistently affirming the convivial competition and mutual respect between different elements of Tokelau society as an arena for the display of genuine authority and valued aspects of personal character. The most interesting aspect of this text, and the focus of Huntsman's analysis of it, is not the chronology of events presented in it but the interactional style in which the local protagonist causes foreigners to "reveal" their real intentions.

Petra Autio's contribution deals with the communicative significance of dance competitions on the Micronesian islands of Kiribati. The dance performances are an aggregate of verbal, musical and bodily expressions, each of which involves codified messages, but the principal importance of dancing as a whole lies in its effect on different kinds of audiences and its enactment of their hierarchical relations. Autio argues that in spite of the ostensibly high position of the "guests of honor," these people are not the ones whose appraisal is sought by the contestants; instead, the songs accompanying each dance aim at giving voice to the whole community of people whom the dancers performatively represent. The formal style of performance thus becomes a metacommunicative comment on the multiple relations which affect the performance behind the stage: the secret instructions of teachers to students, the relations between competing groups, and the relationship of the dancers to the guests of honor whom the dance aims at impressing with its beauty. Even as the formal expression of singers and dancers appears to de-individualize the event of a performance, lending an aura of self-evidence and incontestability to these relations, Autio argues that they add persuasive force to the creative agency of teachers, authors and performers.

In his article Timo Kaartinen describes a dispute in which the self-evident nature of inter-group relations and political leadership comes under question. Instead of being resolved through customary means – an assembly of village elders which involves formal exchanges and oratorical complaints – this dispute evokes mythological reflections about the ancestral relations which constitute a diversity of people as a society. In parallel with the cases discussed by Huntsman and Autio, the main communicative purpose of narrating ancestral history in this case is to comment on the structural basis of authority and the productive potential of different kinds of action. By revealing the ancestral background of different parties to the dispute, narrators offer two related perspectives for evaluating the present situation in terms of broader, cultural categories. Even as each narrative lends plausibility to certain personal ambitions and collective interests, it indicates what actions are clearly destructive to society and therefore devoid of value. In each myth, a primordial dispute or war marks simultaneously the ontological source of authority and the limit of exercising it. Instead of simply providing a charter for present social identities and status relations, the myths thus reveal their internal contradictions which people are forced to deal with in symbolic terms.

The common theme of these three papers is the power of writings, cultural performances and storytelling to reveal the hidden value of different aspects of social being. We can perhaps speak about cultural texts – broadly defined – as horizons of value, signs which mark the discontinuity between taken-for-granted aspects of life and the domains of generative and creative processes. Drawing from Paul Ricoeur's view of writing, Jukka and Anna-Leena Siikala characterize textuality as a meaningful potential in which people recognize their culture. "What is fixed by writing is thus a discourse that could be said, of course, but that is written precisely because it is not said" (Siikala & Siikala 2005: 59).

Crossing boundaries and the idea and practice of anthropology

In his writings, Jukka Siikala has repeatedly stressed the importance of crossing boundaries. Boundary-crossing, as he tells us, is, after all, an essential part of doing anthropology. "The practice of doing fieldwork always means a departure; leaving behind everyday activities at home... and entering a different world" (2001a: 1). Moreover, as anthropologists, after returning from the field, we tend to enter into areal discussions with colleagues who have worked within the same general region. As Jukka notes, interaction between specialists in anthropology is "surprisingly scant compared to the intensity of areal discourse," with the result that these different areal discourses tend oftentimes to be "intellectually incommensurable" (1990a: 5). In addition, there are also, of course, different national and scholarly traditions. In organizing past international symposiums at the University of Helsinki, Jukka deliberately sought to break down these various boundaries by intentionally juxtaposing different traditions and place-bound discussions so as to open up novel and comparatively more fruitful perspectives. As he wrote in his introduction to the collected essays of the 1987 Helsinki symposium on "Culture and History in the Pacific," "My firm belief is that if there is a future for ethnographic analysis, it can [only] be found by crossing the borders of these traditions and breaking the boundaries of areal discussions" (1990a: 8).

In bringing together the essays in this present volume, we have tried to be faithful to this ideal. At the same time, we have also sought to preserve a degree of topical coherence, reflecting in this, too, Jukka's own evolving interests. While the papers in this collection range widely, they all, in one way or another, concern societies of the Pacific, New Guinea, or Island Southeast Asia, and treat in interrelated ways the topics of myth, textuality, history, travel, and cosmology. Similarly, they also, by intent, juxtapose a wide range of different approaches to these topics.

In recent years, Jukka has voiced a growing concern with the idea of anthropology as it is currently practiced and with its future. Here, again, the notions of boundaries and horizons are pertinent and offer a useful point of departure.

"The idea of anthropology," as Bruce Kapferer (2007: 72) has recently written, "is a vast one...potentially open to all forms of human practice and thought." Very little now seemingly escapes an anthropological gaze, with, as Kapferer says, "new topics continually appearing on the anthropological horizon." At the same time, anthropologists have also attacked dimensions of their discipline that appear outdated.

> If anthropologists once concentrated on human groups at the periphery of modernity, were fascinated by the exotic defined as historically or spatially distant from or at the edge of the metropolitan realities of dominant capital, this is no more. Everything is now judged to be in some way or another modern, inside rather than outside (Kapferer 2007: 73).

Thus, if the initial location of the anthropological project was once "at the fringes of Empire," the discipline has since transcended its beginnings and "the horizons of anthropological knowledge are now anywhere and everywhere" (Kapferer 2007: 85).

While welcoming critical self-reflection, Kapferer, like many others, has expressed misgivings about the more radical forms that critique within the discipline has taken, which he sees as potentially endangering some vital elements of the very idea of anthropology itself as it was historically formed. Thus, he notes, some recent reconfigurations of anthropology in relation to current globalization give rise to a myopic "presentism," an exclusive concern with the immediate moment. Here previous anthropological approaches are dismissed as irrelevant, or worse, and the large bodies of ethnographic work painstakingly achieved in the past are ignored or undervalued. Jukka has expressed similar concerns, noting that such radical critiques have more often succeeded in "criticizing the representer, not the representation," with the result that, for some, "exotic field sites [have] become politically incorrect and fieldwork at home becomes more and more popular as part of a self-reflective search for the moment" (Siikala 2007: 21).

The decades since the 1960s, and particularly from the 1980s onward, have brought about dramatic changes in the way in which anthropology defines its object and in its position in the larger intellectual scheme of things. "The classic object of anthropology," as Jukka observes, "has been the ethnographic other, which has been described in holistic terms" (2007: 19). But as narrative constructions of the "other" have come under attack, "constructions of 'self' [have] replaced the holistic approach of previous inquiry," with dramatic consequences. Thus, Jukka argues, both radical criticism within the discipline and conservative politics without have "had the same aim and both [have] undermined the fundamental practice of the discipline." In this, as Jukka notes, anthropology, of course, is not alone. "The whole university system has been transformed through the capitalization of knowledge which has led to an amalgamation of interests among the previously separate institutions of state, industry and universities" (Siikala 2007: 22). Knowledge is now "produced" for its application. "Learned traditions have been replaced by commercial relevance as the criterion for the quality of research at the same time as the administration of academia has been transformed to imitate corporate models of commodity production" (2007: 22). If the modern individual defines his or her identity through consumption, and hence through commodities, he or she, as a consumer, now expects to find his or her own self in these commodities, "not the self of somebody else." Hence, the currently endangered state of anthropological ethnography. Anthropology at home turns into "an anthropology of familiarity…in which the only thing 'new' is in its presentation … If the only novelty in ethnographic description is the way it is said, attention is naturally drawn to the modes of depiction instead of its contents" (2007: 23). The results may, perhaps, be most clearly seen in some versions of current American anthropology where an obsession with the contemporary is wedded to a preoccupation with the literary nature of anthropological representation itself.

The university system, where, since the first decades of the twentieth century, most anthropological knowledge has been generated, is now undergoing a restructuring in which academic interests are subordinated to those of governments and corporations. One result has been to undermine economic support for extended fieldwork and, indeed, within anthropology, the value of ethnography itself (Siikala 2007: 21). As anthropology's scientific practice has always been its stress on the empirical and ethnographic, the primacy of ethnography is such, as Kapferer (2007: 81) notes, "that anthropology is almost synonymous with ethnography." As the discipline's distinctive form of scientific practice, it is, as Kapferer writes, "through the reflexive deconstruction of the anthropologist's own preconceptions in the fieldwork encounter that knowledge is gained." Moreover, the nature of the ethnographic encounter is such that, in a sense, no ethnographic study is ever completed, but, rather, each remains in a state of ongoing debate to which the anthropologist continually returns, by further fieldwork, reanalysis, or by comparison with other materials, both to his own ethnography and to that of others. Thus, "the neglect of…ethnography…, both in the teaching and in the practice of anthropology, risks the very fundamental basis of anthropological knowledge and of its authority as a particular type of science" (Kapferer 2007: 84).

Jukka adds to this by pointing out that in conflating the interests of the university with those of governments and corporations, rather than posing questions, universities are now being increasingly called upon to provide answers to questions posed elsewhere. Not only is the quality of academic research threatened as a result, but for anthropology, its capacity for social critique is lost (Siikala 2007: 23). Indeed, as he notes, these processes endanger the very idea of anthropology itself. "If the ultimate aim of anthropology…is immersion into another culture in such a way as to force one to question received ontological presuppositions," then clearly "one cannot derive the organizing questions of…research from one cultural area only" (2007: 24). If the ethnographic encounter is no longer used to raise questions or to interrogate our received presuppositions, anthropology loses both its critical impact and its ability to overcome the consequences of reductionist analyses, and so becomes, in effect, as Siikala warns, a form of endless repetition. The only way to avoid this is to continue to cross borders and to go on exploring new horizons.

REFERENCES

Dresch, Paul 1988. Segmentation: Its Roots in Arabia and Its Flowering Elsewhere. *Cultural Anthropology* 3(1): 50–67.

Hanks, William 1996. *Language and Communicative Practices*. Boulder: Westview Press.

Hirsch, Eric 1995. Landscape: Between Place and Space. In: Eric Hirsch and Michael O'Hanlon (eds.) *The Anthropology of Landscape: Perspectives on Place and Space.* Oxford: Clarendon Press. Pp. 1–30.

Hoskins Janet 1993. *The Play of Time: Kodi Perspectives on Calendars, History, and Exchange.* University of California Press.

Jolly, Margaret 1994. Epilogue: Hierarchical Horizons. In: M. Jolly and M. Mosko (eds.) Transformations of Hierarchy. Structure, History and Horizon in the Austronesian World. Special issue of *History and Anthropology* 7(1–4): 377–409.

Kapferer, Bruce. 2007. Anthropology and the Dialectic of Enlightenment: A Discourse on the Definition and Ideals of a Threatened Discipline. *The Australian Journal of Anthropology* 18(1): 72–94.

Lévi-Strauss, Claude 1987. *Introduction to the Work of Marcel Mauss*. London: Routledge & Kegan Paul.

Ricoeur, Paul 1976. *Interpretation Theory: Discourse and the surplus of meaning*. Fort Worth: Texas Christian University Press.

Sahlins, Marshall 1985. *Islands of History*. Chicago: University of Chicago Press.

Siikala, Jukka 1982. *Cult and Conflict in Tropical Polynesia. A Study of Traditional Religion, Christianity and Nativistic Movements*. FF Communications 233. Helsinki: Finnish Academy of Sciences.

Siikala, Jukka 1990a. Introduction. In: Jukka Siikala (ed.) *Culture and History in the Pacific*. Helsinki: Finnish Anthropological Society. Pp. 5–8.

Siikala, Jukka 1990b. Chief, Gender and Hierarchy in Ngaputoru. In: Jukka Siikala (ed.) *Culture and History in the Pacific*. Helsinki: Finnish Anthropological Society. Pp. 107–124.

Siikala, Jukka. 1991. *'Akatokamanāva: Myth, History and Society in the Southern Cook Islands*. Auckland: The Polynesian Society in association with The Finnish Anthropological Society.

Siikala, Jukka 1996. The Elder and the Younger – Foreign and autochthonous origin and hierarchy in the Cook Islands. In: James J. Fox and Clifford Sather (eds.) *Origins, Ancestry and Alliance. Explorations in Austronesian Ethnography*. Canberra: Australian National University. Published as part of the Comparative Austronesian Project by the Department of Anthropology, RSPAS. Pp. 41–55.

Siikala, Jukka 2001a. Introduction: Where have all the people gone. In: Jukka Siikala (ed.) *Departures: How Societies Distribute their People*. TAFAS 46. Helsinki: Finnish Anthropological Society. Pp. 1–6.

Siikala, Jukka 2001b. Tilling the Soil and Sailing the Seas: Cadastral Maps and Anthropological Interpretations. In: Jukka Siikala (ed.) *Departures: How Societies Distribute their People*. TAFAS 46. Helsinki: Finnish Anthropological Society. Pp. 22–45.

Siikala, Jukka 2001c. Chiefs and Impossible States. *Communal/Plural: Journal of Transnational & Crosscultural Studies* 9(1): 81–94.

Siikala, Jukka. 2007. Ethnography and the Denial of Difference. In: Minna Ruckenstein and Marie-Louise Karttunen (eds.) *On Foreign Ground: Moving Between Countries and Categories*. Helsinki: Studia Fennica, Anthropologica 1. Pp. 19–27.

Siikala, Anna-Leena & Jukka 2005. *Return to Culture. Oral Tradition and Society in the Southern Cook Islands*. Helsinki: Academia Scientarum Fennica.

Wagner, Roy 1981. *The Invention of Culture*. Chicago: University of Chicago Press.

Urban, Greg 1996. *The Metaphysical Community. The interplay of the senses and the intellect*. Austin: University of Texas Press.

Horizons of Experience

The Future is a Foreign Country

Time, Space and Hierarchy among
the Urapmin of Papua New Guinea

Joel Robbins

Jukka Siikala (1991: 3) begins his study of myth and history in the Southern Cook Islands by noting that "The constant presence of the world beyond the horizon in the two senses of the word, past and abroad, became my main interest during fieldwork." This proves to be a productive focus for a study of Cook Islands social life. The past informs the present there in ways that people must constantly work out, and regular travel beyond the local horizon is an enduring fact of Islander life that puts the problem of defining and maintaining the value of home at the center of people's concerns. Moreover, the two worlds beyond the horizon are, at least as the Ma'uke people see them, fused from the outset. This is so because the past is precisely another country, that of Avaiki, the origin-place from which the Islanders originally came. It is in the tales that tell of how the foreign past became the domestic present that the logics of Southern Cook Islanders' thinking and action are elaborated and made available for people to use in conducting their contemporary lives.

As fitting as this focus on the presence of two worlds beyond the horizon is for the project Siikala carries out in *'Akatokamanāva*, one cannot help but note that another world that would seem to belong to this set of horizonal outliers is missing: the world that lies beyond the present in time and is generally known as that of the future. Anthropological theory has been shaped for a long time and in very deep ways by thinking about how the past informs the present. It has also more recently, under the sign of globalization, reckoned with great energy with how connections to and imaginary constructions of the world abroad shape peoples' lives. But it has had less to say about the role of the future in the construction of social action and social life. To be sure, there is a large literature on millenarian and other future-oriented movements, and it is one to which Siikala has also made important contributions (1982, 2004). But this work has not had the kind of impact on anthropological theorizing in general that work on the influence of the past and the foreign has had. In this chapter, I want to borrow Siikala's initial insight into the importance for present social life of worlds beyond various horizons and consider what adding the world of the future might mean to the ways we think about the problematics of structure, history and change that have always been among his central concerns.

Valuing the foreign future among the Urapmin of Papua New Guinea

> If it is for this life only that Christ has given us hope,
> we of all men are most to be pitied (1 Corinthians 15:19)

The Urapmin of Papua New Guinea are a group of approximately 390 people living in the West Sepik Province of Papua New Guinea. Although never directly missionized by Westerners, everyone in the Urapmin community has been Christian since a charismatic revival movement arrived in the late 1970s and sparked a wave of conversions among those Urapmin who had not already found their way to Christianity by visiting the mission centers Baptist missionaries had set up among neighboring groups. As I have discussed elsewhere, since the revival, Urapmin Christianity is culturally sophisticated and intensely held. It provides the most important set of cosmological orientations for everyone in the community and its impact on almost all areas of Urapmin life is profound (Robbins 2004).

One of the most notable features of Urapmin Christianity is its markedly millennial tone. Urapmin wait expectantly for Jesus' return and are sure its arrival is imminent. Sometimes they give themselves over for a week or more to the kind of anticipatory fervor that one expects of those caught up in a millenarian movement. During these periods, people abandon their gardening and other earthly tasks for a regime of constant prayer and attendance at church services. At other times, in fact most of the time, Urapmin lead more recognizably earthbound lives, but even as they do so they still maintain a meaningful focus on the fact that Jesus might come at any moment. When He comes, they say, He will rapture believers into the sky before battling the Antichrist on earth. At the end of this battle, which will destroy the earth, God will judge everyone. Those who have believed in Him will find heaven, while those who did not will be consigned to hell. Most Urapmin aim at all times to live their lives in ways that will demonstrate their belief in God and earn them entrance to heaven. Yet even in spite of such efforts, humans are bound to sin, and so the Urapmin have developed an elaborate ritual life that allows sinners to recuperate their moral selves and ready themselves for God's judgment. With these rituals dominating community life, and with the Second Coming always on people's minds in more private moments, heaven can rightly be said to be an overwhelming preoccupation among the Urapmin.

From the point of view of the argument of this chapter, the most important feature of the heaven the Urapmin focus upon so intently is that it is over the horizon in several senses. It is over the temporal horizon, at least for earthly people, inasmuch as they will only be able to see it and live in it in the future, after the Second Coming has occurred. It is also over the horizon in the sense of being, in Siikala's terms, foreign. For the Urapmin do not put any store in the idea that heaven might somehow be a metaphorical reference to an earthly state of peace or plenty. It is, rather, located in a distinctively different place than the one they live in now – a place in the sky in which believers will live after this earth has been destroyed in the wake of Jesus' return.

The importance of the quality of being elsewhere to the Urapmin conception of heaven was brought home to me by a conversation I had one day with Rom, one of the most important younger leaders in Urapmin. Rom is a generally unflappable sort. Having attended a local Bible college, he has one of the more extensive Christian educations in the community. As a young man, Rom also worked on a tea plantation in the central Highlands of Papua New Guinea and spent his second year there as a "house boy" for one of the expatriate managers. By virtue of this work experience, he has had more contact with Westerners than most Urapmin. For all of these reasons, Rom is widely respected in the community and has for many years served as its councilor (its elected representative to the government of the district and its unofficial representative to other non-local powers).

Patient, smart and deeply thoughtful, one rarely sees Rom flustered. For this reason, it caught my notice when he returned from the district headquarters in Telefomin one day in a noticeably agitated state. In Telefomin, he told me, he had met with a young man who claimed to be able to make contact with his dead mother. She would take him, he said, underground and reveal to him important information. On the basis of the things his mother communicated to him, he had set himself up as a prophet. One of the things she had told him was that when Jesus comes back, believers will, as has been promised, live in a world where all needs are met and no one is marked as marginal (see below). Yet in one respect things will be different than what Christians are expecting: they will experience this beatific state on earth, in the very places where they have always lived; there will be no heaven in the sky for them to go to, nor even any new place on earth. Rom was deeply disturbed by this vision and felt it could not be true. Uncharacteristically at a loss for words, he could not say much about why the prophet's words seemed to him so wrong. But the extent to which they threatened to play havoc with the structure of the Christian cosmos in which he had lived all of his adult life was evident. The whole episode revealed to me how important it was to his sense of ontological security that heaven was not only in another time but was also in another place.

As it happens, Rom's disquiet at the suggestion that heaven might not be a distinct place is not a singular one. Jacka (2005) reports a remarkably similar response from a Christian man in Porgera Valley in Enga Province to whom he had inadvertently suggested that heaven might not be in the sky. The question both of these cases raise is that of why it is so important for people like the Urapmin to imagine that heaven is somewhere else. Why is it not enough to know that it refers to the promise of the coming of a better life in the future? Why must it also be, as it were, a foreign country? My primary goal in this chapter is to answer these questions. Once that is done, I also want to return to some more theoretically motivated questions that I raised at the outset. If one thinks about it, Christian cosmology as it is understood by the Urapmin and many other Christians is almost the exact inverse of the Polynesian kind that Siikala has worked with. In the Polynesian cosmology, the past is located elsewhere, provides an important source of order, and is hierarchically privileged. In the Christian one, it is the future that is foreign, that sets the ideal terms for the current order, and that is valued above all. At the end, we will have to consider if such divergent cosmologies shape social action and the making of history in different ways.

Spatial hierarchy and the value of being elsewhere

One crucial aspect of Urapmin ideas about heaven is that it is elsewhere than where the Urapmin currently live. Another is that it is a better, more valued place than their current home. In this way, Urapmin Christian cosmology links place and value and thereby hierarchizes space, defining the earth as less valued than heaven. In Urapmin terms, the earth is 'the ground' or 'this ground' (*towal diim*, dispela graun).[1] Urapmin can talk about the 'land' (*bokon*), in reference to places where one might garden or hunt, or even 'ground'(*towal*) as in soil, in neutral or appreciative terms. Thus, for example, they sometimes note that in comparison to some of their neighbors they possess 'good ground' (*towal tangbal*) for growing crops. But the use of 'this ground' or "the ground" in general always implies a contrast to 'heaven' (*abiil tigen* – lit. 'place in the sky') and as such is used to remind people of the relative unimportance of earthly matters. One most commonly hears it used in the construction 'something of the ground' (*towal diim mafakmafak*, samting bilong graun), a construction speakers deploy to suggest to interlocutors that whatever it is they are attaching great importance to at the moment (a pig, a garden, development, etc.) is not really very important at all from the point of view of what should be their ultimate concern. I want to argue in the next section that the way in which the idea of heaven renders Christian cosmology one of hierarchically arranged places is part of what makes that cosmology so compelling to contemporary Urapmin. Before turning to that argument about the importance of cosmological spatial hierarchy, however, it is necessary to explore the ways Urapmin have conceptualized earthly space in hierarchical terms both in the past and in the present.

Traditional Urapmin conceptions of space were also in important respects hierarchical. In the past, the Urapmin were part of the well-known Min or Mountain Ok regional ritual system (Barth 1975, Jorgensen 1981). This system linked all of the communities of the Min region together in a ritual division of labor the ultimate aim of which was to make everyone's crops flourish and their boys grow. Although all the communities involved in the

---

1 Words in the Urap language are given in italics. Words in Tok Pisin, Papua New Guinea's most important *lingua franca* and a language that is important in Urapmin Christian discourse, are underlined.

ritual system had rites of their own to perform, several communities were thought to possess the most powerful sacra and the greatest secret ritual knowledge and thus to be more central to the system than the rest. Urapmin were widely understood by all Min people to be one of these central groups. By their own reckoning they may even have been more important than, or at least equal to, the Telefolmin, who were regarded as paramount by the majority of Min groups.

Contact and the colonial and postcolonial era put a great deal of pressure on the Min ritual system and by the early 1980s it had largely collapsed, taking with it the spatial hierarchy it had formerly underwritten. Christianity was of course the greatest challenge to the ritual system, and it was the revival of the late 1970s that finally made it impossible for it to continue to function. But the traditional ritual system faced challenges not only from Christianity and the way its cosmology reconfigured its spatial hierarchy, but also from the way the colonial government and the world economy redrew the map of the region before Christianity became the predominant force it is today. In fact, it is reasonable to suggest that at least among the Urapmin this first "political" and "economic" transformation of the value-saturated landscape of the Min region in some key respects set the terms in which the Christian one that would come later could be understood as meaningful.[2]

In the way they so often do, at least in retrospect, events of the early contact and colonial period conspired to bolster the authority of the traditional map of the world. The first airstrip was built at Telefomin in the 1940s, and then shortly after World War Two the first government offices and mission station were located there as well. Since Telefomin was widely regarded as paramount center of the regional ritual system, its emergence as the center of the colonial order made good sense from the point of view of indigenous spatial hierarchies. Yet in relatively short order the spatial hierarchy that the colonial order was putting into place ceased to map neatly onto the traditional one. From the Urapmin point of view, the mapping started to fall apart most forcefully once the Baptist Mission began building airstrips in various places around the Min region. Urapmin lacked good ground for an airstrip, and its location, only four to six hours of rugged walking from the station at Telefomin, made it a low priority in any case. As Urapmin was bypassed and airstrips were built in locales further and further from Telefomin, communities that were clearly subordinate in the ritual hierarchy suddenly began to far outrank the Urapmin in the newly important hierarchies centered on Christian sophistication, knowledge of the ways of the new government, and access to cash. With the development of the huge Ok Tedi mine and the associated town of Tabubil to the southwest of Telefomin in the early 1980s, the redrawing of the spatial hierarchy was complete, for now Telefomin itself became a distinctly secondary center and its rank as one of the least developed district office towns in the country became apparent to those like the Urapmin

---

2 Jorgensen (1996) provides a detailed account of how Min regional organization has changed since contact. His article provides a crucial background to my argument here, which is focused more closely on Urapmin historical experience.

for whom it had once been the major regional center of the colonial and post-colonial orders. It was in the run-up to this final transformation the mine would bring that the revival swept through Min country and for all intents and purposes laid the regional ritual system to rest.

I have discussed in detail elsewhere how the collapse of the regional ritual system and the resultant displacement of the Urapmin from the center of their known world pushed them toward Christianity and played a crucial role in laying the groundwork for their unusually thorough conversion to that new religion (Robbins 2004: 88–100). Rather than repeat that historical account here, I want to focus on how the Urapmin thought about the hierarchical ordering of earthly places during the ethnographic present of the early 1990s, the period of my fieldwork. This was a time when the spatial hierarchy configured by the colonial and postcolonial governments, Christianity, and the development of the Ok Tedi mine was firmly in place.

In broad terms, the map of the earthly world the Urapmin worked with in the early 1990s contained three kinds of places: bush areas, towns, and countries. The bush (*sep*)/town (taun) distinction has its roots in a traditional demarcation between the bush and the village (*abiip*). This latter distinction, which among other things would qualify as the Urapmin way of talking about "nature" and "culture," is one in which human beings (*unangtanum* – lit. 'men and women,') very much belong in villages (Robbins 2003). This point is not so well borne out by Urapmin daily life, for almost every family has a house in the bush near their gardens and hunting grounds as well as one in a village, and people spend a lot of time working in the bush and living in their bush houses. But even as the connection between people and villages is not so firmly rooted in quotidian practice, it is forcefully established in mythic understandings. When Afek (lit. 'the old woman') first created Urapmin people, she faced the problem of where to put them on an earth that was already crowded with nature spirits (*motobil*) who inhabited its every corner. In order to solve this problem, Afek cleared the spirits off into the bush, telling them that all of it, all the land and all the game and plants living on it, would be their possessions as long as they left the villages to the Urapmin. To this day, even in the wake of Christian conversion, these spirits are still understood to own the bush. People thus have a heightened sense of danger in the bush (a sense of danger that is also mixed with one of excitement for the possibilities for hunting, gathering, and growing crops that the bush offers), and even as they spend a good deal of time in the bush, there is a feeling of comfort and safety that attaches to time spent in the village. Moreover, as Jorgensen (1981) has noted for the Telefolmin, the Urapmin scrupulously maintain the distinction between village and bush spaces by clearing the central plazas of their horseshoe-shaped villages (*abiip mat*, 'village belly') of all natural growth. Sitting in the doorway of one's house and looking into the village center, one sees nothing but clean, densely packed earth – a scene very much the opposite of that of the riotous display of rainforest growth that greets the eye wherever one looks in the bush.

Much of the pride the Urapmin have in their particularly human accomplishments follows from the work they do to transform aspects of the bush into food and material objects that they can use for living their lives, and particularly for living the lives they live in villages where such food and other objects are shown to and shared with others in the practices of display and reciprocity that are fundamental to human sociality. In this respect, the village is where uniquely human abilities reach their highest expression. It is a place where nature is put in the background and the focus is squarely on what humans have been able to do with it.

The bush/village distinction is still central to Urapmin life, which is why I have been able to write about it in such confident terms. Yet I did not include the village in my list of the three kinds of places that are most prominent on the map the Urapmin currently use to navigate the world. In deference to the way notions of the village still shape Urapmin understandings of their working lives and social arrangements, I could well have included the village. But I left it off because in ways that are very important to my developing argument, the bush/village distinction which was responsible for so much of the meaning of the "village" has been superseded by a distinction between the bush and the town.

Towns are, as the Urapmin reckon them, western or "white" social forms.[3] They are places where the bush is much more completely held at bay than it is in Urapmin villages. In towns, as the Urapmin see it, people hardly have to work to gain food or other goods. Instead, machines do much of the work. And houses in town, made of sawn timbers and outfitted with metal roofs, do not require the constant maintenance that village dwellings need if they are not to disintegrate into nothing more than rotten versions of the bush products that were used in their construction. In these and many other ways, towns have replaced villages as the kinds of places that epitomize the power of human labor to transform the world. They have thus come to represent the very opposite of the bush in the way villages once did.

The Urapmin themselves do not have a town of their own, one that exists on their land. The closest place that counts as one is Tabubil, the town built around the Ok Tedi mine. It has paved roads, lots of permanent materials housing, twenty-four hour power, and well-stocked stores. Although small, it is well-equipped by Papua New Guinea standards with the modern features of town life and the Urapmin see it as very different from their villages. They also know there are many towns that are larger and more imposing in other parts of Papua New Guinea and the world.

The partial supersedure of the village/bush distinction by the town/bush distinction has sharply affected the Urapmin sense of their own humanity. In a world divided into town places and bush places, even Urapmin villages have to be classified as bush. No longer the epitome of what human labor can produce, these villages are more like the unworked jungle than like Tabubil or other towns. With villages relegated to the status of bush, and with no town on Urapmin land, it is impossible for the Urapmin to escape defining

---

3 The black//white distinction is another one that is crucial to contemporary Urapmin thinking and it inflects their geographical imagination in ways I will touch upon but not fully lay out here when I come to discuss the role of "countries" in Urapmin thinking. I provide a more thorough discussion of these issues in Robbins 2004.

themselves in terms of the bush. Unsurprisingly, the Urapmin regularly refer to themselves as a 'bush line' (bus lin) and sometimes even reckon that they are 'big bush' (*bisip*) creatures, those who belong in the higher elevations where even the semi-domestic spaces of human gardens (*lang*) and garden houses (*sep am*) cease to break up the rainforest landscape. The big bush is the least human place of all on the Urapmin map. It is cold and spirit-filled, and people rarely venture into it unless they have to walk through it to get somewhere else or are led there by game they are pursuing. In referring to themselves as bush people or big bush people, the Urapmin suggest that the villages they make, the ultimate fruits of their labor, are not enough to propel them into full humanity. Town people and whites do not want to come to Urapmin villages or to exchange with the Urapmin for what they have made, and so their sphere of sociality is restricted to a world they now see as in its entirety one of the bush. The wider connotation is that they are somehow natural beings who can no longer of their own accord make themselves fully human in the way they were able to in the world as they previously understood it.

Countries (kantri) are the final kind of place that stands out as important in contemporary Urapmin views of the world. Urapmin understand the earth to be divided among different countries and they believe that people inescapably belong to or in the countries in which they are born (Robbins 2004). The United States, Australia, and Papua New Guinea are the countries that are most vivid in their minds. In the present context, what is most important about this aspect of their geographic imagination is that the Urapmin understand countries largely in "racial" terms and that these terms themselves array the countries of the world in a hierarchy of increasing modernity, here understood as the ability to transform nature into humanly usable shapes. Australia and the United States are, in Urapmin thinking, white countries that are fully modern – no one in these countries gardens or hunts, and I have never heard the Urapmin speculate that these countries even have bush areas. It is as if they are made up only of cities. Life in them is understood to be comfortable, free from want and the conflicts want brings. Papua New Guinea, by contrast, is a black country and as such is not as modern as others. Even its major cities – Port Moresby, Lae, Hagen, etc. – are understood to be undeveloped by the standards of white cities. Urapmin often hear about the violence that marks daily life in these cities, and they have a sense of their failure to provide fully human livelihoods for the 'rascals' (raskol) (members of urban youth gangs) and squatters that make up important parts of their populations. Papua New Guinea as a whole, then, even its cities, are identified with the bush when compared with other, white countries. This leaves the Urapmin doubly confined to the not-quite-fully-human world of the bush, since they belong to it both by virtue of the daily lives they live at home and by virtue of the racialized national identities they see themselves as confined to by birth.

The spatial hierarchy of bush, town, and country presents the Urapmin with a distinct problem. How are they to move themselves from the least valued place in this hierarchy to a more valued one? The earthly answer to this question comes in the form of 'development' (*developman*). As it is elsewhere in Papua New Guinea, in Urapmin development is a complex, polysemous notion that is crucial to how people currently see the world. I cannot fully explore its meanings for the Urapmin here, but want to focus on only those aspects that relate to Urapmin ideas about place and spatial hierarchy. In essence, development means a reorientation of one's relationship to the bush. Developed people neither depend on the bush for subsistence nor live in the bush. Instead, they work in mines, stores, or factories, and they live in cities or at least towns that feature permanent materials houses and well-stocked stores. The bush, with all its dangers and contingencies, only appears in town in such radically transformed forms (e.g. store-bought canned foods) as to present no threat to human designs.

As Urapmin see it, their land is so fully bush in character – has so much the quality of the big bush – that they hold out little hope that it could become a developed town. This was brought out quite strongly in a request they made to the Kennecott Corporation when its representatives came to renew a mining lease the company held to search for minerals on Urapmin land. A crew from Kennecott had been coming to Urapmin intermittently for a few days at a time since the later 1980s. By 1991 they had found enough gold and copper to lead them to renew their lease, though not nearly enough to making mining in Urapmin a real possibility yet. Still, Urapmin hopes that Kennecott would build a mine on their land ran very high, and fueled most of the fantasies of development the Urapmin dreamed about at night and discussed incessantly during the day during the early 1990s. People were therefore united in their desire to see Kennecott's license renewed.

To indicate their feelings at the meeting, many of the adults in the community worked together to prepare an elaborate performance to express to Kennecott and the Papua New Guinea government representative who would be in attendance how important it was to them that Kennecott build a mine. At the end of this performance, as a carefully scripted climax, a man and a woman would jump out of the bushes wearing, respectively, a traditional penis-gourd and grass skirt. Rom, the Urapmin councilor whose concerns about the place of heaven I discussed above, would then say: "we surprised you with our penis-gourds and grass skirts. But this is still what we are. If you have a mother and a father [i.e. sufficient resources] tear off our grass skirts and penis-gourds and replace them with trousers. We must become just like you." After several more displays designed to drive home similar messages of need and entreaty, Rom would finish by saying "if you have the power, take our land and destroy it and move us to a town somewhere else."[4]

---

4 As the meeting unfolded, the Kennecott representatives and the government mining warden quickly grew impatient with the dramatic parts of the performance, reminding the Urapmin that they needed to get in their helicopter and go before the predictable afternoon rains arrived – a demand fully predictable from the point of view of the general Urapmin understanding that developed people do not like to spend time in their bushy home. In response, Rom had to think on his feet and reduce the full-fledged performance to a speech. That speech ended in a way not much different from that planned: "Our mothers and fathers gave birth to wearing grass skirts and penis-gourds, if you have a mother and a father, please destroy our land and move us to a town somewhere else." I take it that the fact that this climactic message survived Rom's rapid editing down of that performance is an indication of how important the theme of destroying their land and moving them elsewhere was to Urapmin ideas of what it would take for them to become developed.

The emphasis the Urapmin placed on having their land destroyed no doubt followed to some extent from what they had witnessed during the development of the Ok Tedi mine and the town of Tabubil. During the early 1980s, they saw an area as remote ("bush") as theirs radically transformed into a town. But even more, I think, the idea that their land must be destroyed and they must be moved to new land made sense to them in relation to their thinking about the bush, the town and the nature of humanity. They planned in the performance to represent themselves as fully identified with the bush, naked except for the obviously bush items of their traditional dress. By violently tearing these off and replacing them with clothes made by modern labor, Kennecott would, they suggested, restore the Urapmin to full humanity. In reality this transformation would only be fully brought about when Kennecott used similarly violent means to destroy the Urapmin bush, transforming it far more extensively than the Urapmin have been able to by themselves, and thus liberating the Urapmin to move up the spatial hierarchy to a town somewhere else. The violence or force involved in these processes of transformation represents precisely the human 'power' (powa – a term with no Urap cognate that is now used constantly as a loan word) modern, town people have and the Urapmin lack.

Development in Urapmin is tied to displacement because of how central people's understanding of the postcolonial spatial hierarchy is to their sense of their human marginality. Yet at the same time as ideas about development as a shift in locale help people address this sense by imagining they could move elsewhere, they also have some limitations. First, their notion of development makes the Urapmin dependent on others for any progress they make, since it defines them as lacking the power to destroy the bush themselves or to move themselves elsewhere en masse (or even individually in most cases). Since autonomy in matters of production and life decisions is also crucial to Urapmin notions of humanity and development (a point I can only state but not fully substantiate here), this is a serious drawback to development. Second, development does not address the Urapmin idea that they are trapped within an undeveloped, "black" country, since as the Urapmin see it no kind of development can actually render them a citizen of another country. It is these two difficulties with development as a model for how to address marginality that render a heaven that is elsewhere so important to the Urapmin. Urapmin ideas of heaven provide workable models for getting past precisely the problems of limited autonomy and entrapment within a national identity that development has no answers for.

Heaven is not a place on earth

In keeping with the Protestant tradition from which their Christianity derives, the Urapmin are not given to describing heaven in detail or to elaborating ornate images that portray it in concrete terms (Russell 2006: 20). Its basic features are, however, widely agreed upon. Heaven is, as I have stressed, in the sky rather than on earth, and as a place occupied by human beings, it is also something that belongs to the future rather than to the present or past. When people will live there in the future, there will be among them no hierarchy of humanity based on ability to transform nature or allied distinctions of race or relative modernity. Indeed, transforming nature will not be an issue in heaven, since all needs will be satisfied without work, a condition that will also eliminate conflict between people. Finally, all places in heaven will be equal. As the Pairundu people of the Southern Highlands of Papua New Guinea put it to Jebens (2005: 189), heaven will be "flat," with no differences between the places in which people live and no barriers to travel from place to place. Summing all of these features together, one can say that for the Urapmin, heaven is a place that completely obviates the distinctions (bush/town, more/less human, black/white) that articulate the earthly hierarchy in which the Urapmin are placed in such a disadvantaged position. As Stendi once put it to me, in a phrasing that captures all of this in a pithy opposition made up of terms taken from two of the oppositions that structure this field of ideas, "heaven is in the sky, the ground is bush." From the point of view of heaven, the entire earth and the distinctions of its spatial hierarchy are of little value, for everywhere on earth is the bush and nothing related to the earth has ultimate human value.

The possession of such a heavenly point of view is crucial for Urapmin efforts to think productively about their current situation. Most pointedly, as I indicated above, it allows them to confront the problems left unaddressed by their ideas of development: those of the human marginality of their nation and their lack of ability autonomously to change their place within the earthly spatial hierarchy. Development leaves the first problematic, that of national identity, intact because even if it consists of having a company destroy their land and move them, they will still remain within Papua New Guinea. The destruction Jesus' Second Coming brings will be, by contrast, far more extensive – the entire earth will be destroyed and with it the national system that is such a key feature of its spatial hierarchy. By the time the Urapmin get to heaven, then, national identity will no longer define them, or anyone else, in any way. The second problematic, that of autonomy, is one that goes to the heart of Urapmin Christianity, and one could write about it at much greater length than I have space for here (see Robbins 2004). Suffice it to say for present purposes that probably the key feature of Urapmin charismatic Christianity is that it offers the Urapmin techniques for getting to heaven that they can deploy with no outside help. The presence of the Holy Spirit in their lives gives them the 'power' and 'knowledge' (save) they need to run their own heaven-bound 'Christian lives' (Kristin laip) without relying on any outside human expertise. In the development model, they cannot transform the bush into a fully human place without the help of a "company," a kind of entity they rightly feel themselves to be powerless to control. In the Christian model, by contrast, they assume primary responsibility for transforming themselves into beings fit to dwell in heaven, and the Holy Spirit is readily available to help them work consistently toward this end. On the basis of these features, heaven serves the Urapmin as a very elegant solution to the problem of the way the current earthly spatial hierarchy leaves them with diminished power to realize what they take to be the highest values of humanity.

It should be clear by now that the elegance of heaven as a solution to such problems of earthly hierarchy depends upon it being a distinct place, rather than a metaphor for a certain kind of human life on earth. If it were stripped of its spatial qualities, it would no longer resonate so perfectly with the Urapmin concern with the ways spatial hierarchy defines the human condition. It would cease to be good to think as a language for addressing earthly problems that most concretely present themselves to the Urapmin in terms of various kinds of places and the ranking that holds between them. It was for this reason that Rom was so upset over the prophet's claim that there was no heaven, only paradise on earth. Without the promise of a future that is elsewhere – that is, as it were, a foreign country in a world beyond all countries – Christianity would lose much of its appeal to people who like the Urapmin experience their current marginality most keenly in spatial terms.

Structure, agency, and future horizons

The Urapmin, like millenarians everywhere, live for the future. They live pitched forward, directing their energy not to a valued past but to a future they see as more valuable than anything that has come before. What does this heavy emphasis on the future mean for the way they make their lives? I am only capable of providing a couple of hints of an answer to this kind of question here, but in keeping with the core emphases of Siikala's work, I hope a few speculations along this line might provide a fitting conclusion to this chapter.

First, I want to take on an issue that arises not so much in the anthropological tradition of modeling the relation of structure and history to which Siikala has contributed, but rather in the literature on millenarian movements across the social sciences, another area of focus for him (as I mentioned above). It is often argued that millenarian ideas and the movements they spawn appeal to those who feel relatively deprived in this life and thus find in them imaginary compensations for what they currently lack (the classic formulation is Aberle 1970). One implication of this kind of analysis is that millenarianism renders its followers quietist and thus sustains them in their subservience to the earthly structures that create their marginality; with their eyes so firmly focused on heaven and its imaginary fulfillments, the argument goes, millenarians never effectively confront their earthly problems. Instead, they settle for the comforts of mere escapism.

I want to be careful to differentiate my analysis of the Urapmin concern for heaven from such an analysis. Urapmin ideas of heaven and of the requirements by way of belief and behavior one must meet to gain a place there do not so much feed escapist fantasies as they provide people with tools to reorganize their earthly lives through an emphasis on moral practice (Robbins 2004). Because the Urapmin believe that it is on earth that one must make oneself fit for heaven, and because they also assume everyone has at hand all the tools they need to succeed in this task, their millenarianism generates a good deal of earthly energy people use to fund the kinds of personal and institutional experimentation that transform cultural structures rather than in quietist fashion leave them untouched. While it is hard at this point to determine where these transformations will leave Urapmin culture in the future, it is worth noting that there are those working in other locales who see such future-oriented Christian practice as a spur to major worldly political changes (Martin 1990 is the most influential version of this argument), and as I document elsewhere, change in Urapmin has already been extensive (Robbins 2004). Although not conclusive, I hope these observations are enough to suggest that an intense cultural interest in the future does not of necessity render people effectively passive in the present.

But what of the influence of people's conception of the future on the issues of structure and history that motivated Siikala's focus on the past and the foreign in *'Akatokamanāva*? That is a second and final issue I want to take up briefly in this conclusion. Speaking in very rough terms, one might argue that the most widely accepted models of action in anthropology see people as pushed forward by existing structures. To the extent that this is true, history (in the form of pre-existing categories and values) becomes the ultimate source of motivation. In important respects, the most sophisticated versions of this kind of argument certainly are true. If we credit culture with any force at all, it must shape motivations and action in accordance with the legacy it carries forward from the past within itself. Furthermore, even the kind of future we are talking about here, the kind people project and use to orient action, is one that for any given group of people is defined by their culture and as such is effective in their shared present only inasmuch as it too is part of their tradition. So there is no question of using the concept of the future to somehow completely dislodge the model of structure and action that is central to the work of Siikala and many others.

Yet even in the face of that last point, there remains some question as to whether living for the future in radical and self-conscious terms might orient people to the structure-agency dialectic differently than living largely for the past or the present. Might not people who live for the future think differently about what Siikala (1991: 139) calls the "orientation of individual desire towards the objective structure" because the individual desire itself is culturally defined in a different way? Elsewhere I have argued that many (though not all) kinds of Christians desire to understand their lives in terms of valued discontinuities in the objective structures that guide them (Robbins In Press). They want to see their conversions as radical transformations that leave little of their old lives in place, and they scan the horizon for a coming apocalypse that will similarly reduce to dust the older earthly structures by which they have lived. Many moderns, drawing in part on the Christian inheritance of modernity, also relate to structures by trying to surpass them. My point is not that Christians or moderns actually do overcome the structures that shape their lives. No more than moderns, as Sahlins (1976, 1996) has shown, do future-oriented Christians like the Urapmin succeed in living outside of culture or in making the world anew on their own terms at each moment. But in ways anthropology cannot yet specify, their interest in the future and in discontinuity may lead them to pull history along in different ways than those who are self-consciously more attentive and responsive to its ever-present push.

REFERENCES

Aberle, David F. 1970. A note on relative deprivation theory as applied to millenarian and other cult movements. In: S.L. Thrupp, ed. *Millennial Dreams in Action*. New York: Schocken. Pp. 209–214.

Barth, Fredrik 1975. *Ritual and Knowledge among the Baktaman of New Guinea*. New Haven: Yale University Press.

Jacka, Jerry K. 2005. Emplacement and millennial expectations in an era of development and globalization: Heaven and the appeal of Christianity for the Ipili. *American Anthropologist* 107(4): 643–653.

Jebens, Holger 2005. *Pathways to Heaven: Contesting Mainline and Fundamentalist Christianity in Papua New Guinea*. New York: Berghahn.

Jorgensen, Dan 1981. Taro and Arrows: Order, Entropy, and Religion among the Telefolmin. Ph.D. Thesis, University of British Columbia.

Jorgensen, Dan 1996. Regional history and ethnic identity in the hub of New Guinea: The emergence of the Min. *Oceania* 66(3): 189–210.

Martin, David 1990. *Tongues of Fire: The Explosion of Protestantism in Latin America*. Oxford: Basil Blackwell.

Robbins, Joel 2003. Properties of nature, properties of culture: Possession, recognition, and the substance of politics in a Papua New Guinea society. *Journal of the Finnish Anthropological Society* (Suomen Antropologi) 28(1): 9–28.

Robbins, Joel 2004. *Becoming Sinners: Christianity and Moral Torment in a Papua New Guinea Society*. Berkeley: University of California Press.

Robbins, Joel 2007. Continuity thinking and the problem of Christian culture: Belief, time and the anthropology of Christianity. *Current Anthropology* 48(1): 5–38.

Russell, Jeffrey Burton 2006. *Paradise Mislaid: How We Lost Heaven – and How We Can Regain It*. New York: Oxford University Press.

Sahlins, Marshall 1976. *Culture and Practical Reason*. Chicago: University of Chicago Press.

Sahlins, Marshall 1996. The sadness of sweetness: The native anthropology of Western cosmology. *Current Anthropology* 37(3): 395–428.

Siikala, Jukka 1982. *Cult and Conflict in Tropical Polynesia: A Study of Traditional Religion, Christianity and Nativistic Movements*. Helsinki: Academia Scientiarum Fennica.

Siikala, Jukka 1991. *'Akatokamanāva: Myth, History and Society in the Southern Cook Islands*. Auckland: The Polynesian Society.

Siikala, Jukka 2004. Priests and prophets: The politics of voice in the Pacific. In: M.E. Harkin, ed. *Reassessing Revitalization Movements*. Lincoln: University of Nebraska Press. Pp. 88–103.

Islands without Horizons
Rivers, Rainforests, and Ancient Mariners

Peter Metcalf

> The canoe let its sailors visit not only east and west but also different
> sides of heaven, and opened up a world for its sailors to inhabit, that
> is, to form and to follow their habits (Siikala 2001:32)

A t the end of his introductory chapter in *We, the Tikopia*, Raymond Firth
allows himself a moment of lyricism in a book that is otherwise distinctly
sober-sided. It is not about the uncorrupted lifestyle of the Tikopians, or the
elegance of their social organization, or even the remarkable persistence
of their indigenous rituals. Instead, it is simply about the view from atop
Tikopia's only hill:

> In the evening the shades of the sea vary from a steely grey where the light is reflected
> on it through a pale green of the reef waters inshore to a darker green near the reef
> edge, and an indigo beyond. Sometimes when the sky is stormy the sea has a leaden
> hue of the same tone. On a lowering evening the stark staring white of the surf-line is
> in forcible, almost painful, contrast to the inky black of the sea, and then on a sunny
> day the water has a brilliant ultramarine shade. (Firth 1983: 29 [original 1936])

It is clear that Firth often slipped away to the loneliness of the hilltop, no
doubt to escape the pressure of incessant social interactions in the villages
below.

When I first discovered anthropology as an undergraduate at the University
of Auckland, I was entranced by Firth's vision – including his soulful
contemplation of the sea. I desperately wanted to share an experience like
his, and to a surprising degree I managed to do that. Firth's account of
Tikopian religion (1961, 1967, 1970) is the only one from all of Polynesia
based on firsthand observation of a functioning ritual system. All the rest of
the islands in that vast archipelago had become Christian long before. Half
a century after Firth arrived in Tikopia, I had the good fortune to stumble
onto an island of Malayo-Polynesian people who similarly held fast to their
indigenous religion, even when all around had converted. What I did not
manage to find was a place to escape, a hilltop with a view, because this
island was surrounded, not by sea, but by rainforest.

Islands in the rainforest

My "island" was a clearing perhaps 600 meters long by 200 wide, running along the banks of a river of about the same width, at a place called Long Teru. In this clearing stood one of those remarkable longhouses for which central Borneo is famous. In this case, it housed about 350 people. From outside, its most conspicuous feature was a steep-pitched, shingled, gable roof that ran the length of the building. A couple of meters below the eaves was a floor made of massive planks, as much as ten meters long and half a meter wide. The weight of this structure was supported on sturdy ironwood posts. Along the river side of the house ran an open veranda, the scene of all manner of communal activity, and on the landward side was a string of apartments, whose occupants maintained their own farms and rice stocks. Around this crowded, noisy space, the silent rainforest stretched away for miles in every direction. It took several hours by canoe to reach the next longhouse, upriver or down, and it is because of this isolation that I speak of longhouse communities as islands. Tikopia had almost four times the population, but divided between several villages, none of which rivaled the social density of the Long Teru longhouse. The main point, however, is that in both places there was a sense of being in a world sufficient unto itself. People knew little of what was going on elsewhere, and for the most part cared less. After a few months in the longhouse I had thoroughly absorbed this attitude, and the outside world seemed remote and inconsequential. I might have written an ethnography called *We, The Long Teru*.

Under these circumstances it is not surprising that Long Teru people resented the casual assertion by outsiders – government officials visiting from the coast, for instance – that they lived *in* the jungle. They no more lived in the jungle than the Tikopia lived in the sea. They were not wild animals – or wild people like the foraging Penan – but rather residents of a metropolis that was the essence of everything civilized. The impression of superior breeding was confirmed by the bad manners of coastal people, who would often stride about inside the longhouse as if they were indeed in the jungle. Well-mannered people knew better than to stand threatening over those seated sociably on the longhouse veranda. They knew to approach modestly, crouching with their hands between their knees. This was the first lesson I learned in the longhouse, and without benefit of language. I understood their shocked glances to say clearly enough: was this boy raised in a barn?

The edge of the forest may have been only a few meters away, but it constituted a distinct categorical boundary. For instance, that was where the souls of the recently dead hovered. As I have explained elsewhere (1982), after "loss of breath," human souls slowly transform themselves into benign ancestral spirits, the guardians of the community. In the interim, however, they are unable to find a place either in the community of the living or the dead. In this liminal condition, they may become jealous, and drag others along to share their fate. The rites designed to avoid this outcome lasted all night for many days, during which the veranda was lit brightly with pressure lanterns. Those sitting on the veranda to keep the vigil could see the light dimly reflected off the damp leaves at the forest's edge.

This is not to suggest, however, that the boundary was really that distinct, or that the forest itself inspired dread. Small gardens were strung out along the levee at both ends of the longhouse, and paths led off into the forest here and there. Men frequently went hunting with spears and dogs, seeking deer or wild boar. Often the chase would lead them off in unexpected directions, and hunters frequently got lost. Unperturbed, they would retrace their path, or if that failed, follow streams down to the main river. What they could not do, however, was look around for a fixed point of reference. No landmarks, no prominent hill, not even a view of the stars to navigate by. At the turn of the century the colonial officer most responsible for the "pacification" of the region, Charles Hose, decided to explore the mountains that rise spectacularly along the banks of the middle reaches of the river Tinjar. (Long Teru is located lower down the same river.) He struggled up to the top, discovering along the way a waterfall that he named after his wife, but when he got there, he was cheated of the expansive view that he had expected to find. Instead, there was the forest canopy high above his head just as before, and no way to climb up far enough to see out (Hose 1927: 163–172).

Claustrophobia and cathedrals

Within a rainforest, there are no horizons. In tangled jungle, visibility may be no more than a few yards, and for most Westerners this conjures frightening images of being helplessly hemmed in. Early explorers in Southeast Asia made much of their ordeals, fighting their way through fetid, pathless jungle (King 1995). No doubt there was some mythic heightening in this – local guides would surely have avoided such places. Nevertheless, they did sometimes want to go where indigenous people did not, like Hose struggling up his mountain. Moreover, there are less dramatized accounts, such as those of British soldiers during the "Emergency" in the Malay peninsula, cutting their way through dense jungle in search of the camps of communist guerillas (O'Balance 1966). They report that sometimes they could keep a line of march only by taking a compass bearing on a tree perhaps ten meters away, hacking their way through to it, and then sighting again. It might take a week to travel twenty kilometers.

The mature rainforests of Borneo were not this impassable, however. Where the massive trees soared fifty meters into the air, the canopy cut out almost all direct sunlight below. Most animal life was up there, and one might walk a long way without seeing any near the ground. Walking was possible because the forest floor, though muddy, was covered only with flimsy bushes and creepers. The effect often inspires religious analogies: the quiet, the gloom, the coolness, and above all the massive boles of the trees, as straight as any stone columns, can hardly fail to bring to mind the interior of a cathedral. I remember one occasion when heavy rains caused flooding all along the valley of the Tinjar. The water was almost up to the floorboards of the longhouse, and people had canoes tied up directly to the veranda railings, ready to escape to higher ground. When it finally stopped raining, it was possible to paddle off into the still-flooded rainforest, and drift amongst the massive trees, the water strangely illuminated as if from an inner glow. Years later I visited the temple of Karnak at Luxor, and entering the hypostyle hall, with its massive, closely-packed columns, I was immediately carried back to that flooded forest. There was no claustrophobic feeling at all, yet all one could see in any direction was columns.

A world to inhabit

This illusion of an enormous building, softly lit by diffuse light, makes it obvious why geographical space in central Borneo is not indigenously oriented by the cardinal directions of north, south, east, and west. As Robert Blust notes (1997:39–40), for the ancestral Indo-European speakers, herding their livestock across open plains, the most obvious directional markers were sunrise and sunset. By contrast, the equivalent terms in Proto-Malayo-Polynesian reflect a seafaring mode of life in Southeast Asia: *habaRat, 'west/north-west monsoon,' and *timuR, 'east/south-east monsoon.' These terms also have little application in central Borneo. Sailing is unknown, and impractical on the rivers. Moreover, local weather conditions have more to do with the diurnal cycle of cloud formation over the jungle than anything happening out at sea.

In addition to the monsoon winds, Proto-Malayo-Polynesian has two other orienting features: *lahud, 'downriver,' 'towards the sea,' and *daya, 'upriver,' 'towards the interior.' These clearly *do* apply in Borneo. Indeed, the latter is often used as an ethnic label. In the nineteenth century "Dayak" came to be the word used by Europeans to describe all the peoples of the interior. Across northern Sarawak there is a broad band of communities that describe themselves as "Upriver People," though they use the local Malay lingua franca to express it: Orang Ulu (*orang* meaning 'people' or 'person,' *ulu* meaning 'upriver'). One element of the Orang Ulu, however, call themselves Lun Dayeh (*lun* meaning 'people' or 'person' in their language or languages). So the Lun Dayeh are upriver people three times over. Such redundancies are found across Southeast Asia, but the ethnic labels of northern Sarawak are particularly tangled (Metcalf 2002: 77–108).

Blust refers to all these terms as aspects of "macro-orientation," distinguishing them from another set of terms such as "inside," "outside," "above," and "below," that constitute "micro-orientations." The latter clearly refer to a "field of reference" that is more homely than the monsoon winds, and Blust's account of them in Proto-Malayo-Polynesian is neatly matched by terms used at Long Teru, most obviously in connection with the longhouse itself. However, there are significant contexts that transfer terms between macro- and micro- levels of spatial reference. For example, one end of the longhouse is referred to as the "upriver" end, as contrasted, of course, with the "downriver" end. From the site of Long Teru, the headwaters of the Tinjar

River lie to the south, but the longhouse lies along a roughly east-west axis. This in itself need cause no confusion, since everyone understands that the upriver end of the longhouse is identified by the direction of flow of the river directly in front of the longhouse, and in full view from the veranda. Since the river is flowing from east to west in this particular stretch, the eastern end is the upriver one, and vice-versa.

If one steps outside the longhouse, however, things become more complicated.

Along the riverbank in front of the longhouse are a number of small docks, mostly consisting of logs or whole tree trunks brought downriver during high waters. It is no easy business to capture these logs, since no mere canoe could pull them out of the flood, and it is necessary somehow to attach a line from onshore and then nudge them sideways. Or sometimes some back eddy will bring great bulks of timber, often weighing many tons, charging unbidden towards the longhouse, and their impact can cause major damage. All-in-all, major inundations are exciting times in the longhouse, but they seldom occur more than once a year. Most of the time the river stays within its banks, sometimes higher, sometimes lower, according to rainfall. It rains almost every evening as the day cools somewhat and the diurnal clouds release their moisture, but local rains have almost no effect on the level of the river. Consequently, at such times men will look earnestly "upriver," trying to make out whether the storm clouds are particularly black, and whether lightning can be seen stabbing through them. When they do this, they look towards the mountains, to the south. A man might then instruct his son to move his canoe closer into the bank, in case of rising water. It is at the upriver end, he might say, nodding towards the east.

Moreover, the contrast upriver/downriver (at Long Teru, *krai* and *king* respectively) implies another: inland, i.e. 'away from the river' (*kelajji*) and 'riverward,' or 'towards the river' (*keliko*). All of these terms can be used as verbs, so *krai* means 'to go upriver' as well as simply 'upriver,' and so on. There is a verb 'to go,' regardless of direction (*puloo*), but it is surprising how often the verbs incorporating direction are preferred, even in a localized context. In a land of waterways, however, running the gamut from tiny streams to mighty rivers, choosing the appropriate context can be challenging. Hunting deer and wild pigs, for instance, usually involves "going inland," at least to begin. Once the dogs have located game, however, the chase may lead in any direction, and shouted instructions fly back and forth between the hunters. But did "going upriver" refer to the Tinjar, now far out of sight, or the rivulet we just splashed through? Or are we working our way along a sidestream whose general direction is familiar to the hunters?

It is not at all unlikely that hunters will find themselves disoriented when the chase ends, successful or otherwise. On such occasions, I have seen experienced men point in opposite directions as "towards the river." They laughed about it, but neither was keen on spending the night in the jungle. The expedient of following a stream is a last resort, because there is no knowing how far "back" (*lum*, 'in' or 'inside' – one of Blust's micro-orientation terms) into the forests it will go before circling back towards the Tinjar. It could take days to get home, and sometimes does. As evening comes on, the direction of the sunset may be clear, but that is little help since the hunters have no idea of the direction they traveled during the chase, in terms of compass bearings. At such times, some tricky decisions have to be made.

Vikings of the Borneo sunrise

What is not tricky, however, is navigating *along* the rivers. That is to say, even where negotiating rapids is difficult, finding the way is not. Rivers have the same quality as roads – all you need to do is follow them. Consequently, no one has ever seen any need for the kind of research into indigenous navigation that has been such an exciting aspect of Polynesian studies, starting with Sir Peter Buck's pioneering synthesis (1938). Since then we have seen theories of accidental voyages replaced by sophisticated assessments of the sailing qualities of Polynesian canoes and the resources of their navigators, concluding with computer simulations of techniques of exploration infinitely more sophisticated than simply heading off in a new direction at random (Haddon and Hornell 1936–1938, Sharp 1956, Levinson, Ward, and Webb 1973, Irwin 1980).

Nevertheless, Orang Ulu were and are canoe people. Some years ago, I asked Bob Blust to estimate for me a date upon which the Austronesian-speaking ancestors of the people in that corner of Borneo arrived. Blust's concerns were with comparative, not historical, linguistics, and his meticulous research and brilliant analysis in the 1970s have been invaluable to me over the years. Briefly, Blust found that all the languages spoken in the watershed of the Baram, of which the Tinjar is a tributary, belong to the same subgroup, which he labels "North Sarawak." Note that this constitutes dozens of languages and dialects, spread out over a large area. There is also an important exception: Kayan. This is significant for ethnohistory, but need not concern us here. We might also note that all the languages of Borneo belong to the Western Austronesian branch, and that no traces have been identified of the NAN languages that must have been spoken across the island for the millennia of human occupation prior to the arrival of Malayo-Polynesian people.

For present purposes, the point is that the speakers of proto-North Sarawak arrived on the coast near the mouth of the Baram River approximately 3,000 years ago. The navigational skills they needed to reach this point from the original Austronesian homeland, wherever its exact location, were clearly not so demanding as those required to cross the vast expanses of the Pacific. Even so, they must have been competent seamen with sturdy vessels, probably with outriggers, such as are found throughout the Indonesian archipelago. From the mouth of the Baram they traveled east, towards the sunrise, switching to simpler paddling canoes along the way. This loss of seagoing skills was not, of course, unique to settlers in Borneo. As Patrick Kirch shows (1984:

82), by AD 1000, long-range voyaging in Polynesia virtually ceased, and oceangoing canoes were replaced by smaller ones suitable for only local journeys. All knowledge of sailing disappeared in New Zealand, which constitutes by far the largest islands in Polynesia, if still only a fraction of the size of Borneo.

The distribution of North Sarawak languages, particularly all the many varieties of Kenyah, show that the settlers traveled right across the island. In crossing the central mountain range, they must have walked between the headwaters of rivers on opposite sides, either dragging their canoes or building new ones on the other side. How long it took them to do that, however, is a mystery. No serious archaeology has been conducted in interior Borneo, and it is hard to see how it ever will be, since living sites close to rivers are infamously prone to erosion. When Westerners first encountered Upriver People in the Baram watershed during the mid-nineteenth century, they were generally moving west, evidently attracted by new opportunities for trade with the coast (Metcalf 2001). Oral histories reach back at most another century or two before that, which leaves more than two millennia unaccounted for. Had there been previous oscillations between coast and interior? Or had people moved around the interior in a kind of Brownian motion, bouncing off one another like billiard balls? We simply have no way of knowing.

What is unlikely is that populations simply sat where they were for a couple of millennia. We know that large population movements occurred before contact, not simply between coast and interior, but between different regions in the interior. There is no reason to suppose that they had not done so before.

Islands, ethnicities, and laboratories

There is a further possibility, involving neither oscillating nor rebounding, but fusion. My "island" in the rainforest was not geographically anchored in the way that Firth's Tikopia was. In general, identifying ethnicities in Polynesia is simply a matter of naming islands. Wherever Tahitians came from, there was no doubt at contact who the Tahitians were, and the same applies to all the other islands and island groups. Certainly, there continued to be movement, for instance in the phenomenon that Marshall Sahlins (1985: 73–103) describes as "stranger kings," but this is trivial compared to the incessant movement in the Borneo rainforests. Longhouse communities are mobile, in general relocating about once in every generation. This movement is usually attributed to the demands of slash-and-burn agriculture, but there is more to it than that. To start with, the terrain is far from uniform. On the contrary, there are only scattered niches suitable for farming, that is, with alluvial soils, but not prone to flooding – or at least not every year. These niches often constitute the valleys of tiny tributaries, whose secondary growth has been cut many times throughout several generations by families who are neighbors in the longhouse. The longhouse site may be moved repeatedly, whenever an old structure falls into disrepair, without the farmlands of its inhabitants changing much at all. Most communities, however, also have histories of migrations to different rivers or river systems, in response to the overall geopolitical situation. Each such movement has a knock-on effect, but ethnic groups do not simply replace one another. Instead, they become dispersed and mixed with others, which later fragment into new combinations (Metcalf 2002: 77–108).

It follows that Borneo does not provide the kind of "laboratory" that many ethnographers and archaeologists have seen in Polynesia. On the first page of his study of *The Evolution of the Polynesian Chiefdoms*, Kirch sets out his objective "to dissect the several major processes that underlie the transformations of the various Polynesian societies from their common ancestor" (1984: ix). The proposition is that immigrants arrived with a uniform culture, including technologies and ideas about rank, and that this Ancestral Polynesian Society then developed along a different path on each island or island group, virtually without contact with any other. In this, Kirch followed the approach of Marshall Sahlins (1958) a generation earlier, incorporating all that had been learned in the interim.

Nothing of this applies in central Borneo. There are several linguistic cohesions other than North Sarawak, each implying a different group of settlers, perhaps at different epochs and with different cultural repertoires. Moreover, influences from outside Borneo continued to have major impacts. For instance, rice agriculture did not arrive with the first Malayo-Polynesian settlers, and the process of its subsequent introduction and spread is far from clear. Trade in jungle produce is even older than rice agriculture, and the manufactured goods imported from India and China, such as ceramics and glass beads, play a crucial role in legitimizing rank. In the face of such volatility there can be no study of independent lines of social evolution, and ethnicity, far from being self-evident, becomes the central issue – and a thorny one at that.

Different sides of heaven

Of the maritime origins of Upriver People there is one faint echo: the dead travel downriver towards the sea. This journey is recounted in song cycles that are performed as part of funerary rituals, and indeed the most sacred part. At Long Teru, the crucial song lasts all night on the final day of the funeral, before the corpse is finally removed from the longhouse and taken to the graveyard. It starts by instructing the dead person to get up, to bathe, to equip a canoe with the necessary gear, and then to set off downriver. After that, the instructions take on the format of travel directions, each verse naming a sidestream on the way down the Tinjar, and then the main Baram. Tiny streams too small to have names are pointed out under the generic label Long Bec, and every few verses the deceased is urged to paddle vigorously. This continues all night, but the phantom canoe never does quite reach the sea. Just before that, the deceased is instructed to paddle close along the northern shore of the estuary, and there to find a large river that is invisible to the living. This river leads directly to the longhouse of the ancestors, and rapidly too, since the singers of the death songs do not know the names of the side streams along it.

That the journey is riverine is no surprise; after all one can hardly walk to the land of the dead. More surprisingly, heaven itself is just another watershed. In his collected ethnographic notes, as edited by William McDougall, Charles Hose provides a map of heaven showing the residence of ancestors and deities (Hose and McDougall 1912:II:43).

Indeed, all foreign countries are understood in terms of rivers. I was often asked to name and describe the major rivers of America, and was hard put to answer. I did explain that sometimes the rivers there turned to stone – that being the only way that I could explain ice. (*Ayer batu*, 'stone water' in Malay.) This set them clucking in amazement, and no doubt some thought it was a tall story. On another occasion I showed them a picture of Manhattan, with the Hudson flowing alongside. The skyscrapers I explained as longhouses stood on end. But where, they asked, are all their farms? Surely with so many longhouses at one site, people must have to paddle miles up the Hudson to get to them.

Opening up a world

Living beside major rivers has many advantages. People at Long Teru like to bathe several times a day, and at sunrise and sunset the rafts in front of the house are always crowded with people. It is counted a great hardship not to be able to swim and splash each day, as sometimes happened at the farms when the weather had been dry and the sidestreams well away from the main river were low. Children are in and out of the water all day, and are often warned to stay inside a half circle of bamboos set into the riverbottom next to the bank. This is a defense against crocodiles, not because they could not penetrate the barrier, but because the movement of the bamboos would give warning of their presence.

In addition to the luxury of bathing, the river in front of the longhouse opens up a vista that relieves any sense of being enclosed in the jungle clearing that comprised my "island." The open side of the longhouse looks out over the river, through a screen of betel nut palms along the bank, and when people are sitting quietly on the veranda they are always looking out over the river. By comparison, the view from the kitchens at the back of the house is drab and gloomy. From the riverbank at Long Teru, the Tinjar is about two hundred yards across, and one can see perhaps half a mile upstream and down – still no great distance in comparison to Firth's view from atop the hill in Tikopia, but enough to open up a large area of sky.

This view of the sky also provides the frame, literally, for calling the major omen bird, *plake* (the Malaysian black eagle, *Ictinaetus malayensis*). In the words of an augur:

However small the window of sky,
Of bright sky in front of me,
>   Spirit of Eagle,
That is where you show your feathers, show your pinions,
>   You Spirit of Eagle.
Even if no bigger than a winnowing basket, a cutting board,
>   The blue sky, the azure sky,
>>   The bright sky, the radiant sky,
>>>   In front of me,
>>>>   Spirit of Eagle,
>>   That is where you,
>>>   Show your feathers, show your pinions.

Within this frame, *plake* gives omens by flying in the direction requested by the augur, or by failing to do so. This furnishes another set of verbs of motion, neither macro-oriented nor micro-oriented, in Blust's terminology. Instead, they are oriented to the sky view of the augur. The best possible outcome is for the bird, having answered the call, first to 'fly left,' *ngabeng*, then 'right,' *ulong*. Appropriately enough, the second term is an inflection of *mulong*, 'to live.' Any other result is less encouraging. If the bird flies away, or off at an angle (*ngabut*), no positive outcome is likely. If it should fly across the heads of the augur and other onlookers (*mupok*), then, disaster is unavoidable (Metcalf 1989: 184–213). The world that this view opens up is nothing less than heaven, since *plake* carries messages directly from the Creator Spirit, *Bili Ngaputong*.

Highways into the interior

There is one section of the upper Tinjar where the river runs along the bottom of a ridge of mountains, the Dulit range. It could hardly be described as straight, but its curves are constrained by the mountain rearing up along its left bank. From the river it is possible to see much further than is normally the case, as at Long Teru for instance. Not only are the Dulits themselves clearly visible, but also the central mountain chain that divides the Malaysian side of Borneo (Sarawak) from the Indonesian (Kalimantan). It is as beautiful a place as I know, and almost compensates for the absence of Firth's sea view.

The view along the valley of the Tinjar reinforces a general impression that rivers, like highways, generally lead in one overall direction. They may of course wind, but the traveler need pay no attention to that. Driving a canoe with an outboard motor, one expects to bear first left, then right, advancing in a sinuous manner, but nevertheless steadily. There are exceptions. Sometimes, but unusually enough, a river may flow straight over some distance. Alternatively, when rivers enter the coastal plain their loops can be so convoluted that a boat spends almost as much time traveling away from its destination as towards it.

MAP 1
Viewed from the coast

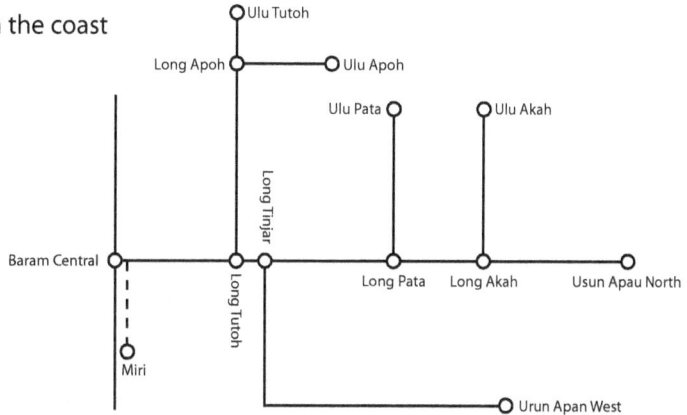

There is a section of the lower Baram where you travel for an hour or so on one of the Chinese launches that haul freight upriver only to arrive almost back where you started, with the river on the other side of a narrow neck clearly in view. The river will in the end break through, leaving another of the great oxbow lakes that are characteristic of the lowlands.

Upriver People seldom comment on the differential windingness of rivers. After all, the traveler is simply going 'upriver' (*krai* in the terminology of Long Teru), and that is that. That being the case, I often wondered if there were a schematized map of the Baram watershed in their minds not unlike the famous one of the London tube system. (The New York subway or the Paris metro will do just as well.) That was certainly how I understood it when I was first finding my way around, using whatever river transport I could find. The advantage of such maps is clarity, which makes them a useful *aide mémoire*. The problem is that they distort geography, or at least geography as Westerners understand it. Tube stations that appear to be far apart are actually close together, and vice versa. Consequently, even for riverine people cheerfully traveling "upriver," there is a price to pay.

MAP 2
Viewed from the interior

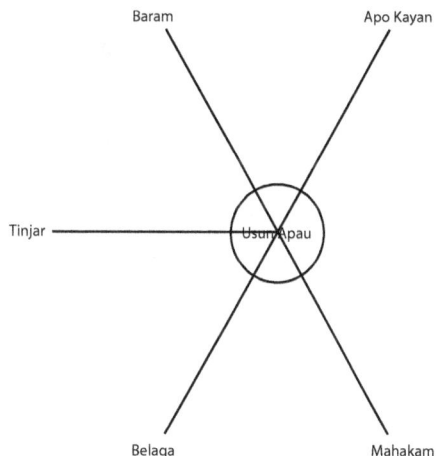

The problem with my idea was, of course, that I was imposing my schematized map, rather than looking for theirs. When I did that, I came up with a different one. The majority of Upriver People have stories of migrations into the Baram watershed that begin in or near an elevated plateau of eroded limestone just to the west of the central massif, called the Usun Apau. As we saw above, this can only be a recent homeland, not an ancient origin, but it now exists as the furthest limit of oral history. From there, the stories tell, they descended at various times down the rivers that flow out of the Usun Apau, principally the Baram, Tinjar, and Belaga. The last of these does not appear on my schematic map because it belongs to a different watershed entirely, joining the mighty Rejang which meets the sea far away to the southwest of the mouth of the Baram. Upriver People in the Baram district are also aware of two large rivers flowing away to the east and southeast, the Apo Kayan and the Mahakam. These rivers do not in fact arise on the slopes of the Usun Apau, but on the east-facing side of the central mountain range. Such details, however, are not what schematic maps are made of.

This mental atlas – as I assume it to be – does better than mine, in that it makes the Usun Apau a hub, rather than a sprawling region. In terms of ethnohistory, it is important to grasp that the headwaters of all these rivers are sufficiently close together that it is no great matter to walk, or sometimes even portage, from one to another. For me, the Belaga valley seemed very remote. To get there required traveling downriver, then along the coast, then up another very long river. Thought of in those terms, the ethnic diversities and cohesions that I found in Baram made no sense. Meanwhile, there are certainly distortions involved in the schematized map implied in the migration stories I collected, ones that that would be seriously problematic for the people on the Kalimantan side of the mountains. On the Sarawak side, however, they were an effective aid to people not equipped with cadastral maps.

The Upriver People used to live upriver

As a final note, I will point out that I have abused the conventions of the ethnographic present in this description. The Long Teru longhouse no longer exists. It was burnt down in 1998, but it was by then almost abandoned anyway. This was part of a wider tragedy, the overall features of which are well-known. Beginning in the eighties, and gathering momentum through the nineties, the rainforests of central Borneo were devastated by industrial logging on a massive scale. Huge fortunes were made by Asian capitalists and corrupt politicians, and wealth was squandered that might have funded steady economic development for generations. Meanwhile, longhouse people followed the logging camps as they ate their way across the landscape, or moved down to the coast to live in shanty towns. Having finally moved irrevocably into a cash economy, they found that they were poor in ways they had never been before.

In the process, people from different longhouse communities were thrown together. Their identity as Upriver People was strengthened, even as their ties to home communities were loosened. The languages of smaller ethnicities began to disappear, and their individual migration stories with them. They were replaced by a heavily truncated but shared account. The Upriver People came from the Usuan Apau – simply that. The effect was to reinforce mental map number 2 (see diagram), and make its distortions irrelevant. Young people born in the cities knew little more about the interior than was contained in it.

There was, however, another tendency, one that viewed Borneo from the outside in, as I had done when I first arrived there (map 1). On one occasion I was sitting in a coffee shop in Miri talking to some teenagers, when I mentioned some Kenyah people that I had met in a small bazaar on the Belaga River. They were surprised to hear that there were Kenyah in so distant a place, far away in the headwaters of the Rejang.

Horizons without islands

My urge to find an island of my own would now be distinctly atavistic. There are a vanishingly small number of places in the world where it would now make any sense to see communities in this way, and central Borneo is not one of them. The wholesale destruction of the rainforest, plus the familiar processes of entry into a cash economy, migration in search of work, penetration of the media, and so on, have obliterated the longhouse societies that I knew in the 1970s. One of Jukka Siikala's major contributions, however, has been to emphasize the mobility of many societies long before the modern era. This is, of course, a phenomenon entirely familiar to archaeologists, but it seems to have escaped the notice of contemporary theorists in cultural anthropology and other disciplines anxious to identify the essence of "modernity." For students of Polynesia, the integration of linguistic and historical data into accounts of cultural diversity has always been an obvious move, and it is in that sense that Polynesia has provided a "laboratory."

In other parts of the Malayo-Polynesian world, however, the laboratory has been a much less tidy one. The island of Borneo covers many times the area of all the islands of Polynesia put together, and it has no internal natural boundaries. Canoe voyages lead into the interior or away from it with equal ease, regardless of prevailing winds. The mountains constitute not so much an obstacle as a hub of transportation. There is no hope of reconstructing pre-historic migrations in all their complexity, with peoples moving back and forth and contingents hiving off here and there. Our view of the past is limited to that of oral history, a couple of centuries at the most. Meanwhile – and this also follows from Jukka Siikala's arguments – these migrations have everything to do with the evanescent quality of ethnicity in Borneo.

REFERENCES

Blust, Robert 1972. Report of linguistic fieldwork undertaken in Sarawak. *Borneo Research Bulletin* 4: 12–14.

Blust, Robert 1997. Semantic change and the conceptualization of spatial relationships in austronesian languages. In: Gunter Senft (ed.) *Referring to Space: Studies in Austronesian and Papuan Languages.* Oxford: Clarendon. Pp. 39–52.

Buck, Sir Peter 1938. *Vikings of the Sunrise.* New Zealand: Whitcombe and Tombs.

Firth, Raymond 1936. *We, the Tikopia.* London: Allen and Unwin.

Firth, Raymond 1961. *History and Traditions of Tikopia.* Wellington, NZ: Polynesian Society.

Firth, Raymond 1967. *The Work of the Gods in Tikopia.* London: Athlone.

Firth, Raymond 1970. *Rank and Religion in Tikopia.* London: Allen and Unwin.

Haddon, Alfred Cort and J. Hornell 1936–1938. *The Canoes of Oceania*, Vol. 1–3. Bernice Pauahi Bishop Museum Special Publications nos. 27, 28 and 29. Honolulu: Bishop Museum.

Hose, Charles 1927. *Fifty Years of Romance and Research, Or, A Jungle-Wallah at Large.* London: Hutchinson.

Hose, Charles & William McDougall 1912. *Pagan Tribes of Borneo.* 2 Volumes. London: McMillan & Co., Ltd.

Irwin, Geoffrey 1980. The prehistory of Oceania: Colonisation and cultural change. In: A. Sherratt (ed.) *The Cambridge Encyclopedia of Archaeology.* Cambridge: Cambridge University Press. Pp. 324–332.

King, Victor (ed.) 1995. *Explorers of South-East Asia: Six Lives.* Kuala Lumpur: Oxford University Press.

Kirch, Patrick 1984. *The Evolution of the Polynesian Chiefdoms.* Cambridge: Cambridge University Press.

Levinson, M, R. G. Ward and J. W. Webb 1973. *The Settlement of Polynesia: A Computer Simulation.* Minneapolis: University of Minneapolis.

Metcalf, Peter 1989. *Where are YOU/SPIRITS: Style and Theme in Berawan Prayer.* Washington D.C.: Smithsonian Institution Press.

Metcalf, Peter 2001. Diaspora vs. Volkenwanderung: The Orang Ulu apparition. In: Jukka Siikala (ed.) Departures: *How Societies Distribute Their People.* Helsinki: Finnish Anthropological Society. Pp. 46–66.

Metcalf, Peter 2002. *They Lie, We Lie: Getting on with Anthropology.* London: Routledge.

O'Balance, Edgar 1966. *Malaya: The Communist Insurgency War 1948–1960.* London: Faber and Faber.

Sahlins, Marshall 1958. *Social Stratification in Polynesia.* Seattle: American Ethnological Society.

Sahlins, Marshall 1985. *Islands of History.* Chicago: University of Chicago Press.

Sharp, Andrew 1956. *Ancient Voyagers in the Pacific.* Wellington, NZ: Polynesian Society.

Siikala, Jukka 2001. Tilling the soil and sailing the seas: Cadastral maps and anthropological interpretations. In: Jukka Siikala (ed.) *Departures: How Societies Distribute their People.* Helsinki: Finnish Anthropological Society. Pp. 22–45.

Mystery and the Mundane

Shifting Perspectives in a Saribas Iban Ritual Narrative

Clifford Sather

Introduction

During the great Gawai Betawai, the most complex of all the curing rituals performed by Saribas Iban shamans, a troupe of *manang*s relates in song the journey of a pair of spirit-bats, Bachelors Entawai and Kusing, as they fly from the earth to the upperworld. This occurs roughly midway through the ritual. Their mission, as described in the songs, is to summon the upperworld god Menjaya, 'Lord of Shamans' (*Raja Manang*), so that he may descend to the longhouse below where the *manang*s are singing and assist them in curing a human patient by means of his invisible presence and the powerful medicines he is believed to bring with him.

In the opening stages of the Gawai Betawai, before the *manang*s begin to sing, a wooden dais (*meligai*) must first be erected by the men of the longhouse over the summit of the longhouse roof (*perabung rumah*). Surrounding this dais, ritual ikat cloths are hung to attract the gaze of Menjaya and his celestial and spirit-shaman companions as, later on, invoked by the shamans' songs, they descend to this world. Here, shortly before their arrival, during the final phases of the ritual, the shamans, climbing by ladder, lay out elaborate offerings of glutinous rice, cooked meat, sweets, fruit, and rice wine for the enjoyment of the arriving host of spirits and gods.

Continuing with the story of the bat-messengers, to reach the upperworld, Entawai and Kusing must first cross a major cosmic divide described in the songs as the *jerit langit* or *jerit tisau langit*, literally, 'the horizon,' or, more poetically, 'the furthest bounds of the sky' (Richards 1981: 128).[1] This divide is characterized as an 'empty void' (*menua puang*) which is likened in the song's imagery to a 'vast uninhabited forest' (*kampung raya*) that is said to separate the earthly world below (*dunya tu'*, lit., 'this world') from the upperworld or 'sky' (*langit*) above. The latter is described, in turn, as

---

1 'Horizon' in its primary, conventional sense of "the line or circle that forms the apparent boundary between earth and sky" (*Random House Webster's College Dictionary*, 2001: 635).

covering over, or enveloping, the earth's surface like the circular lid of a rice storage bin (*tibang*).

What is on the other side of this divide is, for the Iban, a genuine mystery, in the sense that no human being is able to cross this horizon, and so enter into and perceive directly what goes on in the upperworld. It is therefore a realm beyond ordinary human experience. Confined to the earth's surface, human beings can only perceive obscuring clouds and what appear to be vast empty spaces. Even Iban shamans, or, more precisely, their *semengat*, or 'souls,' cannot cross the *jerit langit*, although, in ordinary healing rituals, they freely cross other cosmic divides, including that which separates the living world (again, *dunya tu'*) from the realm of the dead (*menua Sebayan*). Hence, in the songs, the spirit-bats are called upon to act as messengers and perform this journey which the *manang*s themselves cannot undertake.

Given all of this, the songs that immediately follow are remarkable. The mystery posed by what exists on the other side of this horizon is at once banished by means of familiar images of the mundane. In short, there is no mystery at all. The longhouse in which Menjaya lives is portrayed as essentially identical in every respect to the longhouse in which the *manang*s are singing and the way in which the spirit-bats approach and enter it is the same as would be followed by any ordinary Iban traveler. Why should a world beyond ordinary experience be portrayed in commonplace terms?

In an earlier essay (Sather 2001b: 159–169), I briefly discussed the Gawai Betawai and, in particular, this part of the ritual's songs in which the spirit-bats fly to the upperworld and meet the god Menjaya. My more general purpose in that paper was to explore the ways in which Saribas Iban shamans, through their rites of healing, not only import distant landscapes into a familiar longhouse setting, but, through their frequent ritual departures and travels, project local agency outward and so make the invisible other worlds they frequent a part of everyday Iban landscapes.

The book in which this essay appeared, *Departures*, was the product of a research project initiated by Jukka Siikala, and I am especially grateful to Jukka for drawing my attention to something else – which we have just now touched upon – namely, to the fact that, paradoxically, "the structure of these [invisible other worlds as] seen by ritual specialists reminds us very much of the ordinary world around the longhouse" (Siikala 2001: 5). In other words, the imperceptible is not only represented by features drawn from the familiar world, but is itself depicted at times in essentially identical terms.

In this essay, I want to pursue this point. Clearly, to begin with, it raises questions about the nature of ritual imagery. For example, why in ritual is the mysterious, as here, sometimes evoked by using the language of the ordinary? And, inversely, why is the ordinary and everyday sometimes mystified? What are the effects of this reversal of seeming opposites? In addition, this same point raises questions about the nature of shamanism. If shamans, as ritual specialists, are concerned with relations between humans and nonhuman others, how are these relations portrayed and acted upon through the use of contrasting images of mystery and the familiar? By way of framing these questions, I begin with a general discussion of ritual imagery and the role of

Iban shamans as intercessors between humans and nonhumans. I then return to a more detailed look at the Gawai Betawai itself, suggesting how mystery and the mundane are combined in its performance in ways that both reveal and alter the relationships of its participants, both human and nonhuman, with one another and with the world of everyday experience.

Ritual Imagery: Mystification and the Mundane

If, as Stephen Lansing (1983: 81) insists, the aim of Balinese priests is "to mystify with illusion," then clearly Iban shamans, at least in this particular instance, aim at something very different. In this connection, Gilbert Lewis' warning in his classic introduction to the *Day of Shining Red* seems particularly appropriate. After noting that ritual characteristically focuses our attention in ways that often invite us to see things in unfamiliar ways, Lewis (1980: 31) goes on to stress that, despite this, "the anthropologist is not free to assume that everything occurring in ritual aims at mystery and has many meanings." While, for certain purposes, ritual may, indeed, aim to "disconcert, confuse or fascinate," its object may equally well be "clarity, overt meaning and lack of ambiguity" (1980: 31).

In the chapter containing this warning, "Problems of Ritual in General," Lewis notes that all efforts to define ritual and set it apart from other kinds of behavior have failed because ritual is not, in fact, a kind of behavior, but is, rather, an aspect of behavior, one generally identified most especially with its expressive, symbolic, or communicating aspect. But, here we must recognize, Lewis (1980: 6) adds, that oftentimes "the people who perform these behaviours cannot put into words what they express, symbolise, or try to communicate by them." Moreover, expressiveness, by itself, is not enough to distinguish ritual since most behavior has expressive elements. Thus, Lewis (1980: 8) additionally singles out what he calls ritual's "peculiar fixity." To a greater or lesser degree, those who perform rituals assume that there exist explicit rules which, if followed, result in a correct and effective ritual performance. From this, Lewis argues that what is clear and explicit about rituals is the notion that fixed rules exist that govern how they should be done, not what they mean or why they are done. The existence of these rules introduces an element of constraint into the flow of everyday life that produces what Lewis calls an "alerting quality," signaling to those involved that they have entered a special arena in which words, gestures, and actions may have a significance they would not otherwise have (1980: 25).

But how are we to grasp this special significance? While words may be, and frequently are, a major component of ritual, this does not mean that this significance is necessarily formulated in verbal terms, or even that a purely verbal formulation may be possible. "Ritual," Lewis (1980: 8) asserts, "is not exactly like language...nor can it be decoded like one." Instead, it is better seen as a performance, like a play, to which the actors and spectators respond in various ways. In this sense

the 'meaning' of a ritual performance...is [less like] the meaning
of a purely linguistic message than it is like the 'meaning' of an
event. We interpret a ritual...rather in the way we interpret an
event in which we are present or in which we take part; ...we do
not 'decode' it to make sense of it...We are affected by it (Lewis
1980: 34).

It is here, in terms of how we are affected by ritual, that the question of
clarity and mystery arises. Lewis argues that ritual may aim alternatively at
one or the other, although his own concern is chiefly with mystery (1980:
30). One way mystery may be achieved – well-known, Lewis notes, to all
who study rituals – is to remove something familiar from its usual setting,
thereby alerting our attention and inviting us "to discover relations or aspects
of that object or action which [we] would not otherwise or ordinarily see"
(1980: 30). Here, Lewis borrows from Jerome Bruner (1957) the notion of
"gating" and "ungating" perception to describe the way in which a spectator
may attend to something, following it by ordinary logical thought, and then,
suddenly, have his attention deflected to some echo of meaning or tangential
association. Thus, mystification acts to "ungate" perception. Rather than
seeing something in a conventional way, it prompts us to expand our vision
and look for new and possibly unexpected associations. Lewis distinguishes
two devices by which ritual imagery may mystify. One he calls "isolation,"
that is, by removing the object or action from its customary setting, and the
second, "cognitive dissonance," by relocating it in a way that renders it out of
place, in a setting where its presence makes no apparent or obvious sense.

Lewis has less to say about clarity. Moreover, clarity is not precisely the
same as the mundane, although the two obviously overlap. It is therefore
necessary for our purpose here to extend Lewis' arguments and restate them in
somewhat different terms. On the matter of clarity, Lewis argues that if clarity
is the aim of ritual imagery, then, the appropriate device is one we might call
"cognitive redundancy," although Lewis himself does not label it as such, that
is, embedding the act or object in a seemingly familiar context and setting
all around it multiple clues as to its meaning (1980: 30). Although he does
not pursue the matter, clarity in this sense would seem to have the opposite
effect of mystification; namely, it "gates" our perceptions and so invites us to
confine them within conventional limits. Lewis offers no explanation of why
ritual should at times aim for clarity, but, by extension, a possible explanation
may be suggested. While mystification invites us to see ordinary things in
potentially unfamiliar ways, by utilizing mundane imagery and so "gating"
our perceptions, what is, in actuality, beyond ordinary apprehension may be
invested with a seemingly familiar form, making it graspable in everyday
conceptual terms.

The question here is how and to what effect do Saribas Iban shamans
employ these contrasting strategies, and why, in particular, do they sometimes
portray the imperceptible in commonplace terms.

The events of the Gawai Betawai suggest, as we shall see, several possible
answers. To begin with, the songs and ritual events that comprise the first

half of the Gawai, preceding the flight of the spirit-bats, serve primarily to situate the ritual spatially and temporally in the immediately visible here-and-now. Thus, the shamans open the Gawai by singing a series of praise-songs as they enter the patient's longhouse and move through the various parts of the house that will later serve as settings for successive stages of the Gawai. The resulting appropriation of images of these tangible surroundings directly into the songs themselves has the effect of asserting, at the very outset of the Gawai, the primacy of the quotidian world of everyday human life over the unseen worlds of the nonhuman actors who later assume a prominent role in the ritual.

In this, the *manangs* explicitly affirm the primary objective of the Gawai which is to cure and prolong the life of a living human being in this world. To this end, mystery alone is not enough. A major argument of this paper is that the shamans must, in the course of performing the Gawai, demonstrate a mastery of both mystery and the mundane, of the here-and-now as well as of what lies beyond it.

In the case of the Gawai Betawai, the recurrence of affliction and the failure of prior rituals to bring about a lasting cure give rise to a view that the source of affliction may be a more pervasive one, due, in this case, to a lack of divine attentiveness, in which not only the patient, but the whole community is no longer 'visible' (*tampak*) to the gods and so no longer the recipients of their favor.[2] The object of the Gawai is therefore to reestablish this attentiveness by, in this instance, invoking the direct intercession of Menjaya and his spirit-shaman followers. To do so, however, requires that the *manangs* look beyond the here-and-now and so initiate relations with the unseen inhabitants of other worlds. Thus, just before the flight of the spirit-bats, a significant shift occurs within the Gawai, with the flight itself acting as a transition leading into the second half of the Gawai. At this point, the ritual becomes, as we shall see, a ritual within a ritual. Thus, the Gawai recreates, during its second half, an invisible ritual within the immediately visible one, as the longhouse and its human participants are merged in the words of the songs with an unseen raised world and its ritual cast of the spirit-heroes, spirits, and gods. At the same time, there is also, as we shall see, a corresponding shift of vantage points. While the imagery of the first half of the Gawai invests both human and nonhuman worlds with immediately recognizable features, the perspective changes as Menjaya and his unseen followers begin their descent to this world. The focus shifts from the immediate ritual setting of the Gawai to Menjaya's cosmic journey in which the longhouse now becomes the journey's final destination. The viewpoint presented is thus from the outside, from Menjaya's vantage point, looking from afar towards what, for the human audience, is their own familiar world. Significantly, the itinerary of this journey is completely different from that followed by the spirit-bats, reflecting the very different ontological statuses of those who now become the

---

2   In Iban traditional religion, the gods (*petara*) both create life, including that of each individual person, and are able to sustain, extend and end it. Being temporarily forgotten by the gods, invisible, or out of their sight, is therefore a major source of misfortune, just as being seen by the gods is, conversely, thought to be a major source of blessing.

primary actors in the Gawai. The effectiveness of the performance rests, as we shall see, on the ability of the *manang*s to bring together and convincingly orchestrate these differences of perspective.

Finally, at the conclusion of the ritual, events return full-circle back to the longhouse where ritual imagery, once again, affirms the primacy of a now transformed, but, nonetheless, familiar everyday life.

Iban shamans as intermediaries

Iban *manang*s, as intermediaries between human and nonhuman beings, operate within a layered cosmos. Humans (*mensia*) inhabit 'this world' (*dunya tu'*), which they share with other 'living things' (*utai idup*), chiefly plants and animals, and with inanimate physical nature (Sather 2001a: 82). Also inhabiting this world, but perceptually differentiated, that is to say, invisible to human beings, are various kinds of 'spirits' (*antu*), many of them, although by no means all, malevolent (Sather 1978, 2001a: 66–69). Downriver from 'this world,' in another cosmic layer, along an invisible river called the Mandai, is the afterworld of the human dead (*menua Sebayan*) inhabited by the 'spirits of the dead' (*antu Sebayan*) and by the gods of the afterworld (Sather 2001a: 67–89). Above this world is the upperworld or sky (*langit*), the principal home of the gods (*petara*). Finally, interposed between this world and the sky is a raised world, close at hand, but invisible to human beings, inhabited by spirit-heroes and heroines (*Orang Panggau*), supernatural beings whose affairs, depicted in Iban oral sagas, represent an exemplary version of traditional Iban society itself (Sather 1994: 31–34, 1996: 98–99).

In Iban mythology the idea of creation *ex nihilo* is, as Viveiros de Castro (2004: 477) has said of indigenous Amazonian cosmogonies, virtually absent. "Things and beings," instead, "normally originate as transformations of something else." These transformations typically involve differentiation from a previously undifferentiated state. Thus, for the Iban, the gods and spirit-heroes were originally members of a primordial human society present in this world. In time, first the gods and then the spirit-heroes quarreled among themselves and departed, the gods migrating to the sky, the spirit-heroes to the raised world (Sather 1994: 31–33, 2001b: 147). Humans thus comprise those who were left behind, and who have now themselves dispersed and, through migration, differentiated into numerous "tribes." Although now spatially separated and, since their separation, invisible to human beings, the gods and spirit-heroes remain essentially human in terms of motives, consciousness, and volition. They also remain in communication with humans, primarily through the intercession of the shamans and priest-bards. However, both are far more powerful than humans and possess more effective charms and medicines; hence, the importance of maintaining connections and enlisting their continuing favor.

For the Iban, shamanism is a universal or transcendent calling, practiced by the gods and spirit-heroes as well as by human beings. Among the upperworld gods, Menjaya and his sister Ini' Inda are the principal shamans. According to myth, Menjaya was the first *manang* to perform the Gawai Betawai and it was the first ritual he performed after being initiated by his sister (cf. Sather 2001a: 98–99).[3] There are also, in addition to Menjaya, lesser celestial shamans, a number of whom are depicted as participating in the Gawai. In this world, too, various categories of 'living things' such as birds, animals and insects have shamans who, in spirit form, also join Menjaya.

  - In this world, different kinds of beings, both human and nonhuman, while distinguished from one another by outward appearance, are thought to share internally a similar subjective nature. For the Iban, human beings, as well as other objects and living things, all possess a *semengat*, a 'soul' or 'life-force' (Sather 2001a: 51–58). Like its more familiar Malay cognate (*semangat*), *semengat* is present "in all organized things, guiding and coordinating their actions," being in this sense the one component of humanity "that has a counterpart in all other things" (Endicott 1970: 49, 51). Each *semengat* is bound to a distinctive body. It is this external bodily form, and not the *semengat*, that differentiates one kind of being from another. Hence, Iban shamans deal with nonhumans, not by transforming their own bodies, or assuming nonhuman identities, but by freeing their soul and deliberately dispatching it into invisible dimensions of this world or into the afterworld of the dead. Within these dimensions or worlds, souls and spirits, when encountered by the *manang*'s soul, are perceived as having a visible outward appearance as well as an inner subjective nature like that of a human being.

In contrast to the soul, spirits are essentially "bodiless" (cf. Endicott 1970: 56) or, more accurately, are comparatively unbound to any particular bodily form. For the Iban, many spirits, including those who enter into special relationships with shamans and act as 'spirit-helpers' (*yang*), frequently manifest themselves in outward appearance as animals or other natural species. Whenever they do so, their apparent animality, however, is likened to a disguise, donned like a 'shirt' (*baju*), in order to hide their true identity (Sather 1978: 316, 2001a: 82–83). The latter, from both their own perspective and as seen by the shaman's soul, is essentially humanlike. On the other hand, outward bodily form determines their distinctive capacities and dispositions, such, for example, as a predisposition to malevolency, or, as in the case of the spirit-bats, the ability to fly.

As Viveiros de Castro (2004: 465–466) suggests, writing of Amazonian cosmologies, despite their manifest differences of appearance, their "corporeal diversity," humans and nonhumans are believed to share a similar subjective nature, or "spiritual unity."[4] What this view implies

---

3   While, in the Saribas, the Gawai Betawai is specifically associated with Menjaya, Ini' Inda is associated with the Bebangun, the ritual of initiation by which novices are elevated to the status of practicing *manang*s or, subsequently, practicing *manang*s gain recognition of increasing degrees of ritual expertise (cf. Sather 2001a: 29–34). Ini' Inda is also briefly invoked during the Gawai Betawai, immediately after the arrival of Menjaya, but she plays no active part in the ritual (Sather 2001a: 639–641).

4   My argument in this paper is strongly influenced by Eduardo Viveiros de Castro's (1998, 2004) notion of "perspectivism," particularly as he develops it in regard to shamanism. A major implication of Viveiros de Castro's notion is that the presuppositions that follow from "perspectivism" are in many respects diametrically opposed to those of

is that nonhumans possess, at some level, a subjectivity similar to that of human beings. To possess subjectivity is to be a "person," albeit, in this case, a person of differing degrees and kind. To personify is to attribute to others the capacities of intentionality and social agency and whoever possesses these capacities, Viveiros de Castro (2004: 467) argues, "is capable of having a point of view." While for ordinary Iban, animals are normally animals, and not spirits in disguise, and seeing and entering into relations with otherwise invisible souls, the dead, or spirits is considered unusual, very likely even life-threatening, Iban shamanism, by contrast, foregrounds such experiences. Shamans are persons who are capable of crossing ontological divides at will, and so of "adopt[ing] the perspective of nonhuman subjectivities in order to administer relations between humans and nonhumans" (Viveiros de Castro 2004: 468). Only by seeing nonhumans as they see themselves are shamans able to take on this role and act successfully as intermediaries. "Shamanism is a form of action that presupposes a mode of knowing," and, in this case, "to know is to personify; to take on the point of view of that which must be known" (Viveiros de Castro 2004: 469). We will return to this conceptualization shortly as it is a key part of our argument regarding ritual images of mystery and the mundane.

Thus, as we shall see, the use of imagery is one significant way in which Saribas Iban shamans, in their construction of ritual performances, are able to employ this knowledge, and thereby alter relationships with nonhuman others by adopting, through words and actions, their differing points of view. Hence, after Menjaya has been invited and is on his way to the Gawai, the journey is portrayed from Menjaya's vantage point. From this portrayal, the shamans' audience is invited to "ungate" its own perceptions. It is only by being able to see things from a nonhuman point of view that the *manangs* are able to enter into relationships with the nonhuman others whose help they must enlist in order to cure their patients. Iban society is notably non-hierarchical (Sather 1996) and to create a successful performance, the *manangs* must not only claim for themselves, but be able to share this way of seeing with their human audience.

Opening the Gawai Betawai

The Gawai Betawai is, or more precisely, was until a half century ago, typically performed for a patient considered to be either gravely or chronically ill, most often a child, usually as a last resort after all other means of shamanic

---

modern Western thought, which he identifies, by contrast, with a prevailing "objectivism." Thus, in Western thought, rather than presupposing "corporeal diversity," humans, animals, and other nonhuman beings are assumed to share elements of a common corporeal nature, whereas human beings are presumed to possess a unique inner subjectivity, for example, "mind," "reason," or "a capacity for culture," that differentiates them from other beings. As a consequence, the prevailing Western mode of knowing the nonhuman world is not by personification, but by objectification, that is, by seeing others not as "persons," in terms of their own subjectivity, but, rather, as "objects."

healing were exhausted. Unlike ordinary curing rituals, the Gawai Betawai is performed not singly, but by a 'troupe' (*bala*) of shamans consisting of a lead shaman (*tuai manang*), a principal assistant, and a small chorus.

Once a decision is made to hold a Gawai Betawai, the sponsoring family sends messengers to the home of the shaman. The latter then gathers a troupe of assistants and notifies the family of the day that they will arrive. That afternoon, the lead shaman and his party are received in a special welcoming structure erected at the foot of the patient's longhouse entry ladder. Here, mats are spread and the shamans are invited to sit together with their principal hosts while prayers are recited over them and offerings are made to their spirit-guides. Inside the longhouse, men and women form a procession and, accompanied by welcoming music (*gendang ngalu*), descend the entry ladder and escort the shamans into the longhouse. Before they leave, however, the *manang*s sing the first song of the Gawai, a praise-song to the 'welcoming-site' (*menalan*). As they enter the longhouse, they begin a second song, this one in praise of the longhouse itself. After circling the gallery, the procession stops at the section belonging to the sick person's family. Prayers are again recited, this time to bless their medicines and to ask the gods to hear their singing. The shamans then enter the patient's apartment. Here they begin preliminary treatment just as they would in an ordinary healing session (cf. Sather 2001a: 123–132). When finished, the lead shaman announces the outcome of their initial diagnosis and instructs the family to begin collecting the paraphernalia the shamans will need to perform the Gawai.

These include materials for constructing a shrine (*pandung*) on the open-air platform, a smaller shrine on the gallery, and a special ladder (*tangga keling*) to be used by the *manang*s when they climb to the rooftop dais. Most important, however, are wooden planks to be used by the men of the longhouse to construct a large ritual rice-winnowing sieve called a *pelangka*.[5] This ritual *pelangka* is used by the shamans to carry the patient, first to the shrine on the open-air platform, and then, up the special ladder to the rooftop dais. At the climax of the Gawai, when Menjaya and his followers are believed to be present, the lead shaman and his principal assistant carry the patient inside the *pelangka* to the dais and from there lift them both into the air.

Here, it should be noted, various parts of the longhouse have special meaning in relation to shamanic curing. The least serious afflictions are ordinarily treated inside the patient's apartment, while most curing takes place on the communal gallery. Only for the most serious cases do the *manang*s make recourse to the longhouse platform, and, finally, as here, to the rooftop. In addition to the perceived seriousness of the patient's condition, this movement also expresses increasing levels of community involvement and concern (Sather 2001b: 160). In this case, it also links the human to the upperworld.

As soon as the necessary planks have been assembled, the shamans leave the patient's apartment and enter the gallery. As they do so, each is handed

---

5   For a description of the *pelangka* (or *pengusak*) as a farm tool and an account of its use in the winnowing of threshed rice, see Sather (1980: 79–80).

a bushknife and an adze. Carrying these tools, they begin to sing the first song of the main part of the Gawai, the *timang beban pelangka*, or 'praise-song to fashion the rice-sieve.' The words, in this case, directly accompany as well as describe the work of the men on the gallery. Once the *pelangka* is completed, the shamans carry it to the outdoor altar. They then return to the patient's apartment which they praise with another brief praise-song. The women of the family are then asked to prepare offerings. These the *manang*s divide into portions, while on the gallery men play gong music to attract the notice of the gods and spirits. Shortly afterwards, at sunset, as the *manang*s sing, they cast a portion of these offerings to their spirit helpers. As they do so, longhouse members complete the main shrine on the outdoor platform, wrapping it in ritual ikat cloth. With this done, the *manang*s take up the remaining offerings and their medicine kits (*lupung*), leave the patient's apartment, cross the gallery, and carry them onto the open-air platform, where they place them beside the *pelangka* at the base of the shrine, singing as they do so praise-songs to each part of the longhouse they pass through, beginning with the apartment and ending with the open-air platform.[6]

The effect of singing these praise-songs, first as the shamans arrive at the longhouse, then as the work of constructing ritual paraphernalia takes place, and, finally, as the shamans move within the house from one ritual site to another, is to anchor this opening stage of the Gawai firmly in the everyday material world and to connect the words that the *manang*s sing to what the participants directly experience and see all around them at first hand. Words, objects and actions are thus brought into conjunction, imparting to the songs a powerful sense of immediacy. At the same time, however, this overt connection with words makes possible, and also signals, a transition of these objects, actions, and spaces, freeing them from their visible, but previously unmarked everyday moorings, and relocating them, instead, in a now demarcated ritual arena, thereby preparing them for the main events of the Gawai that follow.

A ritual within a ritual

At this point a break is normally taken for an evening meal. Afterward, the *manang*s resume singing, performing a brief ritual called 'to plant the Ayu Tawai' (see Sather 2001a: 491). Next, the shamans, seated on the gallery floor, invoke the familiar spirits of the longhouse, 'Spider' (*empelawa*) and 'House Lizard' (*tichak*), informing them that a Gawai is about to begin and inviting them to attend. The shamans then extend similar invitations, moving outward from the longhouse, first to the inhabitants of the rice fields and forests, then to various spirit-fish (*bunsu ikan*), and, finally, upward to the 'Mountain Shamans' (*manang bukit*) (Sather 2001a: 495–515).

---

6   In some performances of the Gawai Betawai, the *manang*s, at this point, carry the patient for the first time to the *meligai* (see Sather 2001a: 471–89). In other performances, the patient is carried only once to the rooftop, shortly before the end of the Gawai, as related here (2001a: 444).

By this sequencing of songs, and the successive locations in which they are set, the *manang*s begin to shift the vantage point of their audience in relation to the actions which the songs depict. Having first established the location of these events in the immediate here-and-now, their words now gradually dislodge them from these familiar surroundings, shifting them, instead, into ever more distant regions, to the outer reaches of this world, the mountaintops, and finally, just above and beyond them, to the raised world of the Iban spirit-heroes and heroines. The events that now unfold are thus discursively transposed to this raised world, and so, through this transposition, signal the beginning of an unseen ritual embedded within the visible Gawai itself. In this ritual the human audience becomes, in the words of the songs, participants in a spirit Gawai taking place simultaneously in the realm of the spirit-heroes, now represented by the longhouse gallery.

Thus, surveying the principal guests, who are described as seated, just like the human audience, along the upper gallery facing their hosts, Grandmother Tali Liung, a spirit-heroine, asks if the god Menjaya is present among the assembled guests, and

Lalu bejalai Bujang Agang Gemurai	Then Bujang Agang Gemurai walks
Ke punggai puting setak bayam pengabang.	To the opposite end of the longhouse to survey the gathering of guests.
...	...
"Mayuh amat mayuh pengabang,	"There are many guests, indeed,
Mayuh ari beluh tambah enseluang.	More numerous than all the *beluh* fish combined with the *enseluang*.
Tang Galang nadai aku meda' indu' batu.	But I do not see Boulder, Chief of Stones,[7]
Teras nadai aku meda' indu' kayu'."	I do not see Ironwood, Chief of Trees."

Thus learning that Menjaya is not present, Grandmother Tali Liung asks who can be sent to invite him:

"O, nadai meh nemu orang lebih ari' aya'	"Oh, none is wiser than our uncle, Menjaya,
kitai, Menjaya, manang tuai.	the old shaman,
Ke diau di selepai langit landai.	Who lives in the vast expanse of the sky
Mesai kepai buntal menenang.	As big as a puffer-fish fin.
Sapa randa kitai deh Agung Gemurai	Who among us, Agang Gemurai,
Tau' diasa ngambi' iya ngabang?"	Is able to send him an invitation?"

Here, Grandmother Tali Liung's speech offers a first hint of mystery. This it does by a favorite Iban device, a riddle or paradox. Thus, Menjaya's home is both vast and yet no larger than a fish fin.[8]

---

7   I.e., Menjaya. In Iban, *indu'* means, literally, 'woman,' but here it connotes 'the chief' or 'mother of,' the 'principal,' 'grandest,' or 'prime example of' (something). It is a common figure of speech, and later on, the *manang*s similarly describe the ritual *pelangka* as 'chief among sailboats' (*indu' bangkung*).

8   Like Jukka Siikala's people of Ma'uke, the Saribas Iban are well acquainted with

The hosts now call for Bujang Entawai and Kusing and ask them to carry the invitation to Menjaya. The spirit-bats inform their mothers who reply that they have prepared them since birth for just this moment. However, before they can depart, they must first call on Grandmother Mampu Lapu Dan, an ancient spirit-shaman, to ask her for directions to the upperworld. In the songs, the latter answers:

"Enti' nya' nadai ditanya' ka seduai uchu',	"If so, you need not ask, grandsons,
Jalai besai nya' endang agi' nyeruran,	For the main road still runs, as it always has,
Nya' endang jalai lama' agi' betampung	The old road still joins onto the longhouse
tempuan."	passageway."

Her answer thus discloses that the visible world and the upperworld are, in fact, continuous from a spirit perspective and that the point of connection, or entryway into the upperworld, is none other than through the longhouse passageway.

Further reflecting this shift in the relationship of the audience to the events portrayed in the Gawai, the voices represented are no longer those of the *manang*s addressing their audience directly, but, rather, those of spirit-heroes, spirit messengers, and other nonhuman persona, now engaged in dialogues, posing questions, or reflecting on events, which, by virtue of their being present, the human audience is able to overhear and so indirectly witness. Sonically, they become an audience in a dual sense, bearing witness simultaneously to both seen and unseen events.[9] By contrast, the shamans themselves disappear from the events they narrate. In her answer, Grandmother Mampu Lapu Dan refers to something matter-of-fact and visible: the 'longhouse passageway' (*tempuan*), which, for the audience sitting along the gallery, runs in plain sight immediately beside them, in front of the family apartments, ending at each end of the longhouse at its main entryways. Again, her words, like those earlier, while referring to a commonplace feature of the longhouse, at the same time act to detach it, separating it from its immediately visible, commonplace setting, and reveal it in a wider, previously undisclosed context, as a ritual entryway that gives access to other worlds beyond what, for ordinary human beings, is immediately perceptible. The audience is thus confronted with a vantage point explicitly different from its own which, if adopted, permits them access to a co-existent realm of parallel unseen actions.

---

travel. Down through the first half of the nineteenth century, Saribas Iban war parties joined lower-river Malay allies to raid much of the western coast of Borneo. They also made annual expeditions by sea to the islands beyond the Saribas River mouth to collect Conus shells for armlets and to catch puffer-fish (*ikan buntal*) which they dried in large quantities and transported back to their upriver longhouses as a source of dietary protein.

9   The Iban term for 'audience' is, significantly, *peninga*, literally, 'listener' or 'hearer,' from the root, *dinga*, 'to hear' (Richards 1981: 272).

Flight of the spirit-bats

This now brings us to the point in the Gawai where we began this paper. After carefully dressing, Bachelors Entawai and Kusing begin their journey. This concludes almost instantaneously, compressed within a brief four-line stanza:

Nya' baru tebang melingkat pampat di urat!	Now fell the *melingkat* tree and cut its roots!
Nyaduh ka tubuh seduai iya bebai' angkat.	The two rise and start their journey.
Lalu' bejalai tegar seduai iya ngena' sempiar untak tulang,	Traveling swiftly, both with all their might,
Bejalai laju seduai iya baka peluru bangkang.	They journey as fast as bullets made of lead.

Once in the upperworld, Entawai and Kusing orient themselves by tell-tale sounds familiar to every Iban river-traveler. Inhabiting a rainforest environment, the Iban often locate places not by sight, but, rather, by their being "sonically announced" (Feld 1996: 98). In this case, the spirit-bats hear the sound of swiftly-flowing water as it courses around the guide stakes of a fish-weir and conical fishtraps, both unmistakable signs of a nearby longhouse, even though the house itself, at this point, remains hidden from view:

Nya' baru ninga rauh tampun ensenga'.	Now hear the rippling sounds made by the guide stakes of a fish-weir.
Nya' baru ninga riap tampun buba'.	Now hear the bubbling sounds made by the guide stakes of conical fishtraps.
Nya' baru datai di pendai' ili'	Now reach the downriver boat-landing
Bekerangan ka rangki' penumpang bujang.	Covered with pebbles like the shell armlets worn by bachelors.

Reaching Menjaya's landing-place, Entawai and Kusing bathe, as Iban visitors customarily do. They then proceed to the longhouse, where their arrival is described in the following terms:

Lengka' ka dulu' jaku' nya'!	Let us now conclude these words!
Entawai lalu terebai lapu-lapu,	Entawai flies on swiftly beating wings,
Lalu rebap-rebap penerebai Kusing kesindap	Kusing flaps as he flies
Inggap di kerabat tajau baru.	And alights, perching on a modern jar.
Datai Entawai inggap ba' pemanggai sengkayau baju.	Entawai arrives, perching on a clothesline where shirts are hung to dry.

Not only do these words demystify, but the image they present is mundane almost to the point of comedy. Thus, we meet modern jars and laundry, and the spirit-bats themselves, who otherwise speak and behave as human beings, now lapse into bat-like behavior, perching and flapping their wings.

The flight of the spirit-bats plays an important role in the Gawai, bridging the first half of the ritual to the narrative account that follows of Menjaya's descent and arrival in this world. In addition, the flight also recreates, in the spirit ritual embedded within the this-world Gawai, the essential everyday events which immediately preceded, and effectively initiated the Gawai itself, namely the dispatch of messengers to the house of the shaman. Thus, in the songs, the spirit-bats play an identical role to that of the human messengers sent by the sponsoring family to summon the lead shaman. In part, the use of mundane imagery heightens this parallel; but more importantly, it sets the stage for the even more dramatic shift of perspective that follows.

The descent of Menjaya

The songs which the *manang*s now sing are presented from a very different vantage point than those which initiated the invisible Gawai. In contrast to the almost instantaneous flight of the spirit-bats, the tempo of events now dramatically slows to match the movements of Menjaya as he descends from the upperworld. In place of an empty void, there is now laid out before the audience a long road or pathway that runs downward through the upperworld to the earthly world below. A horizon no longer divides these worlds, but, rather, a door, the 'Door of the Sky' (*Pintu Langit*), through which the travelers must pass in order to leave one world and enter the next. More notable yet, the events of the narrative are now constructed in what the *manang*s describe as a 'journey' (*jalai*). This journey, in turn, takes the form of a continuing sequence of named or otherwise identified places through which Menjaya and his followers move as they descend from the sky. In most instances, these places are joined, one to the next, by the use of a formulaic 'leave there' (*kejang ka ari nya'*) (or 'move on a bit,' *nginsit mimit nyungkah mindah*) followed by 'arrive at' (*datai ba'*) (or 'come to,' *manggai ba'*). Through this device, named places are arranged in what the Iban call *ripih*, a correct 'sequential order,' so that their recounting, one after another, serves not only to define a precise itinerary, but to effect, or bring this journey about within the unseen world where it is depicted as taking place. To a degree, the places themselves are less significant than the order in which they are named. Thus, the *manang*s, when singing, may abridge the narrative by leaving out individual places, or expand it by adding new ones, so long as they preserve the correct order between those they include. Otherwise, if they name some of these places out of order, or reverse their location, the journey itself is said to be 'disordered' (*salah atur*) and so 'ineffectual' (*enda'sidi*) (cf. Sather 2001a: 3–4, 189–190, 2001b: 177fn) and will therefore fail to bring Menjaya to the Gawai.

As the *manang*s begin to sing this narrative journey, they arise and start to circumambulate the longhouse gallery. The journey itself takes most of the night to relate, ending with Menjaya's arrival, which, as the *manang*s pace their performance, they time to occur shortly before dawn the following morning. While, for the human audience, the events of this journey are, in a strict sense, invisible, they are, nonetheless, made witness to what unfolds through the shamans' use, again, of dialogue, voice, and visual imagery. But more than this, the shamans' movements, as they sing while walking continuously from one section of the gallery to the next, repeatedly pausing and circling as they proceed, are said to 'mimic' (*nunda'*) the movements of Menjaya and his companions, as they journey from place to place in the songs. While the *manang*s disappear from the songs themselves, they are now visibly present, mimicking the actions of Menjaya and his followers. For Iban audiences, this conjoining of distinct perspectives, human and nonhuman, through the intermediacy of the *manang*s, is the crucial key to the efficacy of the Gawai. While the human and unseen worlds are believed to be identical in many ways, they are also, at the same time, said to be 'upside-down' or 'opposite' (*tunsang*) to one another. Thus, for the Iban, what is 'play' (*bemain*) in this world – that is to say, the singing and acting out of this narrative journey by the *manang*s before a longhouse audience – becomes 'work' or an 'act of doing' (*begawa'*) – efficacious in other words – when simultaneously performed in the unseen worlds by the gods, spirits and spirit-heroes (Sather 2001a: 134).[10] The task of the shamans is to merge these acts of play and work in order to bring to bear the curative powers of these invisible others in this world.

In the songs, Menjaya begins his journey at a large clearing, described as the country of Engkeramba'-baba, a carved guardian figure in human shape who watches over the main road traversed by the shamans as they go about their healing journeys:[11]

Nya' baru tebang simun mutun bedaun!	Now fell the *simun mutun* tree covered in leaves!
Nyaduh ka tubuh Menjaya belabuh nurun.	Menjaya is about to start his descent.
Nya' baru manggai di menalan besai.	Now he comes to a large clearing,
Kena' tipas langgai manuk sabung.	Grazed by the tail feathers of fighting cocks.
Nya' baru manggai di menalan nyapan.	Now he reaches the level clearing,
Kena' tambun ruman padi nibung...	Heaped with the chaff of *nibung* rice...
...	...
Nya' menua engkeramba'-baba	This marks the country of Engkeramba'-baba,
Ngemata ka jeraya bala manang mansang	Who guards the road used by the troupes of
belinggang.	Shamans as they sing their rituals.

The description of this clearing – heaped with rice chaff, guarded by an *engkeramba'*, and so on – identifies it, at once, as the clearing in front of the longhouse entry ladder, the same place, in other words, where the *manang*s were first welcomed by their hosts and began to sing the opening song of the

---

10   The root of Gawai, a 'ritual festival,' is *gawa'*, 'work' (Richards 1981: 96), hence, like their classic Tikopian counterparts, basically, 'work of the gods.'

11   Traditionally, these figures, carved of wood, were erected in front of the entryways to a longhouse or were carved into the top of the entry ladders themselves. Possessing a *semengat*, the *engkeramba'* is believed to warn longhouse members, particularly in dreams, of approaching enemies, including possible spirit intruders, and to restrain the souls of longhouse residents from straying down the entry ladder and so out of the longhouse and into danger (cf. Sather 2001a: 155–156). Literally, *belinggang* in the last line of this stanza refers to the 'rolling' or 'swaying' motion adopted by Iban *manang*s as they circumambulate, as here, the longhouse gallery.

Gawai. Events thus repeat, but from a reversed perspective.

From this clearing, Menjaya enters the main road. After visiting various gardens in which he grows medicinal herbs, he passes through the lands of a series of celestial shamans. Each possesses different kinds of charms and medicines and, bringing these, all join Menjaya as his traveling companions. Hyperbole and mystifying paradoxes now abound. For example:

...	...
Nya'dipangkang Meringai tau' tuai tau' biak.	Close by lives Meringai, who can be both old and young.
Enti' sukat iya biak baka anembiak berembau bujang,	When he is young, he is as youthful as a bachelor,
Enti' sukat iya tuai pala' iya burak ngemunga lalang.	When he is old, his hair is white as the flowering *lalang* grass.
Laban iya ngembuan ḥatu kupak,	This is because he owns a peeling stone,
Serak anak melaban mipau umbang.	Together with a piece of *melaban* bark[12].

In time, the troupe approaches the lower limits of the sky. Now coming to the midpoint of their journey, they pass the moon, the home of Grandfather Ungkok, the Iban Man-in-the-Moon:

Kejang ka ari' nya'	Leave there
Nginsit mimit nyungkah mindah...	And move on a bit...
...	...
Nya' baru manggai di lembang madang tengang,	Now arrive at a valley covered with *tengang* creepers,
Baka kelingkang tedung nerumbu.	Like the coils of a motionless cobra.
Malik ka kiba' baka rampa' nanga Paku.	Look to the left and see the vast expanse of land at the Paku river mouth.
Malik ka kanan baka reban nganti' nunu.	Look to the right and see cleared fields waiting to be fired.
Nya' menua tandang asam penguji,	That is the country of tempting sour fruit,
Dipangkeng Matai ke bejalai atas bumi.	Where Matai lives who journeys above the earth.
Nya' menua Aki' Ungkuk	It is the country of Grandfather Ungkuk
Ke pengusuk tengang tali	Who braids *tengang* fiber into string
Laban iya tan mata jaga enda' tinduk,	So that he may stay awake and not sleep,
Ngemata ka rayuk peranama mandang.	So as to watch over the halo of the shining full moon.

"Journey[ing] above the earth" refers to the apparent movement of the moon across the night sky. Grandfather Ungkuk's shadow is said to be visible whenever the moon is full. On such nights, he keeps himself awake, according

---

12 The *melaban* tree (*Tristania* sp.) continually sheds and renews its thin, paper-like bark and so is associated by the Iban with perpetual youthfulness. The *batu kupak*, or 'peeling stone,' has the same significance and describes a stone charm in the shape of a "peeling," as of tree bark or a fruit skin.

to folk stories, by patiently twining the fiber of *tengang* creepers into cordage. Here, in this stanza, the imagery mystifies the listeners, not by riddling, but, rather, by allusion, by referring intertextually to stories that exist, not in the Gawai itself, but in familiar folktales. At the beginning of the stanza, the party of travelers looks down from the moon to the earth below, to a river mouth and newly cleared rice fields, in this case, to the location of the human longhouse, not yet visible to the travelers, where the Gawai is being sung.

Eventually, Menjaya and his companions reach the Door of the Sky. This they find closed, barring the way to the earthly world:

Kejang ka ari nya',	Leave there,
Nyau manggai ba' pintu langit burak	And come to the door of the white sky
Dipegai mutak-utak, enda' ulih rambak,	Which moves when pulled, but will not open,
Asai ke mabak chagak bedil temaga.	Like the firmly attached swivel-mount of a brass cannon.
Manggai ba' pintu langit kedil	Then come to the thick door of the sky
Dipegai minggil-inggil, enda' ulih rambak getil...	Easy to move, but impossible to open...
"O, enti' baka tu' puntan pejalai kitai,	"Oh, if this is so, then our journey comes to nothing
Baka menasan jalai jelu.	Like the lost track of a [game] animal.
Enti' baka tu' labah kitai,	If this is to be, then our journey is in vain,
Ke deka' ngabang enda' lalu."	For though we may wish to attend the Gawai, we can go no further."

At this point, the wind goddess, a frequent traveler through this part of the cosmos, calls out to Menjaya, who then arises and miraculously opens the door with a pig's tusk charm:

Lalu angkat Menjaya, Manang Linsing	Then Menjaya, Shaman Linsing, rises up
Lalu diseging iya ngena' taring uting babi belang...	And pushes open the door of the sky using the tusk of a piebald pig...
...	...
Peda' lalu tebuka' Pintu Langit lada'	Then see, the Door of the Sky suddenly opens
Ka jalai sida' gelanyang Manang Nyara',	To make way for Shaman Nyara' and the others,
Ke nengua' mansang ngabang.	So that they may continue their journey to attend the Gawai.

Menjaya and his troupe now enter this world. Here they meet in turn a series of bird shamans, followed by animal and insect shamans, ending with the shaman of river turtles. The growing troupe has now reached the longhouse landing-place (*pendai'* or *penai'*), where, in this world, the longhouse domain meets the natural world (cf. Sather 1995: 79). Here, they bathe and, as they do so, magical charms miraculously materialize in their hands and from their fingertips:

Lalu mandi' sida' ba' ai' besungga' undang.	Then they bathe in the river, floating on their backs.
Mandi' ba' ai' ulai ngesai ka tangan tunjuk empat	They bathe in the river-eddies, turning with the current, and float with their four fingers
Megai penchelap batu janggat, gemalai belang.	In which they hold cooling charms, wax-gourd stones, white jewels.
Mandi' Menjaya ba' ai' ulai chiru.	Menjaya bathes in the clear river-eddy.
Peda' tangan tunjuk antu iya	See the little fingers of his hand
Ngenggam penchelap batu idu, ubat gayu,	Grasp a cooling *idu* stone, longevity charm,
Buban pala' ngemunga lalang.	That allows us to live until our hair turns white as *lalang* flowers.

Menjaya and his companions don festival clothing and enter the longhouse where the shamans are singing, feasting as they enter on the offerings prepared for them.

Having completed the songs of Menjaya's descent to this world, the shamans now perform a ritual on the gallery in which they 'ransom' (*tebus*) the patient's life by purchasing a new one from the gods with various kinds of valuables, such as brassware, money, and Chinese jars. This is described as an 'exchange of life' (*beganti nyawa'*) in which the patient's old life is exchanged for a new one. Concluding these songs, the *manang*s again carry the patient in the ritual *pelangka*, taking him from his family's apartment out onto the open-air platform. From here the lead shaman and his assistant prepare to carry him by ladder to the rooftop dais. But, first, before they do so, they sing a song describing the significance of what they are about to do:

Kami Menani tu' nyau deka' nyagu,	We Menani[13] now prepare to lift up
Ka selantang anak andai	And bless this dependent child
Ngambika iya gerai nguan menua...	So that it shall live in good health in this land...
...	...
Kami Menani nyau be-ati	We Menani wish to lift up
Deka' nyagu ka lantang anak indung	And bless this beloved child
Ngambika iya beruntung nguan menua.	So that it shall enjoy success [For as long as it] lives in this land.

With these words, the *manang*s now address their human audience directly for the first time since the opening stages of the Gawai. At the same time, they re-emphasize the purpose of the ritual and so return its vantage point to "this land," that is to say, to the patient and the living human community whose members have gathered to participate in the Gawai.

On the rooftop dais, the *manang*s now sing a song called the Besagu Ayu

---

13   At this point, the *manang*s refer to themselves in the first-person plural, as 'we' (*kami*). They also, however, throughout the songs, use special shamanic names or titles (*juluk*) for themselves, such as Menani, Usam, Chelung, Jelapi', and others. In some cases, their namesakes are the same celestial shamans whom Menjaya encounters as he descends to this world.

as they lift up the *pelangka* (see Sather 2001a: 482). They then return with the *pelangka*, carrying it inside the longhouse and along the gallery as they resume singing. Here, their songs emphasize the extraordinariness of the *pelangka*. Like the longhouse passageway in the earlier song of Grandmother Mampu Lapu Dan, the *pelangka*, their words now tell us, is not what it appears to be. Instead of a common farm tool, it becomes, as they sing, a miraculous vehicle belonging to Menjaya by which its passengers may ascend and descend through the air as if voyaging across the sea in a sailboat:

Tak lepung-lepung pelangka gantung tu'	Gently this sieve floats [in the air]
Tu'ga'ukai pelangka ngapa',	For it is not an ordinary sieve,
Endang pelangka aki' kami...	But is truly the sieve of our grandfather...
...	...
Nya'alai tu'ga'	There, from it,
Tu'ga'belayar ka tikal kanggan gulung!	Unfurl a sail of folded *kanggan* cloth!
Dipelayar ka kami Gelanyang, Manang Chelung,	It is sailed by us Gelanyang, followers of Shaman Chelung,
Ke gilik tasik lelepung.	Across the gently rolling sea.
Tu'ga'tau'ngadi perau indu' bangkung	It thus becomes a boat, chief among sailboats,
Nangga'sabung gigi gumbang...	And bears us against the crests of the waves...
...	...
Dipelayar ka gilik tasik dalam,	It is sailed across the deep rolling sea,
Lalu labuh ka sauh besi balan.	Then drops its smooth iron anchor.
Peda' tali luan lekat,	See, its bow approaches and is secured,
Di pengkalan tanchang ngagai likang.	Tied fast to the landing-place by a cable.

When the shamans' words come to this point where the *pelangka* is secured to the landing-place, they arrive at the gallery shrine and there, for the moment, end their singing and set down the *pelangka*.

Here, as the Gawai nears its end, events return to the site where they began. Just as the Gawai began by recreating events that preceded it, so it ends by foretelling those that will follow, thus firmly anchoring it in the present. The last major event of the Gawai is an act of divination or augury, which, in effect, projects its outcome into the future lives of those who took part in it. In contrast to the varying tempo of its internal narrative, the Gawai is now reconnected with the larger flow of time in this world, first to the coming of dawn, and then to the this-worldly events of its own past and future. Menjaya now orders the sacrifice of a pig and commands that its liver be found auspicious:

Dia' Manang Menjaya lalu bejaku.	Then Shaman Menjaya speaks.
"Kami diatu' be-ati deka' munuh babi.	"We now desire to sacrifice a pig.
Lalu ati babi," ku' Menjaya, "asuh tuchi,	When it is done," says Menjaya, "I order the liver to be pure.

Nadai apa, nadai nama.	Nothing shall be the matter, nothing to worry about.
Awak ka orang ke begawai,	Allow the people who perform this Gawai
Tau' gerai lalu lantang."	To enjoy good health and contentment."

As soon as the pig's liver has been read, the various nonhuman shamans who arrived as guests or accompanied Menjaya are now briefly sent back, each in a few lines of song, to the various places from which they came, ending with Menjaya himself. This takes place on the open-air platform before offerings laid out as travel provisions. Last of all, the *manang*s recall their own souls (*mulai ka semengat*), returning them to their bodies. Significantly, this return is depicted in a way that reflects the general movement of the Gawai itself, as an entry into the longhouse, and from there, in this case, to the top of 'Mount Rabung,' an allegorical allusion to the anterior fontanelle at the top of the head, the invisible entryway through which the soul is said to enter and leave the body. Here house and body appear as analogous forms of embodiment:

Nyaduh ka tubuh aram kitai bepulai semengat kitai semua.	Come, let us start to return all of our souls.
Aram pulai semua kitai,	Let us bring them all back,
Pulai sama sereta.	Return them all at once.
Pulai kitai nepat sangap tutung penyaga.	Return, make straight for the faint, distant sound of a gong being struck.
Pulai semua kitai nepat rumah,	All return, make straight for the lovely house,
Ke reregah manah baka.	Now plainly visible.
Manggai di tempuan semengat bala Usam	Arrive at the passageway, the souls of the followers of Usam
Baka sampan Raja Belanda.	Like the King of Holland's boat.
Lalu nuju pintu ke belagu belinsu jera',	Then take aim straight for the door ornamented with painted designs,
Lalu tama' ke bilik baik	Then enter the spacious family room
Baka tasik luar kuala.	Like the wide sea beyond the river mouth.
...	...
Betatap enggau ubat seribu bansa.	Sprinkle them with water in which a thousand kinds of charms have been placed.
Bepanjah enggau ubat penyangga nyawa.	Over them pour life-sustaining medicines.
"Tu'baru kitai gayu'!" ku' Sentuku.	"Now, with this, may we live long!" says White-crested Hornbill.
"Nadai apa'!" ku Petara.	"Let nothing trouble us!" says Petara.
...	...
Tu' baru semengat bala Jelapi'	Now the souls of the company of Jelapi'
Niki' ke lenggi' lenggang telaga.	Ascend to the rim of the highest pool.
Tak baka renjung semengat bala Manang Empung	To the very heights, the souls of the followers of Shaman Empung
Nampuk di tuchung Rubung tampak nama.	Alight on the top of famed Mount Rabung, visible from afar.

With the departure of the nonhuman shamans, the refocusing of attention upon the longhouse, its inhabitants and the ailing patient, and lastly the recall of the shamans' own souls and, by extension, those of their audience, the vantage point represented by the Gawai reverts entirely to the materially embodied world, a realm characterized, as we have seen, by differentiation. This ontological shift is completed by the *manang*s, who conclude the Gawai by erecting a series of ritual barriers (*pelepa '*), reestablishing the integrity of the longhouse community by setting it apart from the various unseen realms that surround and otherwise impinge upon it (Sather 2001a: 669ff).

Conclusion

A prominent interest in Jukka Siikala's work (1991, 2001) is with the ways in which what exists at a distance, beyond the immediacies of time and place, is made a part of peoples' lives. This same issue is at the heart of the Gawai Betawai. Here, the attentions of the gods are re-focused on this world through a ritually constituted journey that, for a time at least, abolishes the distance that, from the primordial past, has otherwise separated the gods, spirit-heroes and human beings from one another.

The songs of the Gawai Betawai both depict and, for their Iban audiences are thought to activate, events that are perceived to occur simultaneously, at both a seen and unseen level. The most crucial of these events, as we have seen, unfold as a *jalai*, or 'journey.' For the Gawai Betawai, this is a journey undertaken, not by the *manang*s themselves, but by Menjaya, the principal divine shaman of the Iban upperworld, who descends to where the *manang*s are singing in order to intercede directly in the ritual work of curing.

A decision to invoke the intercession of Menjaya is normally made only after ordinary healing rituals have repeatedly failed, causing the members of a community to suspect that the fault may be due to a more general state of malaise arising from the inattentiveness of the gods and their failure to keep the longhouse and its inhabitants within their protective gaze. While a single person may be the center of affliction, the whole community is thus at risk. Therefore, a higher level of community participation is called for to carry out the Gawai Betawai than is the case with ordinary healing rituals. In order to reconnect with the gods, the sponsoring family, together with other longhouse members and guests, must assume the visible roles of their spiritual exemplars, the intermediating but invisible spirit-heroes of the raised world. This occurs through the embedding of an invisible ritual within the overtly visible one. Through the evocative force of the *manang*s' words, both the human audience and the setting in which they are present are transposed from this world to a distant realm beyond immediate experience, where the human participants are able to act, through their unseen surrogates, as ritual hosts to the visiting gods and spirit shamans. In this, the songs invite the audience to "ungate" its perceptions and to see its actions, and those of the *manang*s, not simply as they appear within the visible setting of the longhouse, but also in terms of the presence of unseen others represented in the songs as simultaneously participating in a parallel set of identical events. Through the songs, a human audience thus becomes witness to the parallel actions of nonhuman performers, which, as ordinary human beings, they cannot directly perceive except as they are ritually recreated by the *manangs* by means of the Gawai's performance.

Shamans, to be effective as intermediaries, must "be able to see nonhumans as they see themselves" (Viveiros de Castro 2004: 468). More than this, they must also be able to convey what they see to a human audience in the course of carrying out their ritual intercessions. Unlike ordinary laypersons, shamans not only intercede and enter into relations with nonhuman others, but, additionally, they "are capable of returning to tell the tale," and it is this tale that the *manangs*' songs and actions convey. At the heart of this tale, and the primary site of the Gawai's effectiveness, is a sung journey both undertaken and depicted from Menjaya's viewpoint. Only by adopting this viewpoint, and correctly executing this journey are the *manangs* able to direct Menjaya's actions.

This ritual journey is always, as in ordinary healing rituals as well, a return journey that begins and ends in the longhouse where the *manangs* are singing. In the opening stages of the Gawai, verbal imagery as well as the speech pragmatics of direct address purposefully connect what occurs to the mundane and immediately visible setting in which it takes place. Here, mystery is not the intent, but, rather, the opposite. The purpose is to connect the events of the Gawai with the ritual's overt intent of curing and with the sensate world where the conditions of affliction are experienced. This, however, changes with the beginning of Menjaya's journey. Here, an appeal is made for the intercession of powers beyond the visible world. Unlike most Iban shamanic journeys, this one, however, is made not by the shamans themselves, but by the shamanic gods, and so begins in a world beyond ordinary human perception and, from there, moves back towards the visible, materially-embodied human world. This reversed movement is signaled in a number ways, including by the mystification of what are otherwise mundane objects. For example, the longhouse passageway is revealed through the conversation of spirit interlocutors to be an entryway into invisible other worlds, including the upperworld of Menjaya. Similarly, later on, the *pelangka*, otherwise a mundane implement, ritually fashioned in this case by the longhouse hosts themselves, now becomes a miraculous vehicle by which the patient may be lifted into the air by the *manangs* and so brought into Menjaya's presence. Here, mystification provides a means of connecting the visible with the unseen. Finally, the journey itself proceeds through a series of named places, arranged in a determinant order, the correct reciting of which abolishes distance by transporting the gods, place-by-place, to this world.

In the end, the locus of events thus returns back to the longhouse where the Gawai began. But, in this, ritual is never just expressive. For those who participate in it, it is also expected to do things, to have effects in this world. To succeed in this regard, what takes place during the Gawai on an unseen level must now, at the conclusion of the ritual, be again connected with events in the tangible, materially-embodied world. If this succeeds, then the miraculous charms and other powers that Menjaya and his followers bring with them may work to effect a cure and prolong the lives of those who take part in the ritual. Here, in this connection, the longhouse is made to serve as a metonymic representation both of this world and of the bodily existence of those who participate in the Gawai. Thus in Menjaya's final blessings before he returns to the upperworld, and in the *manang*s' recall of their souls, the longhouse and its human inhabitants are now depicted as transformed and infused with verbal images of ritual coolness, health, long-life, and tranquility (see Sather 2001a: 175–177, 2001b: 169). And so, mystery in the end gives way to the mundane so that the transformative benefits of renewed contacts with the unseen are able to flow once again into this world.

REFERENCES

Bruner, Jerome 1957. On perceptual readiness. *Psychological Review*, 64: 123–154.

Endicott, Kirk 1970. *An Analysis of Malay Magic*. Oxford: Clarendon Press.

Feld, Steven 1996. Waterfalls of Song: An acoustemology of place resounding in Bosavi, Papua New Guinea. In: Steven Feld and Keith H. Basso (eds.) *Senses of Place*. Santa Fe: School of American Research Press, Pp. 91–135.

Lansing, Stephen 1983. *The Three Worlds of Bali*. New York: Praeger.

Lewis, Gilbert 1980. *Day of Shining Red: An Essay on Understanding Ritual*. Cambridge: Cambridge University Press.

Richards, Anthony 1981. *An Iban-English Dictionary*. Oxford: Clarendon Press.

Sather, Clifford 1978. The malevolent *koklir*. *Bijdragen tot de Taal-, Land-, en Volkenkunde*. 134: 310–355.

Sather, Clifford 1980. Symbolic elements in Saribas Iban rites of padi storage. *Journal of the Malaysian Branch of the Royal Asiatic Society* 53(2):67–95.

Sather, Clifford 1993. Posts, hearths and thresholds: the Iban longhouse as a ritual structure. In: James J. Fox (ed.) *Inside Austronesian Houses: Perspectives on Domestic Designs for Living*. Department of Anthropology, Research School of Pacific and Asian Studies. Canberra: The Australian National University, Pp. 65–115.

Sather, Clifford 1994. Introduction. In: Benedict Sandin. *Sources of Iban Traditional History*, Special Monograph, No. 7, Kuching: Sarawak Museum Journal, Pp. 1–78.

Sather, Clifford 1996. "All threads are white": Iban egalitarianism reconsidered. In: James J. Fox and Clifford Sather (eds.) *Origins, Ancestry and Alliance*. Department of Anthropology, Research School of Pacific and Asian Studies. Canberra: The Australian National University, Pp. 70–110.

Sather, Clifford 2001a. *Seeds of Play, Words of Power: An Ethnographic Study of Iban Shamanic Chants*. Kuching: Tun Jugah Foundation and the Borneo Research Council.

Sather, Clifford 2001b. Shamanic journeys and other travels: interplaces and the importation of distant landscapes in Iban constructions of community and self. In: Jukka Siikala (ed.) *Departures: How societies distribute their people*. Helsinki: Transactions of the Finnish Anthropological Society, No. 46, Pp. 144–178.

Siikala, Jukka 1991. '*Akatokamanāva: Myth, History and Society in the Southern Cook Islands*. Auckland: The Polynesian Society in association with the Finnish Anthropological Society.

Siikala, Jukka 2001. Introduction: Where have all the people gone? In: Jukka Siikala, (ed.) *Departures: How societies distribute their people*. Helsinki: Transactions of the Finnish Anthropological Society, No. 46, Pp. 1–6.

Viveiros de Castro, Eduardo 1998. Cosmological deixis and Amerindian perspectivism. *Journal of the Royal Anthropological Institute*, 4–5: 469–488.

Viveiros de Castro, Eduardo 2004. Exchanging Perspectives: The transformation of objects into subjects in Amerindian Ontologies. *Common Knowledge* 10 (3): 463–484.

Lost Horizons at Karimui

Roy Wagner

"…There is no place that does not see you. You must change your life."
— Rainer Maria Rilke

The horizon means many things to us; it is the point of departure for the sun, moon, and stars; it is our planet's way of saying "goodnight" and "good morning;" it is the Lonely Planet Guide to human self-centeredness. When the ancient Polynesians stopped going in search of the horizon, the horizon came looking for them. But the Daribi people of Mt. Karimui, in Papua New Guinea, would simply stand in awe of it, as though some God (which they did not have) had suddenly smiled upon them. There is no word for "horizon" in the Daribi language, and that for lack of physical evidence. When your plane lands at Karimui airstrip, that is the last you will see of the horizon for a long, long time. *Roads* at Karimui, something of a misnomer, exist for the precise purpose of *avoiding* where you are going.

"The sun, the moon, and the stars, and also the clouds," I was told, when I first arrived at Karimui, "they simply come out of the sky and go back in again. That is the only important thing they do, and whatever else they may do is the subject of myth." *Roads*, however, they simply go into the ground, and are never seen or heard from afterward. A surveyor could get by in that country with a purely *vertical* transit, plus a few thousand assistants with machetes.

During my first fieldwork, propelled by some Byronic lust for openness, I used to climb to the highest point in the local terrain, the ruins of our group's two-storey longhouse. "Well, Roy, you aren't the only one," I was told, "we used to come up here all the time. We would see columns of smoke rising from the burning of distant gardens, and wonder what kind of people lived there." Like space aliens, more or less. Actually, of course, those "far distant people" were Daribi, too, and probably relatives of the onlookers. Astrophysics, in that land, would be a matter of watching ants crawl across the ceiling. If, by some swift magic, all the landforms and geomorphic structures were whisked away from the New Guinea massif, one could still trace its outlines in the network of ants (*stinging* ants) that would remain. Forget perspectives. New Guinea goes by introspection. And micro-management. As a matter of record, there are no astronomical observatories in Papua New Guinea, only geo-tectonic ones.

So, on one clear night (the *only* one in June, 2000), I took a group of Daribi youths out to see the stars. We found a clear patch of almost-sky about a half-mile from my tent. With great aplomb (I was once an astronomy major) I was able to point out Alpha and Beta Centauri, and disclose the fantasy of the Southern Cross. The youths stood in shock and awe, and who knows what was going through their minds. "Wow! Everybody knows those things are only fireflies, or maybe lost torches to help hunters find marsupials at night, and there he stands, giving names to them. Only a silly fool of a white man would do that; they even give names to different kinds of *worms*."

End of reverie. Beginning of serious discourse. The precise nomenclature for a place like Karimui is that of an "extinct" (ha ha! Smoke issued from the eastern crater in April, 1986, and deep rumblings were felt) Pleistocene volcano, *with a deeply etched radial drainage pattern* (no emphasis needed for indigenous folk). The cultural implications of this are mind-boggling, and we shall get to them. The purely natural ones are worse.

There is such a thing as a pyroclastic cloud, like the one that took out Pompeii and Herculaneum. Now that all the roads at Karimui have been rendered permanently useless by a nasty growth called "cow grass," the legacy of a failed cattle-project, one can see here and there immense blackened boulders, the size of a house. Nature's artillery. Those unlucky enough to have escaped being deepfried by the very air they stood in would be obliged to take collateral damage. All we know of the past is that it happened; we do not know how many layers of serial human occupation are deposited in thin layers of soot beneath the leaf-choked galleries of rainforest. Though I'll be sure they saw stars – for a brief moment.

* * *

So now for the facts that we *do* know.

Fact: It is usually impossible at Karimui to see anything at all except for leaf-choked galleries of vegetation, tending vertically and almost horizontally. *Fact;* The earliest Patrol Officers to enter the region said that the mud there was like nothing else in their experience. *Fact;* You do not have a field day at Karimui, you have a field trip. *Fact;* The mountain, Karimui, never looks the same way once, let alone twice. *Fact;* There never has been a stable population at Karimui, and the very idea of a social aggregation is something of a misnomer. *Fact;* There are more than enough flies there to cover the living, the dead, all their garbage, the ethnographer, and then some. (Ants, which I have already mentioned, are another matter.) *Fact;* In all the time I spent at Karimui, recording minutely the so-called reciprocal exchanges that are the very essence of the social life (and death), I have never once recorded an exchange that came out anything close to even. David J. J. Brown, an English ethnographer who worked with the Polopa (blood enemies of the Daribi), had exactly the same experience with their exchanges, and concluded that they and the Daribi must be very similar people.

Conclusion (to all of the above): The reason that the Daribi and the Polopa take particular care, though they should not, to make sure that all of their vitally important social exchanges come out uneven, in fact *unbelievably one-sided*, is that if they did not do so, they could not spend days and days, believe me, and even weeks, inventing highly improbable but immensely imaginative reasons for why the exchange did not come out even. Which, of course, they had already taken care of. So there must be a better reason (there is always a better reason, and, if not, they will think of one). And in most cases the better reason would be, besides the fact that they had never studied at the University of Chicago, that if they did not spend challengingly long periods of time enervating the human mind in this way, they would lack for a spiritual life. And then of course, they would have to go back to looking for the horizon again.

End of serious discourse. Beginning of Daribi-style dialectic on the importance of talk for political and ostensibly spiritual purposes, or, in Daribi, *po begerama pusabo po*, 'the talk that turns back on itself as it is spoken.' Sound familiar? It should; it is highly contagious, and your author seems to have caught a good dose of it. It is distantly related to asthma.

* * *

Now for why the long-awaited deliverance of the Daribi people is almost upon us. At some point in 1970 or so, a man named Nezhuguare (which means, literally, something like 'Whenever'), who lived at Nekapo, where one can almost see the horizon (I actually saw a rainbow there once), had a brainstorm. He claimed, on no uncertain evidence (which is the only kind that there is), that it is possible for some highly privileged people, like him, for instance, to *unlock the ground*, look down inside, and see the *real* reality that lurks behind such things as road-finding, false horizons, interminable dialectics, pyroclastic clouds, the University of Chicago, white men ... things like that.

Meanwhile, back in America, I began to get letters from friends at Karimui to the effect that (I quote): "Some men came around. And they had a key. And they unlocked the ground. And we looked down inside and saw cars, buses, trucks, and taxis moving down there. Many people saw this, but some did not." Now this sounds very much like what is called a "cargo cult," or millenarian movement, for of course they did not see traffic jams, accidents, and that sort of thing. It touched off a general cascade of finding lost horizons where one might least suspect them – a sort of figure-ground reversal of business as usual. People buried pigs in the ground, without even eating them first, stopped working in their gardens; something was afoot. Life itself became one-sided.

Things mounted to a head; there was a rumor of a projected uprising in March, 1973, in which all the white people living at the station were to be massacred.

In fact, it never happened (that would be too much like "evening the score").

* * *

Fact: Most of the white people living at the station were the Reverend Kenneth Mesplay and his family. *Fact;* The Mesplays were about to be detained, jailed, and evicted by the Colonial so-called Government for daring to build schools, hospitals, and successful, indigenously run businesses on their own dime. *Fact;* That pseudo-Government, itself about to be evicted from the country, wanted to claim credit for what the Mesplays had done, since it would never lift a finger to do anything of the sort for what it considered to be "primitives." *Fact;* This author, yours truly, would probably have been shot on sight if he had been anywhere in the vicinity, since he had been acting in concert with the Mesplays to disclose a fraud, by which that Colonial Non-Entity was scheming to re-settle 5,000 Chimbus on Daribi ground.

* * *

Now for the real reason why the massacre never happened.

Fact: Nezhuguare was not a primitive at all, but too damn sophisticated for his own good. Or anybody else's. *Fact;* In March, 1973, he couldn't find the keyhole. *Fact;* The key itself had been obtained by illicit means, being the kind of token key that Australian families give to their sons upon reaching the age of twenty, signifying the Freedom of the House. *Fact;* In this case it was the Freedom of the Chicken Yard, since the young Patrol Officer (Australian) in question had used his key as collateral to seduce a young Daribi maiden in his private guano patch. *Fact;* Anyone, for whatever purpose, who deigns to commit such a pleasurable act in such deplorable circumstances is not a chicken-shit coward at all, but a *Holy Martyr*, who deserves to go *straight to heaven. Fact;* The girl? I guess she got to know Nezhuguare really well, which is more than he ever did.

Conclusion: This is another fine example of uneven exchange at Karimui, and what it leads to, the talk that turns back on itself as it is spoken. Who else would look for cultural conception in a chicken yard?

* * *

There are two kinds of time at Karimui. There is the ordinary kind, like the 80s and 90s in America, when the measures of time merely accumulate like a senseless music, and people generally fall apart. And there is the extraordinary kind, like the 60s and 70s in America, when everyone secretly wishes that nothing will work, and then acts surprised when their wishes come true. In 1988 some Daribi people burned the government station down, because, as they put it, "We think that government is a bad idea." When they tried to raise the Papua New Guinea flag at Karimui, in celebration of Independence, it refused to go up the mast, and the assembled multitudes jeered "Papua New Guinea *duare.*" Which means, in over-polite language, "Papua New Guinea *sucks.*"

Now what has all of this to do with the invisibility of the horizon? Plenty.

It goes back at least to the great Allied air raid on the Japanese concentration at Wewak, which began on August 17, 1943: an event that the Daribi connected with a bizarre code of laws that they received from Papua a short time afterward.

If you lay a ruler on a map, connecting Port Moresby, where the big American bombers were based, with Wewak, the straight edge will run right across Karimui. And that is how the Daribi people, who did not even know what aircraft were, first saw them. "All day long they came, in straight lines, flying nose to tail, many, many of them, with a drone that covered everything. Then later they came back in the same way, and we noticed that some of them were flying with difficulty, as though they had been damaged." Right across the sky, from one non-existent horizon to the other and back again, with a roar that turns back upon itself as it is broken. "And right after that came the Talk of Koriki."

Armed Constable Koriki was a Pawaiian speaker from the Purari River, and an indigenous war hero. The explorer Ivan Champion described him this way to me in a letter:

> Koriki was the most remarkable bushman that I ever knew. He had a remarkable sense of direction. He came from the middle Purari and he seemed to know a 'trade language' he shared with the people round Karimui. (Champion; personal communication, 1971.)

Captured by the Japanese and interned, Koriki broke free and made his way back to Allied lines. Sent to "interrogate deserters" (we know what this means) at a place back of Kerema, where a group of his own people are known to live, he is said to have "run amok" and attacked his ANZAC commanders with a bayonet (I would have used grenades). After that he was remanded to his own village on the Purari, and he sent out a series of seven apocalyptic pronouncements as "laws," predicated upon a forthcoming "end of the world" (Wagner 1979).

Witnesses were able to recount them to me in detail, with an imagery connecting fire, kinship, and sexual intercourse (but not chickens). The one that the Daribi acted upon went like this: "[As for] married women and young women, never mind, let them be; widows, however, they still have fire in their loins, take them!"

The first reaction to the Talk was to perform the *habu* rite, which sets up an artificial antagonism between men and women. Daribi generally did this when things came unstuck. The second, contingent, reaction was to begin the programmatic mass-raping of widows, always in large supply around Karimui.

Gang-rape is usually reserved for women captured in warfare and those that their husbands have "thrown away." But in this case, "Some men did this, others just watched," as I was told. "You don't understand, Roy; this didn't just happen once, it came many, many times, and eventually we got tired of it." What did they do about it? They sent a war party down below the invisible horizon on the Purari, and took out Koriki.

The search for the horizon comes in many parts, most of them frankly disoriented. An American B-24 crew, whose plane had crashed in the highlands, came down through Karimui on their way to the coast, using their parachutes as shelter. They reported much yelling and yodeling at Karimui, and a lot of fighting seemed to be going on. "Oh, those guys," said the Daribi in response to my inquiries, "see, at that time we were fighting about which direction the white man would come from."

The people of Masi remember a white man coming into their village from the south, where, as he indicated by signs, his plane had crashed. "He had a tiny rifle stuck into his belt, the like of which we had never seen before. He kept gesturing for directions to get to the highlands, and we showed him. That night he slept on the verandah, instead of inside where it was warm, and in the morning he took off back in the direction he had come from. We think he did not trust us." Nor, it seems, the horizon either.

Patrol Officer H.E. Clark came from the south, too, probably in 1951, with a large party of carriers. The Masi people had set an ambush on the road for their enemies, the Pawaiians (many of whom are light-skinned), and when Clark appeared instead, they shot him in the temple with an arrow. "We will never forget this," the Masi said, "because a constable shot our bowman *right through the tree* he was standing behind, with a rifle. Wow!" The patrol dropped their heavy cargo-boxes on the spot, and whisked Clark back to the coast as fast as they could travel. Leaving all the "cargo," which the Masis broke open with axes. "We were very foolish, then, because we threw the tins of meat away in the bush." Foolish, maybe, but not unpatriotic; a later patrol, come to make amends, found them wearing undershirts, and their leader draped in the Australian flag. (Clark survived this adventure, but died later when he fell off a dock in Daru.)

Who needs a linear chronology, anyway? When Ivan Champion encountered the Daribi at Mt. Suaru ("The Bomai") in 1936, he photographed them dressed in *habu* attire. As he and his party continued their trek, searching for Mt. Karimui, they were startled by a huge party of armed men, running after them. He expected an attack, but they were coming, in all innocence, to tell him he was on the *wrong road*. A *right road* would be lonely, in those parts.

* * *

Direction matters very much to the Daribi. In fact, *everything* matters (probably because there is so much of it). Their first encounter with white people, we think, was with the Australian prospectors Michael Leahy and Michael Dwyer, on June 17–19, 1930. When I asked Leahy about this, I was stunned by his response: "So, Roy, you were one of the first people into Karimui." Daribi witnesses to the event told me that they had been worried about the *direction* the two had come from, since the Creator Souw (said to have had light skin) had left them going in the *opposite* direction. Making the land (*to nigare*) as he went. Ebinugiai of Karuwabu: "We thought they were coming back to *unmake* the world, because their loose clothing looked like the sheddable skin of Souw. We set spies on them, because we were afraid they would cut the supports of the sky." (Notice he did not say "horizon." How could he?)

* * *

Fact: At a séance in 1968 I told the medium that my mother had died. A lot of women gasped: "We didn't think you people died!" *Fact;* The best maps I could obtain in New Guinea, in June, 2000, showed a modern, vehicular road going straight across the twin volcanic cones of Mt. Karimui. *Fact;* Despite Nezhuguare, or possibly because of him, there are *still* no four-wheeled motor vehicles at Karimui. *Fact;* There are not two, but *three* species of cassowary at Karimui, the one a-fowl (e.g. unbeknownst to ornithologists) being a *subcompact* variety called *harogo tori*, which lives, plus or minus the vehicular road, on the upper reaches of Mt. Karimui. Opposite to the elevation of Nezhuguare's traffic directions.

Startling conclusion: A compass, at Karimui, would have to include an artificial horizon in its design. Most do, but in this case that surrogate horizon would have to encompass an even more ephemeral direction-finder to help the Daribi figure out where they are coming from, and where everyone else is going. As for cassowaries, we have never figured out whether they are pretending to run when they fly, or pretending to fly when they run, or even whether they are mortal or merely subject to long fainting-spells, but in any case they would do better with wheels, or possibly roller-blades. Except, of course, at Karimui, where they would be best advised to go underground.

* * *

Time turns itself around, like the talk that tells of it, and fits itself automatically to the shape of the day. The single day is the microcosm of all happening, like an egg laid at sunrise that broods all day long, and suddenly you have an omelette, perhaps with a bit of cassowary for flavoring. Let's take a sample.

In the rather awkward light of early morning, a voice is booming out. "*Awe*," Daribi for 'Yes!' It is the local *genuaibidi*, or important leader, giving the order of the day. Like a threat that no one fears, or a promise never kept. He faces the house; he suspects the weather; he comments like a talk-show host; he warns of foul play. "Now things have come to a pretty pass," he intoned one morning, "now look what your mistakes have brought us to: a bush owl has carried Roy's cat up into a tree!" Then he tells everyone what to *do* about it.

Fear not; this is but the long crepuscular period in which we are learning to understand one another. After about two years' living there, one begins to develop fantasies about it. My most accurate one was like the nursery story about Henny Penny, Goosey Lucy, and "the sky is falling." One hears about it at first light: "For some reason, we don't know why, and we don't know how, *the sky is falling*. Now what are we going to do about it? I want all you able-bodied men to get your axes and go out there in those trees and cut supports for the sky! No slacking – bring your lunch and get out there. *Now*."

At about ten or so in the morning all the able-bodied men are out there with their axes, perhaps in a disused garden, perhaps along the road, which was never quite finished. Sounds of chopping are heard; sometimes the men chorus their delight as a huge tree goes crashing through the vines that used to hold it up. No one asks how you can tell whether the sky is falling or not when you can't even see the...horizon.

At about one o'clock precisely half the men are still chopping, though perhaps the sky has decided to take a break. The rest of the guys are lazing around, munching on sweet potato, poking the fire, or commenting on the look of the weather or why bush owls carry pussycats up into trees. "Perhaps they don't know any better."

By three o'clock only a few men are left standing. On the treetrunks, musing, perhaps. "Anything as big as the sky would take a long time to fall," or else "Bush owls, you see, they have no real experience of cats, and perhaps they thought it was a marsupial." The rest of the men are moving surreptitiously about, pretending not to look for firewood to take home to their families. The nether part of the sky is beginning to look cobalt blue.

By four o'clock nothing is left in the clearing except a few trees, still patiently holding up the sky. Or wondering why anyone would bother to cut them down. Most likely it is raining, but on some days a cool, crisp wind comes up around the western edge of Mt. Karimui, the heavens clear, and all the people of the household get out and cook their evening meal together in the ground. They make uneven exchanges; they worry about owls, but before anyone can get into the delicious parody of trying to explain how and why, they fall fast asleep.

Horizon-people, like the Tuareg and the Polynesians, have a positive gift for *depth* of any kind – incredible genealogies and long-distance travel. They enjoy immensely being so far away from where they are now. Horizonless ones, like the Daribi, have it the other way around. They have a precocious shallowness that is so originally a part of its not being there that any sort of complication is something of a relief. Though of course inventing anything so complicated and full of moving parts as the *zero* would be considered an act of betrayal. Incest? At least they take responsibility for it, which is more than we ever did. Also, *rainbows*.

* * *

Dobubidi, the eponymous ancestor of the Dobu people at Karimui, was born with a pair of beetle-wings, with which he was able to deceive his relatives in incredible ways and beget a lineage upon his own daughter. His talents in this respect were the legacy of his grandfather *Abupagai* ('Father-Begotten'), a rainbow-like hybrid being who "left his bones in a special place behind a waterfall," moisture-phoenix that he was, and who "*flies on top of the storm*," overdetermines the deluge. He overmakes the rain, masterminds the lightning, and personally superintends the terrible *mazhuku* winds that rip through the rainforest.

And who are we fooling, we anthropologists? None of this, by any stretch of the imagination, or analogic extension, is anything like the *society* or social entity that was disclosed, or perhaps scared out of hiding, by Thomas Hobbes and John Locke, and later "domesticated" by the social-contract argument of Jean-Jacques Rousseau. Remember that Hobbes called his brainstorm "A Mortall Godde" or "The Leviathan," and that Rousseau was chasing rainbows. We have no evidence at all that the Monster has gotten any less feral than in Hobbes's day, or that our "globalized" economy will ever make it out of the debtor's *prism* of Rousseau's reflection.

What does "society" do that a rainbow could not do better? Abupagai was "explained" to me as a *hoa-bidi*, an elemental transfiguration of a gifted savant into the natural forces and uniformities that he could only imagine while still alive. "See that mountain peak over there, the one we call *Kebinugiai* (e.g. 'Named for the Cassowary') that was once a hunter who knew the land so well that after his death he *became* the ground he used to hunt over." Who needs the construction of social realities when you can become a natural one after your death, and then go hunting for people instead of merely trying to understand them.

We have a tendency to use our well-proven and world-famous natural forces to think about everything, including the technologies that were responsible for them in the first place. We see the machine in the person and the person in the machine. The Daribi, like the composer Sibelius, perform this magic with the landscape itself. Might the Daribi want to reverse our anthropological insight on this, and claim that we have some prodigious *hoabidi* of our own, which we fail to recognize as such? Let us try what the *hoabidi* Albert Einstein would call a "thought-experiment." Our world runs on electric current and its many "electronic" specializations. But all of this depends upon the correct behavior of an *Abupagai*-construct called "the electron," an underdetermined artefact of uneven exchanges that "flies on top of the charge." What if Werner Heisenberg's Uncertainty Principle were elevated from its status as the undercurrent of doubt to that of an epiphenomenal natural force? Then none of our so-called electrons, either individually or collectively, would be able to determine its precise location and velocity at the same time. And all of our scientific and practical constructions, to say nothing of our current events, or even scientific currency, would vanish quicker than a bunny. Or a Daribi horizon.

* * *

Fact; The true significance of the Uncertainty Principle has yet to be determined; at certain times Heisenberg was very uncertain about it. *Fact;* None of the expensive electric generators installed at Karimui station has ever worked consistently, and the station itself seems powerless to prevent this. *Fact;* We do not know how many *hoabidi* are at work at Karimui or what their specialities are. *Fact;* The "uncertainty" *hoa* seems to have invaded the traditional Daribi numbering system. *Fact;* The Daribi number-marker *si* is entirely self-relative in its usage, and means both 'two' and 'half' at the same time. This is evident in the Daribi attempt at clarification, the incalculable number called *sidari-si*, the 'two-together-two.' *Fact; Sidari-si* decouples the fantasy of number itself from the (heuristic) action of counting (you can't *count on* it), so the only other numbers traditionally recognized at Karimui were "one" and "three." It follows from this (if anything follows from anything at Karimui), that "one" and "three" (e.g. all the other numbers). – *The Conundrum* plus or minus *its own being there* – are figure/ground coefficients of an implicate inversion of *sidari-si*, that might be called *si-tedari-si*, or 'two-other-two.'

* * *

Conclusion #1: Daribi would not know what to do with even numbers even if they had them, which they do not. *Conclusion #2*; As David Brown pointed out a long time ago, this situation is a direct result of the utter necessity of uneven exchanges. *Conclusion #3*; The *hoabidi* of Gödel's Proof was obviously responsible for the Daribi near-mathematic, since the algorithmic equivalent of the Proof, "Using logic, this hypothesis cannot be proven to be true," matches (evenly) with "the talk that turns back on itself as it is spoken." *Conclusion #4*; Go back to #1 – this one obviously does not count, for all of the above (or below) reasons. *Corollary*; At least we have figured out what Catch 22 really means.

* * *

This brings us to the problem of named and unnamed children. The only time I was ever invited to name a Daribi child, I, in my ignorance, ventured the name "Abupagai." This was rejected with much head-shaking. Children without names are a general nuisance: they *don't count*. Children with names are a *particular* nuisance (they *can't* count), and run the risk of identity theft, bad omens, and possible even numbers. Much of the problem is understandably connected with a kind of uncertainty principle regarding the essential nature of children themselves. A child is regarded as a wound from within (this is fairly obvious in the case of the mother, but even more so in that of the father, who is obliged to go hungry while his mate is in the birthhouse). Often, since names go by analogy, some other injury to a parent is nominated to stand proxy, as a sort of godparent, so there are plenty of kids running around with names like "Bitten-By-A-Pig," "Struck-By-A-Tree," or my favorite, "Killed-By-The-Road."

But I digress. In spite of all the ingenuity, there are still a lot of unnamed children at Karimui, and Daribi have a rather uneasy solution to this. A child may either be named for the fact that it has gone unnamed, and given the name *Poziawai* ('Unnamed'), or else, in a rare streak of positive thinking, called *Poai* ('Named'). We think there are about as many *Poai* as there are *Poziawai*, but are uncertain, given the 50% child mortality before age 5 at Karimui, so they must be distributed *sidari-si*.

Why not just call them all "Larry," as in "Corollary," and move on? In

June, 2000, I asked my friend Danu just why it is that Daribi equate the name of a person, or their shadow or reflection, with the soul, or animating principle, called *noma'*. "Stand over there, in the sun, Roy, and stare at your shadow on the ground," was his reply, "and then look up at the blue sky and tell me what you see." I did as I was told, looked up, and saw the retinal afterimage of my erstwhile silhouette – a rods-and-cones effect – shining up against the blue.

"Luminous beings we are," said the Yoda. That would make our ordinary flesh-and-blood semblance something of an undeveloped negative, and the actual *physical body* into what the Daribi's neighbors, the Wiru, call the "picture-soul" of the person. What's in a name, compared to photosynthesis? It was the Patrol Officer Ernest Mitchell who first suggested that the Daribi were a *negative people*. Possibly he got this idea from the fact that the morphological structure of their grammar comes apart into respective negative and positive alternatives for practically anything that can be said. (Example: future negative imperative: *Nage me dwaidwai po uramo*, 'You shall not, in future, say negative things.') More likely he got the idea from the fact that shadows are basically horizontal, even when standing at attention.

* * *

Ernie's predecessor, the first Patrol Officer stationed at Karimui, had to be dismissed from his post after he was found on his veranda, staring in the general direction of Mt. Ialibu (e.g. where the horizon might be, if it should ever deign to put in an appearance). But before that unfortunate event, he had written in his notes (I paraphrase): "The Pawaiian natives, to the east of the station, claim that there is a part of the person that survives death. But the Daribi natives, to the west of the station, say that that is nonsense, and that when people die they simply go into the ground and that is all." Checking on this with my friends, I got no disagreement; they would nod their heads and say "see, their faces disappear."

There are no such things as *dead persons*, clear? And there is simply no disputing this fact ("Who, *me*? A *negative person*? *Not* on your life") The basic trouble with what the Daribi call *izibidi* ('die-person' as opposed to 'dead-person,' which would be *bidi iziare*) is not that they do not exist, but that they insidiously and evasively *only pretend not to exist*, while in point of fact they are really and categorically non-existent the whole time. (Where, oh where, is Gödel's Proof, or for that matter Russell's or Epimenides's Paradox, *when you don't need it*?) The *izibidi* is not a ghost; why else would it turn its back on itself when it is unspoken? It is only those things, and especially those things, that never did exist, never could exist, and never will exist, that give this kind of trouble, and make the blood go like water in our veins. It is always someone else pretending, or even pretending they are not pretending, as the case may be. What is fear but the (pretended) absence of non-fear? What is infinity but another lame excuse for the (non-existent) horizon?

Are *izibidi* and *hoabidi* different aspects of the same conundrum, like fractal coefficients of a general inability to survive death, or comprehend the wholeness of time? Most of what would pass for ritual or religion elsewhere are actually attempts to control the mind-boggling anomaly in this. Daily life is full of omens and precautions to re-adapt the sane individual to what amount to bursts of uncontrolled hysteria (in the case of the spirit medium) and superbly managed coups of curing and divination (in the case of the shamanic adept).The *habu* rite is a diabolically clever dramaturgical ploy involving whole communities in the effort to domesticate a potential *hoabidi* gone wild. The *izibidi* that victimizes pigs and children is no longer just an *izibidi*, whatever that may be, but a potential serial killer or worse. What is the quick definition of a landscape gone wrong; something like a waterfall without its rainbow, right? The men performing the *habu* offer themselves as sacrifice to the *hoa's* possessive mania, and what they get in return is something of a tropical depression – the *hoa* follows them back to the house in the form of a rainstorm. Shades of *Abupagai* (I experienced the full wrath of this during my self-sacrificing participation in a *habu* at Tiligi' in 1968).

Jesus wants me for a rainbow. Time is anything but linear in the light of a mortality that makes play with timelessness; the measures of things redistribute themselves paradoxically in a pattern rather like that of *sidari-si* and *si-tedari-si*. The *si* (note that this also means 'season' in Daribi) that comes together with itself, and the one that parts with itself. The problem goes beyond the ordinary terms of control and structure, and bears upon an innate incohesiveness of human categorization: what if *izibidi* are not only not the persons they once were, and not even the piece of landscape or thunderstorm they might actually become, but something totally different than we could imagine, that takes form only through our inability to imagine it? What if all *izibidi* are just living people pretending the dead, who have other fish to fry, like the hermetic DNA of our bodies, pretending itself another life outside of the cell? What if "culture" itself were a basically inert facade that comes to life only when the ethnographer, the Patrol Officer, and the missionary happen to be looking?

May I share a vignette with you? It is New Year's Eve – December 31, 1963. Torrential rain is drumming on the tin roof of Karepa Mission Station, and inside Ken and Rosalyn Mesplay, yours truly the ethnographer, and Patrol Officer Ernest Mitchell, are sitting at a table, playing a boardgame. The game, common enough in those days, is called "Careers." Meanwhile, back along the mountain, the Daribi are sitting, warm and cozy, beside their firepits. One of them gets an idea: "Say, it occurs to me that some of the Patrol Officers are not real Patrol Officers at all, but just pretending." Another one chimes in: "Well, if that's the case, then maybe Roy and the Mesplays are just pretending, too." A general discussion ensues, with much smoke, laughter, and quizzical glancing, and finally: "But what are they all pretending?" Silence. Then a voice: "Well ... maybe ... *us*."

* * *

Fact: Time is the pretended form of memory because memory is the pretended part of time. *Fact;* The problem with time is not that it does not exist, but that it does, because all the time we can remember is still with us, and has not passed at all. Time is a wound from within; anthropology is a *wormhole*. *Fact;* As Kurt Gödel patiently explained to Albert Einstein, his theories had nothing to do with time, except to *pretend* it as space. *Fact;* It was at about that time that Einstein gave up on his theories, and only went to his office to talk to Gödel. Who, as a matter of *fact*, only went to his office to talk to Einstein, since, without that magical ingredient called "space," which was, after all, Einstein's forte, neither one of them could *remember* where their offices were. End of continuum.

Beginning of horizon

Conclusion #1: "Space is the only *kind* of time that is still left around, and that really matters" (Wagner 2001: 254).

   Conclusion #2: "Time is the difference between itself and space; space is the similarity between them (Wagner, ditto).

   Conclusion #3: A rainbow is like a false horizon come true to life, "written on the wind and inscribed in running water" (Catullus). I cite Catullus here only to show that a rainbow is not what we think it is, nor even what *Apupagai* (bless his bones) thought it was, but more like a woman at the point of climax, "coming colors in the air" (Rolling Stones: "*She's Like a Rainbow.*")

* * *

And this, at the point of climax, leads us to another fact.

   Fact; What happens to those who *go*, rather than *come*, in their climaxes? As I was flying out, at the end of my first fieldwork at Karimui, a *double rainbow* formed around my plane, and escorted me, like a portable orgasm, all the way to Goroka. The Daribi with me viewed it with alarm, but not me; my time had *come*.

* * *

Is it possible that the horizon was somehow *rained out* over Karimui, or detonated by some ancient pyroclastic cloud? More probably what we have here is an *auto-mimetic* (e.g. self-imitating) phenomenon, like the orgasm itself, that comes of its own accord when you least expect it. To find out the answer to this and other tantalizing mysteries, one would need an absolute master of horizons like Jukka Siikala. The Polynesian horizon would make infinity think twice about its destination, and provide Jukka himself with the rainbow he deserves. What kind of rainbow would that be? Well, you know, and the Daribi do too – the kind of *double rainbow* that would make immortality itself seem anti-climactic.

Long live the *Sisu*!

REFERENCES

Wagner, Roy 1979. The talk of Koriki: a Daribi contact cult. *Social Research* 46: 140–165.

Wagner, Roy 2001. *An Anthropology of the Subject: Holographic Worldview in New Guinea and Its Meaning and Significance for the World of Anthropology.* Berkeley: University of California press.

Means of Travel and Models of the World

Old Men and the Sea

Antony Hooper

The themes of "age" and "manhood" both seem appropriate for this congenial Festschrift occasion. So also is the sea, given that it has for years been Jukka's haven from many everyday cares – and because of the fishing. My paper begins with the fishing, more particularly with an account of sixteen exciting and occasionally ecstatic days of skipjack fishing on the Tokelau[1] atoll of Fakaofo, over 35 years ago. It concludes with some thoughts about what fishing meant in Tokelau all those years ago – and, surprisingly, what it still means today in spite of all the changed circumstances of life on the atoll. It always meant food, of course. But more than that, it gathered together and displayed the prowess and authority of older men, as well as the virtues of generosity, reciprocity, cooperation and humility, which were seen as the core of male identity. These are of course all things that Jukka has long known. I hope that this paper might go some way towards reassuring him that he is not alone in this understanding.

In 1971, Fakaofo had a population of about 650, divided between some 70 households. Although there had already been a good deal of emigration to New Zealand (with a population drop of about 200 since 1961) and there were about 30 administration-paid wage and salary workers on the atoll, the village was still very much a neo-traditional one, with practically everything under the control of an entirely male council of elders. The per-capita annual income was under NZ$50, and much of the people's subsistence came from local production of fish, breadfruit, coconuts, *cytosperma*, pandanus, pigs, chickens. The only links with the outside world were provided by a ship from Samoa every three months or so. Houses were made of local materials; there was no electricity and only three outboard motors. Transportation was by locally-made canoes, of which there were about 60. Fishing was an important subsistence activity. It was almost entirely a male pursuit[2], governed by the weather, making use of some widely-known techniques, and based upon

---

1   Huntsman and Hooper 1996 is a general historical ethnography of the group.
2   Women often joined in expeditions to harvest *tridachna* inside the lagoon, and were the main harvesters of octopus from the reefs.

traditional knowledge of fish behavior throughout the lunar and annual cycles. The gear, however, was as modern as the people could afford, which meant nylon monofilament lines, store-bought hooks and swivels and stainless steel trace. Two main items of the traditional gear survived – circular Polynesian hooks (forged iron rather than shell) and pearl-shell lures rigged to lengthy wooden or bamboo poles.

On the evening of Sunday 18 April, the Fakaofo elders met to decide what should be done about the large flocks of feeding seabirds seen around the island. It was coming up to a time known locally as "days of the ō," usually between the 23rd and the 25th of the synodic lunar month, when large aggregations of the small reddish baitfish known as ō often appear in the sea just outside the barrier reef.[3] Since skipjack and other tuna are closely associated with these aggregations, the elders decided to send out three canoes the following morning to watch for the ō and keep an eye on the birds. The canoes returned at mid-morning on Monday 19th and reported having seen small aggregations of ō and large flocks of feeding birds well out to sea. They had caught some small *caranx*, cut them open and found ō in their stomachs. The elders called a meeting of all men late that afternoon at which the crews out in the morning described what they had seen at sea.

Anticipation and a subdued excitement could be felt all through the village. No such large schools had been seen around the atoll for a generation or so. For the men, the excitement was charged with anxiety and a mood of high seriousness. From the outset, it seems to have been generally assumed that the only way to catch the skipjack was the traditional way, with organized expeditions using poles and pearl-shell lures. That, however, was a very special skill, demanding a long apprenticeship and with the definite possibility of ridicule and shame for those who mishandled things, causing a whole school to panic and sound. But because the skipjack had been absent for so long, a whole generation of men had come to maturity without this apprenticeship, much less with having had a *kau kumete* ceremony performed on their behalf, entitling them to be known as *tautai* 'master fisherman' with the privilege of commanding a canoe crew from the stern seat and handling the rod, doing all the fishing.

On Tuesday 20th, seven canoes went out, returning about mid-morning with the same reports of birds working well out to sea, and with one canoe having caught a single skipjack. That evening there was a crowded meeting of elders and men, at which the talk was all about fishing, with the men questioning the elders closely about the exact meaning and significance of a number of things, for example:

• The difference between the named ways of bringing a hooked skipjack into the canoe,
• Whether skipjack were *hā* 'taboo' in the same way that billfish and turtle were, and how many skipjack could one catch before being obliged to

---

3   The ō are reddish in color and between 3 and 5 centimeters in length. They have recently been identified as damselfish (*Lepidozygus tapeinosoma* Bleeker).

"take them to the village" to be divided amongst the whole population.
• Whether it was permissible for men who had never gone through a *kau kumete* ceremony to fish for skipjack,
• How a *hā* placed on the ocean to prevent any form of fishing other than for skipjack could be lifted.
• If it really was one of our customs (or one brought in from outside) that a man whose wife was pregnant was prohibited from swimming to catch mating turtles. And whether the custom was of any use.
• Similarly, was it true that pointing to indicate mating turtles at sea would make them sound and disappear?
• The meaning of six or seven technical fishing terms.

The elders decided that the same four canoes would go out the following morning while the remainder of the men should stay ashore for village work. A call was made around the village that night announcing that the ocean was now *hā* and only skipjack fishing could be done.

Four canoes went out on Wednesday 21st. One caught six skipjack, which were shared and eaten at sea by the canoe crews. The same four canoes were out on Thursday 22nd. Marlin and porpoise were evident under the scattered flocks of birds, and only 20 skipjack were caught and "taken to the village" to be shared amongst the whole population. This was hardly a large catch, however, and since the skipjack seemed to be petering out the elders announced in the evening that *kāiga* 'family' lands across the lagoon would be "open" on Friday and Saturday for people to visit and make copra. On Friday 23rd, in spite of this "opening" of the lands, four canoes went to sea, catching 30 skipjack, of which 20 were "taken to the village." There was a meeting of elders and men in the late afternoon. The elders had obviously decided that it was time for some concerted instruction, and gave speeches on the following topics:

• The need for skipjack fishing to be organized, with men fishing not just wherever they liked, but taking instruction from the oldest fisherman present, who should also be the first to enter a school and start casting.
• The care needed to prevent hats, paddles, hooked fish or anything extraneous from falling into the water, thus causing the school to disappear.
• This was rather scoffed at by another elder who emphasized that this was all of little use if people did not in fact fish together in a unified way so that in the end there would be enough to feed the village.

Elders also announced that the family lands would be "closed" again tomorrow, countermanding the previous arrangements.

On Saturday 24th, nine canoes went out, but there were only three skipjack caught. Sunday 25th was given over to church as usual. Then early in the morning of Monday 26th, five sails were hoisted at the northern reef, plainly visible from the village. There was a noisy excitement amongst the women, who knew that a lot of fish must have been caught because the canoes were returning so early. They formed a large gathering at one of the lagoon bays as the canoes formed a line offshore and the crews raised their paddles twice in unison, indicating a catch of 200. Women waded out with drinking nuts, cordial, biscuits, any sort of food to present to the crews, grabbing the fish and taking them in procession to the center of the village for division. There were 160 skipjack all told. There was a call for a meeting of elders and men in the late afternoon. This was a crowded session, beginning with thanks to all the fishermen who had been out. The women had by this time prepared baskets of cooked food which they took in procession around the meetinghouse and then, breaking all protocols, marched straight into the middle of the gathering, laying the food on the floor. The older women made mock-heroic speeches and there were dances, skits and a great deal of hilarity. The men then ate, and after that the elders announced that they had come to a decision that no outboards were to be used anywhere near a skipjack expedition (referring to one man who had used an outboard on his canoe, not while actually fishing, but to get his canoe out across the lagoon to the open sea.) One of the more mature men pleaded with the elders to teach the younger men all these things of the sea, and asked for the elders to arrange a *kau kumete* ceremony. There was also some general discussion of many points, including:

- Different ways of holding a skipjack rod,
- Whether fishermen should avoid sleeping with their wives the night before going out for skipjack (Yes. It makes you weak. And besides, that was our custom in the old days.)

On the following day, Tuesday 27th, ten canoes left the village at 3:30 a.m. for the long paddle across the lagoon to the northern reef. They assembled at the lagoon edge of the reef and then, at the very first light, slipped through the breakers in the tiny channel out to the open sea. Skipjack were everywhere, just outside the reef, feeding voraciously, and several canoes were soon foundering under the weight of fish landed.[4] Back over the reef in the lagoon the canoes were gathered together under the direction of an elder and the catch counted as 547. Then back to the village and a repeat of the previous day's reception. On this day, one of the younger men, actually a very good fisherman, had made a couple of mistakes while fishing by dropping hooked fish back into the water; this was noticed by one of the older fishermen, who yelled to him what every young fisherman dreads, "Scram back to shore!" He quickly did so, and that evening went and apologized, with tears, to the older man.

On Wednesday 28 April, 11 canoes went out, doing everything according

---

4   This was the only time that I ever went (as a paddler) on a skipjack canoe, and it remains unforgettable. The fish were breaking in large patches of the surface, disappearing suddenly and then coming up in different places. Terns were screaming and diving all around the canoes as the *tautai* standing at the stern were steadily jerking the skipjack in. With only three or four inches of freeboard the bilges were soon awash with water, blood and froth as the fish, each weighing a couple of kilos or so and very much alive, set up a loud drumming noise as they thrashed against the canoe sides.

to the book, under the direction of a very old and frail elder, but one who had had a reputation for skipjack fishing as a younger man. But only 177 skipjack were landed and taken to the village. On this day there was a very inexperienced younger man in his own canoe out trying his skill and making a mess of things. The frail elder yelled angrily from his canoe, "[You've been] shitting on shore, shitting on shore! And now you come [to shit] at sea! Scram!" On Thursday 29 April the same 11 canoes went out, again led by the frail elder, everyone being punctilious and waiting for him to begin fishing before they did (which turned out to be the wrong decision, since he went to the wrong school). 112 skipjack were landed and taken to the village, with the usual food brought by women to feed the crews. Then a large meeting of elders and men was held in the afternoon, with the usual session of questions and answers, but also some very direct public scolding of younger men for their mistakes. In particular, the man scolded at sea the previous day was called out before the whole gathering and told that he was utterly lacking in proper respect for not immediately sitting down, shipping his rod and getting back to shore when told to do so. Another man who had also made mistakes had his ancestry and proper upbringing questioned, and then both were delegated to go out on the lee shore (where there were no skipjack schools) the following day. There was also a very impassioned speech from one of the older men about the need for *āva* 'respect and politeness' in all fishing, both at sea and on the reefs, waiting for direction from older men, not crossing water where other men were fishing, and so forth.

On Friday 30th, 11 canoes went out, paddling from the village through open sea the long way round to the northern reef because of the tide times, trolling for squirrel fish on the way. These were later given to women (for their own consumption) who would bring food out to the crews when they returned. 77 skipjack were landed and taken to the village. A decision was then made by elders that the family lands across the lagoon would be opened the following day and men could please themselves whether they went there, or out to sea.

On Saturday 1 May, eight canoes were out and back by late morning with 123 skipjack, taken to the village. Sunday 2 May given over to church, and in the evening a long meeting of family heads about some administration business which had been postponed for weeks because of the skipjack activities. On Monday 3 May, six canoes were out in the early morning, some of them having left right after the previous night's meeting closed, and came back in dribs and drabs in the late morning, with none of them having caught skipjack. At the large gathering of men in the meeting house that afternoon there was little directed discussion, just yarning about fishing in general. Again on Tuesday 4 May, eight canoes went out into a large easterly swell, but returned with no fish. That evening there was a call made around the village that a *kau kumete* ceremony was to be held the following day. This had been a sudden decision taken by the elders, though not an entirely unexpected one. There was some grumbling about there not being really enough time to prepare food, but general agreement that perhaps it was better to do it this way – suddenly and without wasting time.

The *kau kumete* occupied most of the daylight hours on Wednesday 5 May and involved the whole village. Previous *kau kumete* ceremonies (none had been held for a generation) had always been initiated by families on behalf of one of their young men and had involved the family in taking food to the elders in exchange for the elders accepting the young man as a proper person to be a *tautai*, a 'skilled fisherman,' worthy of taking the stern seat in a canoe on the open sea. The elders were expected to give blessings, detailed instructions on technical details, and presents of pearl-shell lures.

This was apparently the first "group job," held because everyone thought it somehow appropriate, even though many of the young men were far from being expert fishermen. The whole day was firmly under the control of the council of elders. Thirty-nine men were involved, most of whom were about 30 years old, although three were over 40. Their families contributed 495 baskets of prepared cooked vegetable foods (over 600 kilos), 13 cooked pigs, 12 tins of cabin bread, one chicken and $6 in cash. It was the culmination of two rather extraordinary weeks in which a whole age-group of men had listened to some 18 hours of instruction at formal meetings, heard countless other tales in less formal contexts, and had a bit of practical experience. And still the elders could say, with a mixture of sorrow and compassion, that they had hardly even begun their proper instruction – a view which all the novices readily agreed with. The following is a summary of the lengthy speeches given by the elders:

Elder 1 began by explaining the significance of the gathering, its ancient base, its rarity nowadays, and the high seriousness with which it was regarded. He emphasized that it was done as a "blessing" for young men. He praised the men for their efforts over the previous days, and the families for the large amounts of food brought.

Elder 2, taking his cue from this Christian blessing, began by reciting the well-known pagan prayer asking for a plenitude of all natural products, and spoke of "the most important thing"– respect and courtesy between men at sea, and the value of generosity. "Let your hands be open on the ocean. Do not close them. If your hands are open, you will be known for it." He then referred to the *ika ha*, or 'sacred fish' (billfish and turtle, which when caught must be taken to be divided among the whole village, a practice that is still followed), exhorting all inexperienced fishermen to leave them alone if they encountered them at sea because they were dangerous – in the elder's words, "the death of men." He went on to detail stories of the dangers involved in catching them.

Elder 3 began by explaining that his words were the *fakapuku* of a father, (the term referring literally to the feeding of a young bird by its parents, and widely used to refer to the way in which a father passes his fishing knowledge on only to a true son, and to no others). He spoke of long-lining techniques and the noosing of *pāla* (*Acanthoccybium solandri*).

Elder 1 stepped in again to emphasize that all these things were really too complicated for brief explanations and exhorted the novices to go out with older fishermen to learn exactly how things are done. He also got on to the noosing of *pāla*, and the dangers involved, embellishing his speech with many examples.

Elder 4 emphasized the need for care and attention to the welfare of crew members, and then gave a long detailed story whose moral was the absolute necessity of "being open-handed at sea." He then presented the novices with the pearl-shell lures which had been collected together by the elders, apologizing for their poor quality but explaining that it was the best they could do at such short notice. Everyone then ate.

When the meal was finished a small canoe was brought up from the shore to the ground outside the meetinghouse, and three elders in turn climbed into the canoe, and, using a makeshift rod with a line and coconut attached to it to represent a skipjack, demonstrated the named techniques for bringing a hooked skipjack into the canoe.

While this bald summary really gives very little idea of the richness and technical complexity of the operations dealt with, or the rapt attention of all the men involved, it does give some idea of the major themes. Firstly, the ceremony was not in any sense a venue for open discussion, but rather an affirmation of distinctly Tokelauan techniques. The very structure of the occasion emphasized the authority of elders, making explicit at least some of the knowledge and experience which legitimated that authority. Secondly, all the speakers emphasized the need for care and skill, especially dealing with turtles in the water and with powerful, fast fish like marlin and *pāla*. Thirdly, the speeches all extolled the virtues of cooperation, protocol, etiquette and generosity, all of which are summed up in the phrase *āva i te moana* 'respect [one another] at sea.'

Then it was all over. There were no more skipjack around. The rods were put away and men got on with making copra. Nobody talked much about the skipjack anymore.

* * *

All that happened, as I have said, over 30 years ago. The elders who guided the skipjack operations in 1971 are all now dead, as are, sadly, many of the younger men who so eagerly sought their advice and took part in *the kau kumete* celebration. There have been some sizable schools of skipjack in the waters around the atoll since then, although none of them have been as large as those of April 1971, and there have been no more organized communal expeditions to bring them in. The skipjack rods and lures[5] are still there, stored in the house rafters, and are sometimes taken to sea by those who know how to use them. But the 60 canoes have now effectively disappeared from Fakaofo, being replaced by aluminium dinghies with outboard engines, from which it is impossible to fish for skipjack in the traditional way.

---

5 The pearl-shell shanks of these lures (minus their tortoise-shell hooks) have recently taken on a significance as women's ornaments in Tokelau dance troupes – expanding, perhaps, on an older use as items of marriage exchange.

In spite of these changes, however, the store of traditional fishing knowledge that so suddenly came up for open discussion in 1971 has not simply disappeared and been forgotten. If anything, it has been amplified and even written up in various forms. I have myself tried to play a part in this. Back in New Zealand later in the 1970s my colleague Judith Huntsman and I played my audio tape of the *kau kumete* ceremony to an elderly Tokelau man who had left Fakaofo many years previously. Once a catechist on the island, he was a staunch traditionalist and a renowned skipjack fisherman. He listened very intently and declared (in a most respectful and indirect way) that the speeches were wholly inadequate. He asked for a tape recorder, and, a few days later, sat before it and recorded some two hours of the kind of speech that he thought should have been made. This is full of some mind-numbing detail, and is transcribed (double column, text and translation) in 60 A4 pages.

The same man produced other written texts having to do with fishing and the annual cycle of lunar months together with a description of the preparation of pearl shell for the making of lures which was published by the NZ Education Department.[6] The headmaster of the Fakaofo school published two articles on fishing in the local newsletter, and another, younger man, has written a 70-page single-spaced A4 document in Tokelauan on Fakaofo fishing. Yet another man, an elder, has written a manuscript with details of 100 named fish, with notes on their habits and the methods used for catching them.

All these efforts, however, have been dwarfed by the recent completion of a manuscript of about 80,000 words written by a group of elders from another Tokelau atoll, Atafu. The elders began this about ten years ago, meeting regularly in a hall in the Wellington suburb where they all lived. One of their number wrote down their thoughts in longhand, which was later transcribed by a few of their computer-literate children. Some of the elders died during those ten years, but the manuscript is now about to be published, helped by funding from a New Zealand national heritage organization.

* * *

What might be said about all this? What is the source of the clear, unequivocal authority wielded by the male elders over almost every aspect of village life? Why the fetishization of fishing? The question of authority is embedded deep in the 19th century history of the island, which was, in pre-Christian times, the center of power in the group, and the seat of the sacred *aliki* 'king.' That polity effectively collapsed under outside influences in the 1860s, but not before it had, by local decree, been transformed into a gerontocracy.[7] Although there have since been a few modifications made (again under outside administration influences on what is now called "governance") in the 1970s all women's organizations on the island were ancillary to those of

---

6   Perez 1989.
7   The transformation is described in Hooper 1994.

men, and women did not hold office in village-wide organizations. Fakaofo was male-centered and hierarchical.

Women had a separate domain of influence and authority, derived from post-marital residence being ideally (and very largely in practice) uxorilocal. As the Tokelau saying has it, "women stay, men go on the path." Each household, then, was (and still is) built around a core of related women. Their husbands might live there, but also have no real authority within the house; that authority rests with "brothers" of the women. Men in fact spend a lot of time outside of where they "live," working under the control of the council of elders and spending at least two (and often) four days of working together under their direction. A generation or so ago, communal fishing was a regular part of the work, and, as with fishing everywhere, experience and local knowledge were invaluable. Certainly the elders' control of events surrounding the 1971 skipjack schools had an element of mystification around it. But the events did more than hide the reality of that control, in Maurice Bloch's terms. They also served to create that reality – one that younger men had never experienced, but which they imagined was important for their standing as men.

But there was a great deal more to it than knowledge of techniques. All the advice, encouragement, homilies and rhetoric, whether spoken or, nowadays, written down, are suffused with five pervasive themes:

- The value of cooperation, doing things together rather than individually.
- Social control, especially by the elders.
- Physical skills and accomplishment–very highly rated as in sports and dancing.
- Safety, and responsibility to the young.
- Honor, deference and generosity.

Many of these ideals survive – in Tokelau as well as among emigrants in New Zealand – where they are, at the same time, being steadily transformed into heritage.

.

REFERENCES

Bloch, Maurice 1974. Symbols, song, dance and features of articulation: is religion an extreme form of traditional authority? *European Journal of Sociology* XV (1): 55–81.
Hooper, Antony 1985. Tokelau fishing in traditional and modern contexts. In: R. E. Johannes and K. Ruddle (eds.) *The Traditional Knowledge and Management of Coastal Systems in Asia and the Pacific.* Jakarta, UNESCO. Pp. 7–38.
Hooper, Antony 1994. Ghosts of hierarchy 1: The transformation of chiefly authority on Fakaofo, Tokelau. *History and Anthropology* 7(1–4): 307–320.
Hooper, Antony and Judith Huntsman 1991. Aspects of skipjack fishing: some Tokelau "words of the sea." In: A. Pawley (ed.) *Man and a Half: Essays in Honour of Ralph*

Bulmer. Auckland: The Polynesian Society. Pp. 249–256.
Huntsman, Judith and Antony Hooper 1996. *Tokelau: a Historical Ethnography.* Auckland: University of Auckland Press/Honolulu: University of Hawaii Press.
Perez, Peato Tutu 1989. *Ko te Koloa a Tokelau.* Wellington, Department of Education.

The House and the Canoe

Mobility and Rootedness in Polynesia

Harri Siikala

For a non-islander looking at a world map, the islands of Polynesia may seem isolated dots in the deep blue of the Pacific Ocean. Anthropologists once even considered the region to be a naturally insulated "laboratory" for the study of evolution and distribution of cultural and linguistic traits. For Polynesians themselves, whose fondness for traveling is well documented, the ocean was no confining element, however. In their view the horizons opened up to a vast "sea of islands" (Hau'ofa 1993), with inter-island social networks reaching far and wide. Despite this mobility Polynesians maintain a tremendous sense of place, a reverence for points of origin. This dual nature is manifest in key symbols Polynesians use to conceptualize and organize their societies. In this paper I will take a comparative look at two such ordering tropes, the house and the canoe. Both objects embody group identities by accumulating histories that trace a spatiotemporal connection between the present social order and that of the ancestors. By being containers of persons, they are constructed as total social bodies; composite bodies that encompass all the individuals they contain. Like a founding ancestor who stands for his descendants or a chief who stands for his subjects, the house and the canoe stand for the people whose history they objectify. This pervasiveness of genealogical associations linked to houses and canoes can be traced to a larger Austronesian pattern. Yet, if both tropes articulate origins of social groups, they do this according to very different principles.

By virtue of their function, the house and the canoe stand in a complementary opposition to each other. This opposition is reflected in the way they embody social collectivities. In Polynesian oral traditions society is commonly depicted as a social totality fixed by a point of origin, or as a mobile whole that is differentiated through political segmentation and geographical dispersal. When the fixed point of origin is emphasized, social hierarchy is established by the rootedness of the group to the land it occupies. Unbroken genealogical continuity is crucial in establishing claims to power and rights to land. Here, the house figures as a central symbol that expresses historical continuity and authenticates the group as a territorial unit. On the other hand, when mobility of the social whole determines its origins, authority is established in migration legends that map the movement of the founding ancestors. These legends take two basic forms: stories of migration from an origin island to the present home, and stories of conquest where the present social order is established through predatory acts of an outside usurper. In these origin myths the canoe represents the mobile social whole, and its captain and crew become the founding ancestors of the social group or the chiefly line.

Though at a general level the house seems to represent rootedness and unity, and the canoe, mobility and segmentation, they do not constitute separate symbolic domains. Their complementarity is expressed in the ways the two categories overlap and transform each other. Still, for the sake of analysis I propose to make a distinction between schemes where the spatial fixity of the house receives more emphasis and ones where the migration canoe comes into a greater relief. I call the former "origin societies," as its people claim to be indigenous to their land, and the latter "settler societies" as the people think of themselves as immigrants. I am not proposing that these are two discrete types of social organization, but rather offering the categories as heuristic tools in hopes of shedding light on the different but complementary social processes. Though, for the sake of clarity, I stress the differences between the categories and impose upon them an artificial coherence, it is clear that features of both types are likely to be present as competing narratives in any Polynesian society.

Origin and settler societies can perhaps be placed on a rough historical trajectory. Polynesian cultures developed in the western "homeland" of Samoa and Tonga from which they expanded to the east (Kirch 2000: 208). While Western Polynesians commonly consider themselves autochthonous, Eastern Polynesians generally trace their origins to a mythical island of Hawaiki that lies to the west. Hawaiki can be seen as a reference to Samoa or Tonga (Kirch and Green 2001: 96). Thus, the island groups where canoe symbolism is most pronounced seem to be those that have been settled most recently, though such a simplistic conclusion sheds little light on the complexity of the cultural systems.[1] In the first part of this paper I will examine Samoa as an example of an origin society. In the second part I will take a comparative look at the settler societies in Eastern Polynesia. Through contrasting the two types I attempt to show that the house and the canoe cannot be understood apart from each other, for they articulate a basic social and cosmological dialectic between mobility and stasis.

Transformations of genealogy: From ramage to house society

Before analyzing origin and settler societies I'll give a short review of the theories concerning the composition of Polynesian social groups. The classic

---

1 For example, the systematic relations of gift exchange and marriage alliances that the Tongan maritime empire maintained with Samoa and Fiji form their own complex pattern, see Kaeppler 1978, Kirch 1984, Gell 1993.

model for the Polynesian conical clan is given by Raymond Firth (1982 [1936]), who in his work on Tikopia called the non-exogamous descent groups "ramages." The ramified lineage is segmented according to primogeniture and the different subgroups are ranked according to their genealogical proximity to the patrilineal line of the founding ancestor (Sahlins 1958: 139–142). Firth later claimed that the patrilineal Tikopia were an exception, and redefined the ramage as an ambilineal corporate descent group where membership is obtained ambilaterally (Firth 1968: 213). This system of kinship reckoning is unrestricted in that both group continuity, determined by the lineage, and group membership, determined by the parents, can be traced relatively freely through either sex. Firth (1968: 209) distinguished such optative kin groupings from definitive groups, where individual choice does not enter into establishing membership. Fictive kinship, adoption, and ability to trace kin through affines contribute to the fluidity of the system. Firth's redefinition of the ramage is part of a larger theoretical shift that focused on the cognatic nature of Polynesian groupings. When it became apparent that formal analysis of descent could not account for the variety of social formations found in such societies, operational analysis of kinship and praxis theory, with their emphasis on strategies and individual decision making, superseded the earlier theories (Howard and Kirkpatrick 1989: 54, 59).

For Firth, the problem of social cohesion that cognatic descent groups presented was that eventually everyone can trace kinship to all other groups, and loyalties and rights should become hopelessly dispersed (Firth 1968: 211). In practice, the destabilizing effects of the optative descent system are countered by the organization of the society on two different planes. On the wider scale, society is made up of unrestricted descent groups, but on the ground level it is organized by residential household groups (Goodenough 1968). Since individuals belong to larger ambilineal groups, they are able to move between residences to which they can trace kin, while the localized landholding units remain relatively stable. The connection of an individual to the land and to a house must be demonstrated by residence. Otherwise claims to titles and rights made on the basis of kinship tend to "grow cold" in a few generations (Firth 1968: 212). Though the ramage appears to be a descent group and legitimizes itself genealogically, "a person chooses membership in a particular ramage, either for himself or his children, by settling on its house site, cultivating its land, or participating in significant activities" (Lambert 1966: 642).

These theoretical departures from the strictures of formal kinship analysis can be seen as precursors to the current rethinking of house societies (Carsten and Hugh-Jones 1995, Gillespie and Joyce 2000). Lévi-Strauss (1983) suggested that the house could be viewed as a form of social organization that unites seemingly antagonistic principles of kinship reckoning. The house provides continuity through "holding on to a fixed or movable property and through the transmission of names, titles, and prerogatives which are integral to its existence and identity" (Carsten and Hugh-Jones 1995: 7). Just as in a ramage, membership is gained through participating in the "actions involved with the preservation of the joint property" that defines and socially reproduces the house (Gillespie 2000: 2). As a physical structure the house "naturalizes" differences in rank by representing them in an objectified form (Carsten and Hugh-Jones 1995: 11). Thus, analysis of house symbolism provides a useful starting point for looking at emic symbols of social organization that are not strictly reducible to biological kinship.

Though Polynesian societies can be analyzed according to a house-based model (Kirch and Green 2001: 202), I would argue that the house can be fully understood in this region only in relation to the canoe. They both naturalize rank and provide an objectified symbol for the genealogical continuity of the group. If houses attach people to the land they inhabit and thus organize residential groups, canoes organize groups by defining their movements and anchoring them to a point of origin. In this paper I look at three types of houses and canoes I consider most symbolically salient in Polynesia: ones that are owned by chiefs, ones that are dedicated to gods, and ones that are used in large communal undertakings (meetinghouses and voyaging canoes). The three categories overlap in significant ways, as I'll demonstrate below. Rather than simply reflecting biological kinship, the symbolic efficacy of houses and canoes hinges on their ability to relate parts to wholes in mytho-historical representations of social hierarchies. In their material existence they provide a shared substance through which the group becomes embodied.

Part One: Samoa as an origin society

The origin myths of the Samoan people differ from those found in settler societies of Eastern Polynesia in that Samoans claim to be autochthonous; their social order is not organized according to migration sagas. When pioneering New Zealand ethnographer Peter H. Buck, also known as Te Rangi Hiroa, had to give a speech at a Samoan welcoming ceremony, he alluded to the common Asian origins of the Polynesians and praised the courageous voyages of their seafaring ancestors. To this a chief replied, "the Polynesians may have come from Asia, but the Samoans, no. We originated in Samoa" (Buck 1959: 294). Buck defended his claim by referring to the Biblical story of Genesis to convince the devoutly Christian Samoans, but still received the same answer. Flustered, Buck remarked that he must then be in the Garden of Eden. An affirming silence followed his retort. This anecdote illustrates the strong link Samoans have to their land as a center of the social universe. The name *Samoa* itself can be translated as 'a sacred center' (Allen 1993: 36). This centrality, I will argue, is reflected in the relationship between the house and the canoe.

Mythical origins of houses and canoes

In the oral traditions of Samoa the origins of houses and canoes are intertwined. Tagaloa-Lagi, the god of the sky and the creator of the world, instigated the building of the first house and canoe. In the beginning Tagaloa could not decide which he should start with, and versions of the myth differ on which was constructed first. According to one variant he chose to begin with the canoe, but then realized that the trees of the forest could not provide adequate shelter from the elements (Holmes 1974: 52). He solved the problem by deciding to build the canoe inside the house. The first house was built from people who climbed on each other's shoulders to form wall posts and parts of the roof. This structure was well shaped, but it lacked support. To remedy this, Tagaloa brought three fish from the sea and made them into central posts. The frame had to be further reinforced by more people who formed the ridgepole, arched gable beams, and the cross above the central posts. After the house was completed, Tagaloa decided that it should be made from wood rather than people, and from all the available materials he picked the breadfruit tree. The god was now too old to build any more houses and chose various members of his family to carry on the tradition of housebuilding.

This myth employs several widespread Polynesian motifs. The linking of the house and the canoe is striking. There is a fundamental ambivalence about which came first, the social totality in the form of a mobile canoe or the social totality in the form of a stationary house. The dilemma is resolved by positioning one inside the other. The potential for mobility is encompassed within the fixed parameters of the society. The first house is a total social body that is literally made up of people.[2] The structure of the collective house-body is at first shaky and has to be reinforced until it is stable. Paradoxically, to achieve this, a mobile element from the sea is introduced. The fish are identified with the three central posts that structurally play the most significant part in holding the building upright as well as being ceremonially central.

The myth also identifies the first house with two types of actual buildings. In the end Tagaloa decides to substitute wood for the people, and chooses breadfruit trees (*ulu*) as the correct material. The use of this wood points to the house being a *fale tele*, 'a guest house' or 'a meeting-house where chiefly councils take place' (Buck 1930: 69). These houses are still the ceremonial and political centers of Samoan villages. The myth also implies that at first the house was a canoe shed (Holmes 1974: 53). The canoe shed, which does not have central posts (Buck 1930: 12), was then transformed into a *fale tele* through the inclusion of three fish-posts. Thus the shed can be seen as a mediating figure in the symbolic transformation of mobility and immobility, an intermediary form between a canoe and a guest house.

Another origin myth tells of Sa Tagaloa, the family of Tagaloa, who descended from the heavens to build the first canoe for the paramount chief of Manu'a (Mallon 2002: 48). After they finished the canoe, the workers proceeded to build a great house for the chief without consulting their divine father. The angry god destroyed the house and scattered the carpenters who spread throughout Samoa. These men became the founding ancestors of the powerful guild of *tufuga*, 'master carpenters.' Such carpenters build only better classes of houses and boats, and can ask exorbitant prices for their work. The origin of the carpenters' craft is also explained in stories where Tagaloa

2 The corporal associations are also found in the iconography of Samoan tattooing where central elements correspond to parts of a house (Gell 1993: 99).

appears merely in an advisory capacity. In the beginning, according to them, there was no standard form for a house, and all carpenters specialized in one shape only (Riddell 1930). Chiefs were having trouble finding workers with the necessary skills to build what they wanted, and so a great meeting was held to establish a uniform shape. After a fierce debate the carpenters decided to consult Tagaloa-Lagi, who pointed to the sky and said they should model the houses after it. Henceforth the domed roof of the house is likened to the heavens extending to the horizon.

The process of building the first house out of people could be interpreted as a transition from an initial period of instability to a fixed—and architecturally solid—social order. The movement from chaos to order is also apparent in the second myth where the form of the house is collectively decided. This is a mythical precedence for establishing *fa'a Samoa*, 'Samoan custom,' by the collective decision of a council meeting. The correct form is authenticated by the divine advisor, and establishes a structural analogy between the most visible part of the *fale tele* and the realm of the sky-dwelling god. The association between the rounded dome of the house and the sky can be linked to a common Polynesian motif. The chiefly posts that connect and separate the sky and the earth are mediating elements that open up a space for the social world of humans. It is the potency of the chiefs, here represented by the three fish, which holds together the house that is the society.

The guest house as a diagrammatic icon

Three distinctive features of traditional Samoan houses still persist in contemporary architectural design: round ends, open sides, and a single undivided room under each roof (Neich 1985: 19). Traditionally the important types of houses for which one would consult a master craftsman included the *fale afolau*, a large rectangular guest house with rounded ends that is structurally similar to a canoe shed, and the *fale tele*, the round guest house where *fono*, or 'chiefly councils,' take place. The traditional *fale tele*, 'big house,' is higher than other structures surrounding it. Three central posts support its beehive-shaped roof, and a line of wall posts circle its perimeter. These posts do not actually carry the weight of the roof, and are structurally less significant than the central posts. According to Buck (1930: 56), the erection of the wall posts was beneath the dignity of the *tufuga* carpenters and was left to the unskilled labor of the family or the village. Ritually, however, the wall posts are key elements of the house for they mark the seating positions of chiefly titleholders at *fono*. They are sometimes referred to as "heads of chiefs" (Buck 1930: 58). This might explain why the posts are erected by kin rather than outsiders. During ceremonies the floor of the meeting house is covered with pandanus mats. These mats are feminine goods that served as the most prestigious item of exchange, and fine mats that symbolized the genealogies of their owners were stored in the rafters of the guest house (Tcherkézoff 2002). The size of a *fale tele* indicated the rank of a chief through his ability to mobilize resources for the payments involved in hiring the *tufuga*. The number of collar beams on the roof of the guest house had to adhere to the internal hierarchy of the village: no chief could have more beams in his roof than the highest ranking chief of the village (Buck 1930: 97). Through its size and build, the *fale tele* represents a symbol of chiefly prestige.

The social structure in Samoa is governed on all levels by a hierarchy expressed in the circular arrangement of the chiefly *fono* (Mead 1969: 10–11). The *fono* organizes the precedence of titles that are owned by families. This social ranking is expressed formally in two ways: in *fa'a lupega* formulas that recite the chiefly names and titles that come together in a *fono*, and in the seating order mapped onto the floor plan of a guesthouse. The *fa'a lupega* functions as a mnemonic device for ordering the parts of the social hierarchy, and forms a greeting that must be recited at the beginning of every *fono*. Each hierarchical level of the society is ordered by this system of precedence. These include the great *fono* of all Samoa, the district *fono*, and the village *fono* where most local things of practical importance are decided (Mead 1969: 10–17). As a setting for these gatherings, the *fale tele* functions as a diagrammatic icon of the society. It represents a space within which the hierarchically differentiated parts of the social whole can come together according to a historically defined order of precedence (Parmentier 1987: 107). As such it offers a contextually malleable ideal schema for differentiating rank within chiefly councils (Duranti 1994: 60).

The schema that the meetinghouse objectifies delineates a dichotomy between centers and peripheries. The house itself functions as a center of spatial organization within the village and is usually located near the sacred village green (*malae*). Though round, the house is said to have two sides, a back, and a front. In the ideal scheme the chiefs are seated next to their posts on the two sides, while councilors, called "talking chiefs," sit in the front. The lowest ranking people attending the *fono* sit at the back. The center post of each of the respective sides locates the most prestigious position. Household complexes within the village are oriented towards the *malae* and the guest houses in a radial pattern, so that their front is the more central and prestigious area while the back is the more peripheral (Shore 1982: 48, Neich 1985: 9, Duranti 1994: 62). According to Bradd Shore (1982: 79), the front is the seaward side of the house, while the back is the landward side. From the perspective of the whole village, however, the front/back orientation seems to be lined to face the coastal road, so that those household complexes that are on the landward side of the road face the sea, while those on the side of the sea face the land (Allen 1993: 36). This is important, for both deep sea and deep bush are associated with masculinity, expansion, and aggressiveness, while the *malae* and the guest house are associated with femininity, stasis, dignity, and social control (Shore 1982). The paradigmatic symbol of social order and hierarchy, the guest house, is feminine. It is associated with the sister of the chief. The gender associations of spatial organization correspond to a distinction made between mobility and immobility: "associations of stasis and movement with women and men respectively are fundamental facts of Samoan ideology about gender" (Shore 1982: 227). These associations are crucial for understanding how titles are arranged in the ultimate expression of social hierarchy, the *fono*.

Chiefs, talking chiefs, and social mobility

Titled men who partake in the chiefly councils are called *matai*. They are divided into *ali'i,* or 'chiefs,' and *tulafale,* 'talking chiefs.' The *tulafale*, who are the "foundation" or a space upon which a house stands, specialize in oratory and function as advisors for the chiefs. They speak on behalf of the *ali'i* at the chiefly assemblages, and represent a more active side of political power (Keesing and Keesing 1956). While the *tulafale* have secular authority (*pule*), the *ali'i* have *mana*, or 'sacred power.' All of the titles are linked to descent bilaterally and achieving a title depends on the decision of the *fono* to grant it. A person of high rank is likely to hold multiple titles, and titles can become divided between numerous people by the decision of the *fono*. Usually the titles are only achieved relatively late in one's life, so there is never an absolute identification between a particular individual and a particular title. If a *matai* does not live up to his title, the *fono* may take it from him. The spatial ordering of the guest house serves as a powerful reminder of the relationality of statuses. If a visitor sits down on a place that indicates a lower status than he is entitled to, he will be treated according to this position (Duranti 1994: 58). In building a guest house the Samoans emphasize the fact that the wall posts can be easily removed and replaced (Buck 1930: 57), an assessment that seems to correspond to the fluid movement of individuals in the system. Though persons may move within the hierarchy and between households, rank is always encompassed in a relational system of precedence.

Though Samoan *ali'i* trace their *mana* to the gods, this power is not a constant property of an individual (see Shore 1989). The volatile *mana* must be demonstrated by functioning effectively as a chief. The splendor and size of a *fale tele* could thus be a direct justification of a claim to power. Rather than being associated directly with the chief, *mana* was associated with his sister. The relationship of the chief and his sister was marked by ritual avoidance and mutual respect. "A man's sister has the power to place a curse of barrenness upon him, thus cutting off his line, which in Samoa (and indeed in any Polynesian society) would be an act of utmost gravity" (Howard and Kirkpatrick 1989: 70). As we saw from the spatial organization of the village, the immobile center of social order is feminine, while the mobile periphery is masculine. Accordingly, the sister is central in relation to the brother. The relationship between a chief and his sister can also be mapped onto the relationship between a chief and a talking chief (Shore 1981). The *ali'i* is immobile and feminine while the *tulafale* is mobile and masculine. "The *Ali'i* merely sits (*nofonofo*) whether in the *fono* house or the *malae*, while the orator speaks for him and 'moves about' doing his bidding" (Shore 1982: 242).

In-turned hierarchy

As Peter Buck discovered, Samoans claim to be indigenous to the land they inhabit. Rather than emphasizing mobility in the constitution of social precedence, Samoan origin myths emphasize the rootedness of the social groups to the land. The family group (*aiga*) is "totally defined by this reference to origins: it is the name, the land, the funerary site, the 'house of the name' (where the chief, invested with the name, receives guests)" (Tcherkézoff 2002: 35). This rootedness is often marked by chiefly graves situated next to guest houses near the edge of the *malae*. By erecting a burial monument to their parents, descendants can solidify their claim to the land (Tcherkézoff 2002: 45). While funerary monuments bind the benevolent ancestral spirits to the land, they are also said to be canoes that take the chiefs to the land of the dead where they become posts for the house of gods (Mead 1969: 51, Mead 1968: 245). This double identification of high-ranking ancestors with the land and the realm of gods marks the power that is embodied in chiefly graves. Political authority, with its rights and obligations, is immobile and spatially fixed. It is coded in the history of the bonds of kinship embodied in the houses and burial sites of founding ancestors. The older and more detailed the history, the more solid the authority it represents.

Outside aggressors, when they appear in Samoan mytho-history, are not integrated as such into the social hierarchy, though internal conflicts were commonplace and marriage alliances to the neighboring islands were systematically maintained. When the highly stratified maritime empire of Tonga colonized the islands of Upolu and Savaii, the Samoans revolted. According to the legend, warriors stole the anchor of the paramount chief of Tonga (Ella 1899). They fashioned war clubs out of it, and used them to drive out the invaders. The Tongans were driven out by the very object that anchored their canoe to the shores of Samoa. In another myth, a foreign conqueror does not sail a canoe, but a whole island. According to the myth, the island of Manono was brought from Fiji when its ruler, a chief called Lautala, sailed it to Samoa on a voyage of conquest. After cruising about the archipelago trying to find a good place to engage the Samoans, he finally settled between Upolu and Savaii. "Many Samoans were killed, for Lautala was a great warrior. At the conclusion of fighting Lautala and his men counted their fallen enemies. There was such an immense number that Lautala called a halt (*nono*). This is why their island was called Manono" (Stuebel 1976: 58). This motif of the warlike floating island will be seen again in the analysis of settler societies.

In the legends where Samoan chiefs themselves were the voyagers, the named canoe passes from father to son. Thus it functions much like the guest house in marking and embodying genealogical continuity. Legendary migration sagas are often concluded by the canoe returning to Samoa (Stair 1896). This theme of return establishes Samoa as a center to which the canoe turns back after exploring distant peripheries. In comparison to the Tongan empire, the Samoans did relatively little long-distance voyaging. Most of the traveling at the time of European contact was done within the Samoan archipelago (Haddon and Hornell 1936: 223). The most significant form of travel in Samoa involved ceremonial journeys (*malaga*) that were made between villages and islands (Grattan 1948: 25). These journeys were a "highly institutionalized part of communication behaviour" that "facilitated interaction beyond the local setting" (Keesing and Keesing 1956: 58). They organized the high-level council meetings between villages, districts, and islands. Such councils gathered whenever important decisions had to be made that involved groups beyond the village. The whole social hierarchy was mobilized in a visiting party, as all significant titles were represented. The link between voyaging canoes and chiefly councils seems to be underlined by the fact that the planks that made up the hull of a canoe were called *fono* (Pratt 1977: 151).

Overall, the Samoan hierarchy seems to be inward-focused. At its feminine center are the *fale tele* and the chief with his sister. The talking chiefs, on the other hand, represent an active side of political power. They are mobile and masculine, and mediate the relations between the inside (center) and outside (periphery). Mobility takes place within the larger hierarchical system that encompasses the whole of Samoa and maps relationships between families, villages, districts, and islands. Though individuals may move relatively freely by aligning themselves with any households to which they can trace kinship, political power is always contained in the relational system of the *fono*. The system becomes integrated through the institution of the *malaga*, or 'visiting parties.' Though genealogies are tied to the land and the household by the architectural complex that both consolidates and differentiates the social whole, what solidifies the larger hierarchy is the constant interaction between the constituent groups. This interaction is maintained by the mobility of the talking chiefs. In this respect the talking chief, whose very name has connotations of permanence rather than mobility, is like the mythical fish that stabilizes the great council house of society.

Part Two: Settler societies of Eastern Polynesia

I will now turn to the settler societies of Eastern Polynesia to examine the dialectic between the house and the canoe in societies where cosmological origins of social orders relate to the segmentation of expansive political systems. As I have argued in the case of Samoa, houses that become associated with chiefs and founding ancestors represent a relatively fixed point of origin. Canoes, on the other hand, become symbols for social wholes that are mobile.[3] Like houses, canoes stand for particular social groups they represent in the mythological origin structure by being containers of people whose history they objectify. Canoes define social boundaries by tracing paths between islands which would drift apart without such inter-island voyaging, and so marking their genealogical or political proximity. There is no intrinsic reason to give the house primacy as an ordering trope, and for the seafaring peoples of Polynesia, whose main geographical orientation hinges on the dichotomy between the land and the sea, the canoe represents a complementary symbol of social unity and differentiation.

---

3 For an analysis of the complementary opposition between rooted houses and mobile canoes in Island Southeast Asia, see McKinnon 1991.

Hawaiki as the root of society

The mythical origins of social orders in settler societies are usually traced back to a primordial dispersal of a foundational social whole (see McKinnon 1991, Schrempp 1992, Fox 1996). We have already seen a version of this dispersal in the Samoan origin myth for the carpenters' guild. In Eastern Polynesia the social whole existed on the mythical island of Hawaiki, where the dead return at the end of their lives (Buck 1959: 20). Hawaiki was the abode of gods and cultural heroes, but it suffered from overcrowding and a bloody civil war ensued. This prompted some to embark on hazardous canoe voyages to find new lands to settle. These first chiefs, who were descended from the gods themselves, became the founding ancestors of new social hierarchies, and the paths that they traced on the seascape in their journeying are symbolic extensions of genealogical continuity of the ruling lines. The tribes of the New Zealand Maori attain their distinctive identities in migration sagas where "the order of social structure is...established by the progression through the landscape of the tribal and clanic ancestors" (Sahlins 1987: 58). Named features of landscapes were linked together in ritualized lists that are similar to genealogies in determining the boundaries of political districts (Schrempp 1992: 77–78). In the Cook Islands, the word for "path" (*ara*) is also the word for "genealogical lists" (Siikala 1996: 46). These genealogical paths can be likened to the Austronesian botanical metaphor that conceptualizes society in terms of roots, trunks, and tips (Fox 1995: 218, 221).

Hawaiki is the sacred source, or the root, of the society and its politico-religious authority. If chiefs trace their genealogies to the gods through time, the society traces its origins to Hawaiki through space. It is a base from which the society grows out and upwards. Because of this, Polynesian social formations are sometimes called ascent rather than descent groups (Kirch and Green 2001: 224). Though the branching structure of the botanical metaphor implies segmentation, it is often the trunk itself, or the main lineage, that is said to move and extend from island to island (Beckwith 1970: 487). Thus it is the continuity of the mobile lineage, rather than its segmentation, that is often emphasized when genealogical ranks are being validated. Their movements are recorded in migration legends that serve as charter myths for the social order. In these legends the mobile canoe is identified with the figure of a wandering younger brother of a chief, or a predatory warrior who comes from the sea.

The politics of segmentation

The origin structure found in the migration legends that chart the dispersal of Polynesian hierarchies can be linked to a larger Austronesian pattern of founder-focused ideology that validates claims to power (Bellwood 1996). According to James Fox (1995), the modes of social differentiation that operate within this origin structure include two formal systems. The first is "lateral expansion" and the second "apical demotion with concomitant predatory expulsion" (Fox 1995: 223). In the bilateral societies of Polynesia where the principal criteria for status differentiation is relative age, the younger brother of a ruler can move away to establish a new settlement with its new order of precedence. This lateral expansion gives rise to multiple origins and an emphasis on place and the journey in the construction of political identities. In the mythological scheme, the canoe journey undertaken by the younger brother erases the junior status based on the original primogeniture.

In contrast, hierarchical societies that are based on a tighter exclusivity of social reckoning have singular origins that establish the authority of the ruling class, as one line retains status and guards origin narratives in the form of restricted genealogies (Fox 1995: 223). This system of apical demotion leads to the predatory expulsion of high-ranking people when the system gets crowded (Fox 1995: 225). They are forced to journey onward and establish new hierarchies with their followers. Such a system is centered more on names of ancestors than places, and strictly separates the ruling class from the commoners. The first system seems to be characteristic of large islands that have space and resources to spare, while the latter is characteristic of smaller places where the management of limited resources gives rise to more rigid hierarchies (Bellwood 1987). As social orders become increasingly hierarchical, systems of lateral expansion can turn into systems of apical demotion.[4] Fox identifies the ruling elite of Tonga, Samoa, and Hawaii as classic examples of systems of apical demotion.

The two systems of dispersal and differentiation that Fox outlines are ideal types. The form in which they appear in migration myths can be better understood from the perspective of the political positions they validate. These sagas structure not only internal hierarchies, but relationships between groups or discrete parts of societies. The order of arrival from the mythical homeland generates a social differentiation that is analogous to primogeniture, but when the expansion is directed at lands that are already occupied, it functions to separate newcomers from indigenous people. The founder-focused ideology is then transformed into an invader-focused one (Bellwood 1996: 32). In such a case society can have multiple origins that divide its population into indigenous land people and immigrant sea people (Sahlins 1976: 25). The chief traces his lineage to a foreign usurper and is associated with the sea, while the commoners are associated with the conquered people of the land. Though the chiefs are higher in political precedence, as late arrivals they are also junior to the land people. This scenario could be further complicated with the arrival of multiple waves of immigrant groups. "The multiple origins of groups, their social categorizations as indigenous versus immigrant groups, and the contestation of precedence" generate ever shifting political positions (Fox 1996: 12).

Marshall Sahlins' (1987) famous analysis of Polynesian stranger kings demonstrates how the chaotic *mana* of the warlike divine chief is channeled into the society through a marriage to an indigenous woman of high rank. The stranger with divine origins is domesticated by virtue of this union, and the society is able to benefit from the procreative power of the gods that is rendered safe. In a Cook Island origin myth the conquering immigrant chief is referred to as Darkness-From-The-Sea and the indigenous woman

---

4   For an archeological analysis of this process in Hawai'i, see Hommon 1986.

112

he marries is named Coming-Of-The-Gods-Through-Her (Siikala 1991: 23, 31). The descendants of this first chief are clearly marked as descendants of gods. Sahlins has emphasized that the myths that give chiefs different origins from commoners should not necessarily be taken as representations of literal history, but rather as "indigenous schemes of cosmological proportions" (1987: 76).

Canoes as symbols of society

The symbolic link between canoes and segmentary social groups is clear in the settler societies of Eastern Polynesia. Tahitian high chiefs were sometimes referred to as masts of a canoe, while lesser chiefs were called by the term that designates the outrigger (Oliver 1974: 1038). The society was commonly likened to a canoe, on the prow of which the chief was metaphorically seated (Oliver 1974: 1039). The Tahitian word for "canoe" also means a "clan or a family group" (Andrews 1979: 190). The same is true for New Zealand and the Cook Islands where the term for canoe stands for a tribe (Reed and Karetu 1984: 68, Buse and Taringa 1996: 554). Both New Zealand and Cook Island Maori traced their descent to the crews of the original voyaging canoes that colonized their home islands (Crocombe 1964: 25).

In both New Zealand and the Cook Islands, "canoe" refers to the largest social grouping. The Cook Island canoe was further segmented into "people of the same belly or womb" and smaller household groups called "people of the same door" (Siikala 1991: 76). In the widest sense the former category referred to all of one's consanguines, and in a more narrow sense to those kin with whom one is expected to have close reciprocal relations. The latter term referred to a family living in one household, the door standing as a metonym for the house. The transformation of the canoe into a house is clearly articulated in the oral traditions of the Cook Islands. In Mauke the whole population was said to have inhabited a single building in the time of the ancestors. This mythical "house of eight-hundred people" was called *are orau* (Walters 1985). *Are* refers to a house, while *orau* means 'the whole area, the length and breadth of the land everywhere,' 'a large sea-going canoe shed,' or 'a gathering place of the people' (Buse and Taringa 1996: 73, 290). The corporate body of the ancestors is first united in a single canoe and then under the roof of a single canoe shed that stands for the territorial unity of the entire island or geographical area. As I argued with the origin myth of Samoan houses, the shed mediates between the mobile canoe and the fixed meetinghouse.

Over time the social group determined by the origin canoe is broken up into separate households. A new "canoe" can be created by the arrival of immigrants or by a process of social segmentation at a higher than household level. In New Zealand the canoe was further segmented into tribes called *iwi* ('bones') that descended from individual crewmembers of the ancestral canoe, sub-tribes called *haapu* ('pregnancy') that descended from the sub-tribal founders, and the smallest household units called *whaanau* ('birthing') (Awekotuku 1996: 30–31). Here, the process of segmentation is represented as a process of organic growth from the body of the founding ancestor.

Houses and canoes as total social bodies

As objectifications of the social orders they mediate, houses and canoes are commonly analogous to the human body (Tilley 1999: 40, 113). Carsten and Hugh-Jones have argued that "the contrast between body and the house can be made to relate to differences in scale and relations of encompassment between the individual and society or between levels of social grouping" (1995: 42). This is especially true for the three types of houses and canoes that stand for total social bodies: those owned by a chief, those dedicated to gods or ancestors, and those that serve collective enterprises. These categories are connected by virtue of being in some way paradigmatic expressions of social totality. Patrick Kirch (2000) has claimed that the development of East Polynesian ritual complexes with their monumental architecture can be traced to a common Austronesian process by which dwellings are gradually transformed into temples or holy houses. Houses that grow old become associated with their former inhabitants who, in time, become venerated ancestors. The tradition of burying people, especially chiefs, in their former houses or near them is a common one in Polynesia. As we saw, in Samoa the chiefly graves were located near the guest houses and legitimated claims to group membership. Houses of Polynesian divine chiefs could turn into temples because chiefs were earthly counterparts of ancestors and ultimately of gods.

Chiefs are also focal points for any collective enterprises, in so far as these enterprises are symbolically submerged in the patterns of heroic history that the chief embodies (Sahlins 1987: ch.2). As far as the history of the society is a history of chiefs, chiefly houses and canoes can stand for all other similar structures. Separate parts of the social hierarchy come together in the body of the founding ancestor or the chief who represents him. In a limited sense, the chief stands for the original cosmological totality that existed on Hawaiki. "The original ancestor is now instantiated, not as one body but as many bodies into which his one body has transformed itself" (Gell 1998: 140). A clear example of this is the Tahitian myth where Ta'aroa creates the world and other gods by dividing up his own body, which is the original cosmological continuum (Henry 1928: 340). This is followed by a chaotic period during which the things thus created multiply and start to stabilize. "The universe is a genealogy, which is to say a total cosmological project of sexual reproduction" (Sahlins 1987: 13). But this genealogy is created by the segmentation of a shared substance, the original body. Houses and canoes are material extensions of this shared substance. Like the chief, they are composite bodies that occupy a higher level in the hierarchy of the cosmological genealogy.

Though important canoes in New Zealand might be nominally owned by chiefs, they were communal property (Best 1976: 21). Named war canoes of chiefs were often main symbols of collective prestige and power. Such canoes would have individual histories attached to them, and they represented legendary events of warfare in an objectified form. In New Zealand such canoes were explicitly associated with the body of a chiefly ancestor (Neich 1996: 98). This canoe-body had to be entered in a correct ritual manner, so as not to violate the threshold that separated the living from the dead. The hull of the canoe represented the spine of the ancestor, and was associated with the genealogy of a descent group. In the 19th century a shift occurred in New Zealand as the focus of tribal pride and symbolic elaboration moved from the war canoes to communal meetinghouses that developed from chiefly dwellings (Neich 1994: 90). The body symbolism of the canoes is still clearly apparent in these buildings. The meetinghouses have a head, eyes, mouth, arms, hands, fingers, brains, and a stomach; the ridgepole represents the main line of ancestors and forms a spine, while the rafters represent the junior descent lines and form the ribs (van Meijl 1993: 202). The descendants are thus metonymical extensions of the bodies of ancestors, and as they congregate in the stomach of the house-body, they return to an original state of embodied unity. This unity is not homogenous, but internally differentiated by the juxtaposition of the different parts of the ancestral body. Like the canoe, the meetinghouse had to be entered in a correct manner, for its door, too, marks a threshold between two realms of existence (van Meijl 1993: 209).

The thresholds of both houses and canoes were demarcated by *tapu* restrictions that fixed a temporal boundary between the secular present and the ancestral past. By being containers of collective bodies, these structures became containers of the past; a past that was potent with *mana* embodied in the coming together of the people, an efficacious approximation of the original unity. Hence moving into a house or a canoe meant moving upwards in the cosmological hierarchy. The *tapu* surrounding such movement is analogous to that which separates chiefs from commoners. Both prevent different levels of hierarchy, or different levels of social encompassment, from collapsing into each other. In Eastern Polynesia – just as in Samoa – people were often buried in canoes or burial chests associated with canoes (Mead 1928: 21, 26, 35; Awekotuku 1996: 102). These were vessels in which the deceased were said to return to Hawaiki. As in Samoa, this journey establishes a connection between the living and the dead. In Eastern Polynesia, however, the journey in death replicates in reverse the mythical migration, which established the original separation of the world of humans from that of gods. In this sense, it is another movement between parts and wholes through which *mana* flows into the realm of the living. Wholes or multiplicities (*Hawaiki*, 'ancestors,' 'chiefs,' 'social groups') appear as bodies that can only have *mana* if they are successfully set apart from the individual existence of their parts.

According to the origin myths of the first temple in Tahiti, it was made by the god Ta'aroa from his own body (Oliver 1974: 77). Thus it is metonymically associated with the god by being a physical part of him. Here we see clearly how parts are attached to wholes in a genealogical scheme as lesser entities to greater ones, or restricted concepts to more encompassing ones.[5] The Hawaiian temple was "the archetypal house, which embodied in

5   This relates to Louis Dumont's formulation of hierarchy as "encompassment of the contrary" (1980: 239), which has particular salience in Austronesian ethnography (see Jolly and Mosko 1994). Dumont's prime example of this encompassment is the Biblical story of how Eve was created from Adam's rib. "This hierarchical relation is, very

the most perfect form the meanings that are embodied in lesser degrees by every house in the society" (Valeri 1985: 302). It, too, was equated with the human body; its inauguration ceremony included trimming a thatch hanging above the door that represented the navel cord of the building. Thus the house is born into the world like a human being. The parts of the house are again equivalent to the parts of a man, and the ridgepole was a central symbol of genealogical continuity. The relationships between the house-parts correspond to social categories of rank and gender, and the overall spatial organization represents a system of social differentiation that makes the Hawaiian house a diagrammatic icon of the social order (Valeri 1985: 302). The vertical and phallic house posts are masculine and signify high rank, while the horizontal floor is feminine. The front and the top are associated with males, while the rear and the back are associated with the females. The microcosm of the house represents the macrocosm of the society at various levels of social encompassment. "A commoners' house is equated only with his family, but the house of a chief is equated with the social group he rules" (Valeri 1985: 303). The spatial differentiation of houses and canoes was manifested in things like seating orders and provided a template for social precedence. In certain Hawaiian temple rituals, chiefly canoes were represented by men who sat in rows as if they were sitting in a canoe (Valeri 1985: 285).

Marae as the mediating space between sea and land
The spatial organization of meetinghouses and guest houses typically provided a directionally oriented schema for distinguishing rank and for marking the status of hosts and visitors. Meetinghouses, chief's houses, and temples were nearly always positioned adjacent to an open-air ceremonial ground called the *marae*, as was already shown in the case of Samoa. The *marae* structures ranged from village squares found in Western Polynesia to temple complexes with stone pillars or platforms in Eastern Polynesia (Bellwood 1987: 36). The *marae* is usually located on the seaward side of the village or adjacent houses. In New Zealand it is associated with the sea, distant mythical time, and the god of war, while the meetinghouse is associated with the land, a more recent ancestral past, and the god of peace (van Meijl 1993: 197). The whole complex can be seen as a representation of a linear progression or a journey from *po*, 'the dark and violent night of gods,' to *ao*, 'the day of men and the established order of the society' (van Meijl 1993: 207). Visitors arriving from outside the community are greeted at the *marae* and are assigned to the more sacred side of the meetinghouse, which is also the side of the sea. As a ritual ground the *marae* enabled humans to "receive the gods in a benefiting manner" (Henry in Oliver 1974: 95). In Tahiti the sea itself served as a *marae* for a wanderer or an exile who owned no land and thus did not have the use of a household *marae* (Oliver 1974: 96). They would conduct their rituals on the seashore and pray towards the sea.

---

generally, that between a whole (or a set) and an element of this whole (or a set): the element belongs to the set and is in this sense consubstantial to it; at the same time, the element is distinct from the set or stands in opposition to it" (Dumont 1980: 240).

The basic Polynesian orientation of sea versus land is congruent to the stranger king motif described above. The ambivalent power of gods, or *mana*, enters the world of humans from the sea and can be traced to the mythical time of original cosmological differentiation. Though it may manifest as a life-giving power of growth that stabilizes the social order, it is also associated with war and death. The procreative potency of the warlike wandering chief must be safely channeled into the society by making him immobile through alliance and ritual restrictions (Sahlins 1987: 91). The sacred chief, whether he traces descent to the same origins as the people or not, continues to manifest the two sides of divine efficacy, and thus the hierarchical system always retains the possibility of further segmentation. Chiefs can always rise to power through usurpation, the success of which is its own legitimization for it demonstrates *mana*. In stratified Hawaii the chief remained a wanderer. "Without a territorial base, the ruling chief was obliged to move continually over subject land, living off tributary offerings of each in turn" (Linnekin 1990: 92). Thus Hawaiian chiefs were compared to "sharks that travel on land" (Sahlins 1987: 79), mobile predators from the sea. The divine chiefs were (metaphorical) cannibals who, like sharks, ate the people, and in doing so incorporated their subjects into their bodies.

Stabilizing the cosmos: Mobility comes to rest

I have attempted to outline some common symbolic dimensions of houses and canoes in Eastern Polynesia. Both are embodied icons of social hierarchies that unify as well as differentiate what they represent. Social differentiation is often linked to a primordial event where a cosmological totality was broken up. This partitioning produces the discrete categories that make up society (Schrempp 1991). According to a Cook Island origin myth "all of [Hawaiki] was broken up and scattered into small parties...and every fragment possessed a canoe. Islands were floating around like fish, and there was no solid place for society" (Siikala 2000: 22). For social order to exist, the movement of primordial chaos has to cease, the canoe has to come to rest. In Society Islands' mythology, Tahiti was originally a giant fish inhabited solely by a band of warriors (Oliver 1974: 53). The warriors managed to stabilize the wandering fish-island by cutting its sinews with a magical adze, and later became chiefs. This traveling island of warriors is analogous to the Samoan myth of Lautala and Manono. In another Tahitian myth the primordial mobility is represented by the shifting sands of the first island, which are stabilized by the growing roots of trees that represent chiefly genealogies (Henry 1928: 344):

> *There were tens of roots.*
> *There were hundreds of roots.*
> *There were thousands of roots*
> *There were myriads of roots.*
> *Roots that spread upwards, roots that spread downward,*
> *Roots that spread inland, roots that spread seawards.*
> *As roots spread they held sand; the land became firm.*

In this metaphor the principles of differentiation and stabilizing unification are intertwined. The genealogical paths of geographical dispersal also hold the land together. Without keeping in touch through constant visits that reaffirm reciprocal relations, islands can drift apart. Mobility and rootedness are complementary in Polynesia, one does not exist without the other. Hence the house as a symbol for the society cannot be understood apart from the canoe. Together they order oppositions between mobility and rootedness, the sea and the land, the realm of gods and the realm of humans, and foreign and autochthonous origins.

Conclusion: Comparing Samoa and Settler Societies

I have argued that Samoa represents an origin society where the house and the canoe are intertwined social symbols. The canoe is submerged in the house for it appears only to induce fixity. Social hierarchy is turned inward, and long-distance voyaging is largely restricted to an integrated system of *malaga* traveling parties. I have contrasted this example to the settler societies of Eastern Polynesia, where the canoe receives more emphasis, social hierarchy is turned outward, and mobility results in lateral expansion or stranger kings. To make further sense of this contrast, I suggest that we pay attention to the different ways in which *mana* is defined in the two systems. In Samoa, *mana* is associated with the immobile sister of the chief who holds power over his fertility. The sister's line also has a right to veto any decisions made by the line of the brother. The containment of the volatile *mana* is centered on the relationship between a chief and his sacred sister. This relationship is marked by a heightened incest taboo. In contrast, settler societies seem to associate *mana* with the initially aggressive, mobile chief. The containment of chiefly *mana* is centered on the relationship between a stranger king and his indigenous wife. This relationship takes the form of an alliance that channels the volatile procreativity of the gods safely to the society.[6] In the Samoan case, *mana* is associated with land and the fixed feminine center defined by the guest house. In the Eastern Polynesian examples, *mana* is associated with a mobile masculine canoe that comes from the sea.

A further point of contrast can be drawn between the uniquely integrated system of the Samoan *fono* that makes power highly dispersed, and the more centralized systems where power is inalienably personified in the chiefly line. Samoan chiefs are not divine the way Tongan or Hawaiian paramount chiefs are. The title system of Samoa "rises up hierarchically into an arena of uncertain kingship at the top" (Marcus 1989: 194). The relational nature of power in Samoa prevents close identification of individuals with seats of power, and hence the motif of heroic segmentation where the younger brother breaks away from the group is largely absent. Samoan chiefs cannot be stranger kings. A chief may move up or down within the system, but he

---

6 For a discussion of different sexual associations of *mana* in Eastern and Western Polynesia see Shore 1989: 156–163.

cannot move beyond it. The power of individual families may wax and wane but it does not entirely break away from the system of titles. Though the motif of genealogical differentiation and geographical dispersal is apparent in the myth of the carpenters' guild, such segmentary expansion does not validate new systems of chiefly power or create a multiplicity of contested origin narratives.

The concept of the house society has enabled us to step beyond the strict confines of kinship and has given us a way to look at social formations from the emic point of view. Focusing attention on the house has shed light on the ways in which individual bodies are related to collective bodies through conceptual schemes coded in material surroundings. In the cognatic societies of Polynesia, social order is embodied in objects that accumulate genealogical histories. These histories are not reducible to descent, nor is the household the only framework for them. I have suggested that in Polynesia the canoe is complementary to the house, and that one cannot be fully appreciated without the other. The history of Polynesian societies is a history of pathways that is written on the shifting contours of a symbolically coded landscape where space and time mark the proximity between gods and humans. If houses provide fixed points in the landscape, canoes allow societies to move, extend, and segment. As objectified history, both houses and canoes are things that people can grasp. Here genealogical manipulation is not about biological descent, but about pathways, proximity, and collectively shared bodies.

The focus of my interest has been on analyzing how the house and the canoe get different values in the overall cultural system where one or the other figures more prominently. A distinction can be made between the kinds of meanings they receive in origin societies and in settler societies in relation to time and space. The Samoan god Tagaloa could not decide which to build first, the house or the canoe. This is because in Samoa the dialectic between mobility and stasis is a synchronic process. The two objects must exist simultaneously. In settler societies the canoe is prior to the house. It is transformed into the house through the intermediary figure of the canoe shed. Here the dialectic is diachronic. The canoe of the aggressively mobile stranger king must come to rest.

Origin societies tend toward reproducing one hierarchical system through internal mobility. In Samoa the canoe reproduces political relationships within the system, as it links all the regions to the great *fono*. In contrast, the pathways of settler societies produce new orders of precedence and new hierarchies either by lateral expansion or by usurpation. In these societies the canoe creates new hierarchies through political segmentation and geographical dispersal. The two symbols of social order do not represent binary opposites; their boundaries are blurred. The canoe forges unity by creating proximity between separate groups and by unifying the descent group through a shared origin. The house, on the other hand, differentiates society internally and facilitates segmentation by setting regions against each other. Both symbols contain the implicit potential of their opposites.

REFERENCES

Allen, Anne Guernsey 1993. Architecture as social expression in Western Samoa: Axioms and models. *Traditional Dwellings and Settlements Review. Journal of the International Association for Study of Traditional Environments* 5(1): 33–45.

Andrews, Edmund 1979. *A Comparative Dictionary of the Tahitian Language.* Chicago: The Chicago Academy of Sciences.

Awekotuku, Ngahuia Te 1996. Maori: people and culture. In: D.C. Starzecka (ed.) *Maori Art and Culture.* Chicago: Art Media Resources. Pp. 26–49.

Beckwith, Martha 1970. *Hawaiian Mythology.* Honolulu: University of Hawai'i Press.

Bellwood, Peter 1987. *The Polynesians. Prehistory of an Island People.* London: Thames and Hudson.

Bellwood, Peter 1996. Hierarchy, founder ideology and Austronesian expansion. In: James J. Fox & Clifford Sather (eds.) *Origins, Ancestry and Alliance.* Canberra: Research School of Pacific Studies. Pp. 18–40.

Best, Elsdon 1976. *The Maori Canoe.* Dominion Museum Bulletin No. 7. Wellington: A. R. Shearer.

Buck, Peter H. 1930. *Samoan Material Culture.* Honolulu: Bernice Pauahi Bishop Museum.

Buck, Peter H. 1959. *Vikings of the Pacific.* Chicago: The University of Chicago Press.

Buse, Jasper & Rautiti Taringa 1996. *Cook Islands Maori Dictionary with English-Cook Island Maori Finderlist.* Canberra: Department of Linguistics, Research School of Pacific and Asian Studies, Australian National University.

Carsten, Janet & Stephen Hugh-Jones (eds.) 1995. *About the House. Lévi-Strauss and Beyond.* Cambridge: Cambridge University Press.

Crocombe, R. G. 1964. *Land Tenure in the Cook Islands.* Melbourne: Oxford University Press.

Dumont, Louis 1980. *Homo Hierarchicus: The Caste System and Its Implications.* Chicago: University of Chicago Press.

Duranti, Alessandro 1994. *From Grammar to Politics. Linguistic Anthropology in a Western Samoan Village.* Berkeley: The University of California Press.

Ella, S. 1899. The war of Tonga and Samoa and origin of the name Malietoa. *Journal of the Polynesian Society* 8: 231–234.

Firth, Raymond 1968. A note on descent groups in Polynesia. Andrew P. Vayda (ed.) *Peoples and Cultures of the Pacific. An Anthropological Reader.* New York: The Natural History Press. Pp. 207–217.

Firth, Raymond 1982. *We, the Tikopia. A Sociological Study of Kinship in Primitive Polynesia.* Stanford: Stanford University Press.

Fox, James J. 1995. Austronesian societies and their transformations. In: Peter Bellwood, James J. Fox & Darrell Tryon (eds.) *The Austronesians: Historical and Comparative Perspectives.* Canberra: Research School of Pacific Studies, Australian National University. Pp. 214–228.

Fox, James J. 1996. Introduction. In: James Fox & Clifford Sather (eds.) *Origins, Ancestry and Alliance.* Canberra: Research School of Pacific Studies, Australian National University. Pp. 1–17.

Gell, Alfred 1993. *Wrapping in Images, Tattooing in Polynesia.* Oxford: Clarendon Press.

Gell, Alfred 1998. *Art and Agency. An Anthropological Theory.* Oxford: Clarendon Press.

Gillespie, Susan D. 2000. Beyond kinship: an introduction. In: R. A. Joyce & S. D. Gillespie (eds.) *Beyond Kinship. Social and Material Reproduction in House Societies.* Philadelphia: The University of Pennsylvania Press.

Gillespie, Susan D. and Rosemary A. Joyce (eds.) 2000. *Beyond Kinship. Social and Material Reproduction in House Societies.* Philadelphia: The University of Pennsylvania Press.

Goodenough, Ward H. 1968. A problem of Malayo-Polynesian social organization. In: Andrew P. Vayda (ed.) *Peoples and Cultures of the Pacific. An Anthropological Reader*. New York: The Natural History Press. Pp. 133–149.

Grattan, F. J. H. 1948. *An Introduction to Samoan Custom*. New Zealand: R. McMillan.

Haddon, Alfred Cort and J. Hornell 1936–1938. *The Canoes of Oceania*, Vol. 1–3. Bernice Pauahi Bishop Museum Special Publications nos. 27, 28 and 29. Honolulu: Bishop Museum.

Hau'ofa, Epeli 1993. Our sea of islands. In: E. Waddell, V. Naidu & E. Hau'ofa (eds.) *A New Oceania: Rediscovering Our Sea of Islands*. Suva: University of South Pacific. Pp. 2–16.

Henry, Teuira 1928. *Ancient Tahiti*. Honolulu: Bernice Pauahi Bishop Museum Bulletin 48.

Hommon, Robert J. 1986. Social evolution in ancient Hawai'i. In: Patrick V. Kirch (ed.) *Island Societies: Archaeological Approaches to Evolution and Transformation*. Cambridge: Cambridge University Press. Pp. 55–68.

Holmes, Lowell 1974. *Samoan Village*. New York: Holt, Rinehart & Winston, Inc.

Howard, Alan & John Kirkpatrick 1989. Social organization. In: Alan Howard & Robert Borofsky (eds.) *Developments in Polynesian Ethnology*. Honolulu: The University of Hawaii Press. Pp. 47–94.

Jolly, Margaret & Mark Mosko (eds.) 1994. Transformations of Hierarchy: Structure, History and Horizon in the Austronesian World. A special issue of *History and Anthropology* 7(1–4).

Kaeppler, Adrienne 1978. Exchange patterns in goods and spouses: Fiji, Tonga, and Samoa. *Mankind* 11: 246–252.

Keesing, Felix M. & Marie M. Keesing 1956. *Elite Communication in Samoa. A Study of Leadership*. Stanford: Stanford University Press.

Kirch, Patrick 1984. *The Evolution of the Polynesian Chiefdoms*. Cambridge: Cambridge University Press.

Kirch, Patrick. 2002. *On the Road of the Winds. An Archeological History of the Pacific Islands before European Contact*. Berkeley: University of California Press.

Kirch, Patrick & Roger Green 2001. *Hawaiki, Ancestral Polynesia. An Essay in Historical Anthropology*. Cambridge: Cambridge University Press.

Lambert, Bernd 1966. Ambilineal Descent groups in the northern Gilbert Islands. *American Anthropologist* 68(3): 641–664.

Lévi-Strauss, Claude 1983. *The Way of the Masks*. London: Jonathan Cape.

Linnekin, Jocelyn 1990. *Sacred Queens and Women of Consequence. Rank, Gender, and Colonialism in the Hawaiian Islands*. Ann Arbor: The University of Michigan Press.

Marcus, George 1989. Chieftainship. In: Alan Howard & Robert Borofsky (eds.) *Developments in Polynesian Ethnology*. Honolulu: The University of Hawai'i Press. Pp. 175–209.

Mallon, Sean 2002. *Samoan Art and Artists. O Measina a Samoa*. Honolulu: The University of Hawai'i Press.

McKinnon, Susan 1991. *From a Shattered Sun. Hierarchy, Gender, and Alliance in the Tanimbar Islands*. Madison: The University of Wisconsin Press.

Mead, Margaret 1928. *An Inquiry into the Question of Cultural Stability in Polynesia*. New York: Columbia University Press.

Mead, Margaret 1968. The Samoans. In: Andrew P. Vayda (ed.) *Peoples and Cultures of the Pacific. An Anthropological Reader*. New York: The Natural History Press. Pp. 244–273.

Mead, Margaret 1969. *Social Organization of Manu'a*. Honolulu: Bernice Pauahi Bishop Museum.

Meijl, Toon van 1993. Maori meeting-houses in and over time. In: James J. Fox (ed.) *Inside Austronesian Houses. Perspectives on Domestic Designs for Living*. Canberra: Research School of Pacific Studies. Pp. 194–218.

Neich, Roger 1985. *Material Culture of Western Samoa. Persistence and Change*. Wellington: National Museum of New Zealand.

Neich, Roger 1994. *Painted Histories. Early Maori Figurative Painting*. Auckland: Auckland University Press.

Neich, Roger 1996. Wood-carving. In: D.C. Starzecka, ed. *Maori Art and Culture*. Chicago: Art Media Resources. Pp. 69–113.

Oliver, Douglas L. 1974. *Ancient Tahitian Society*, Three Volumes. Honolulu: The University of Hawai'i Press.

Parmentier, Richard J. 1987. *The Sacred Remains. Myth, History, and Polity in Belau*. Chicago: University of Chicago Press.

Pratt, George 1977. *Pratt's Grammar and Dictionary of the Samoan Language*. Apia: Malua Reprinting Press.

Reed, A. W. & T. S. Karetu 1984. *Concise Maori Dictionary*. Hong Kong: Literary Productions Ltd.

Riddell, E. R. 1930. Samoan Stories. Unpublished Manuscript. Sydney: Mitchell Library.

Sahlins, Marshall 1958. *Social Stratification in Polynesia*. Seattle: University of Washington Press.

Sahlins, Marshall 1976. *Culture and Practical Reason*. Chicago: University of Chicago Press.

Sahlins, Marshall 1985. *Historical Metaphors and Mythical Realities. A Structure in the Early History of the Sandwich Islands Kingdom*. Ann Arbor: The University of Michigan Press.

Sahlins, Marshall 1987. *Islands of History*. Chicago: University of Chicago Press.

Schrempp, Gregory 1992. *Magical Arrows. The Maori, the Greeks, and the Folklore of the Universe*. Madison: The University of Wisconsin Press.

Shore, Brad 1981. Sexuality and gender in Samoa: conceptions and missed conceptions. In: S. B. Ortner & H. Whitehead (eds.) *Sexual Meanings. The Cultural Construction of Gender and Sexuality*. Cambridge: Cambridge University Press. Pp. 192–215.

Shore, Brad 1982. *Sala'ilua. A Samoan Mystery*. New York: Columbia University Press.

Shore, Brad 1989. Mana and tapu. In: Alan Howard & Robert Borofsky (eds.) *Developments in Polynesian Ethnology*. Honolulu: The University of Hawai'i Press. Pp. 137–173.

Siikala, Jukka 1991. *'Akatokamanāva. Myth, History and Society in the Southern Cook Islands*. Auckland: The Polynesian Society in association with the Finnish Anthropological Society.

Siikala, Jukka 1996. The elder and the younger: foreign and autochthonous origin and hierarchy in the Cook Islands. In: James J. Fox & Clifford Sather (eds.) *Origins, Ancestry and Alliance*. Canberra: Research School of Pacific Studies. Pp. 41–54.

Siikala, Jukka 2000. This is my beautiful line of chiefs. *Suomen Antropologi* (Journal of Finnish Anthropological Society) 25(1): 15–28.

Stair, John B. 1896. Early Samoan voyages and settlements. In: John B. S. Shirley (ed.) *Report of the Sixth Meeting of the Australian Association for the Advancement of Science, held at Brisbane, Queensland, January 1895*. Sydney: Australian Association for the Advancement of Science.

Stuebel, C. 1976. *Myths and Legends of Samoa. Tala o le Vavau*. Wellington: A. H. & A. W. Reed Ltd.

Tcherkézoff, Serge 2002. Subjects and objects in Samoa. Ceremonial mats have a soul. In: Monique Jeude-Ballini & Bernard Juillerat (eds.) *People and Things. Social Meditations in Oceania*. Durham: Carolina Academic Press. Pp. 27–51.

Tilley, Christopher 1999. *Metaphor and Material Culture*. Oxford: Blackwell Publishers.

Valeri, Valerio 1985. *Kingship and Sacrifice. Ritual and Society in Ancient Hawaii*. Chicago: University of Chicago Press.

Walters, Richard 1985. *Preliminary Report of Archeological Investigations on Ma'uke, Cook Islands*. Auckland: University of Auckland.

On the Ideas of a Boat

From Forest Patches to Cybernetic Structures in the Outrigger Sailing Craft of the Eastern Kula Ring, Papua New Guinea[1]

Frederick H. Damon

Introduction

To honor the place that Jukka Siikala has made in the international world of anthropology I will describe the ideas inherent in the boats in my region of interest, the northeast corner of the Kula Ring in Milne Bay Province, Papua New Guinea (See Map). For many of us, Jukka is from a distant land, far over the horizon, out of sight and nearly out of significance until the transformations in communication technologies of our own time. Like the boats in my region, he has been the instrument which has brought his work and his place very much into our presence. He managed this by the international flavor and reach of his writing, by the parade of outsiders he has brought into his village, and by his turning up in our houses, universities and national meetings. Like every significant anthropologist, he has made the distant a part of us. The boats of the Kula Ring do the same.

Consider the names of reference of the two boat forms that dominate the western and eastern half of the Kula Ring. Their formal names are, respectively, *masawa* and *anageg*. Yet many people on the eastern side of the Kula Ring, those who use the *anageg* form, call the western craft (*masawa*) *tadob*. This means 'cut thing (wooden) from Dobu.' The idea of that boat is located on an island far over the horizon. Yet virtually everyone knows that the actual boats are built by all the communities that use them, stretching from Iwa in the north-central Kula circuit down through the Trobriands into and around the actual island of Dobu. By contrast, at least some of the people from the southern side of the Kula Ring, Gaboyin or Koyagaugau Island in

1 Acknowledgements. This paper draws from Chapter 4, "A Story of *Calophyllum*" of my ms, Trees, Knots and Outriggers (*Kaynen Muyuw*): Environmental Research in the Northeast Kula Ring. Both that work and this particular phrasing of its data follow from extended conversations with a variety of colleagues too many to name. However of special note are André Iteanu, Stéphane Breton, Pierre Lemonnier, Roy Wagner, Carlos Mondragón, Lee Newsom, Anne DiPiazza and Erik Pearthree and Nancy Coble Damon, and continuing conversations with Adrian Horridge, Jack Morava and Simon Bickler.

The Kula Ring
Standard English names in parentheses.

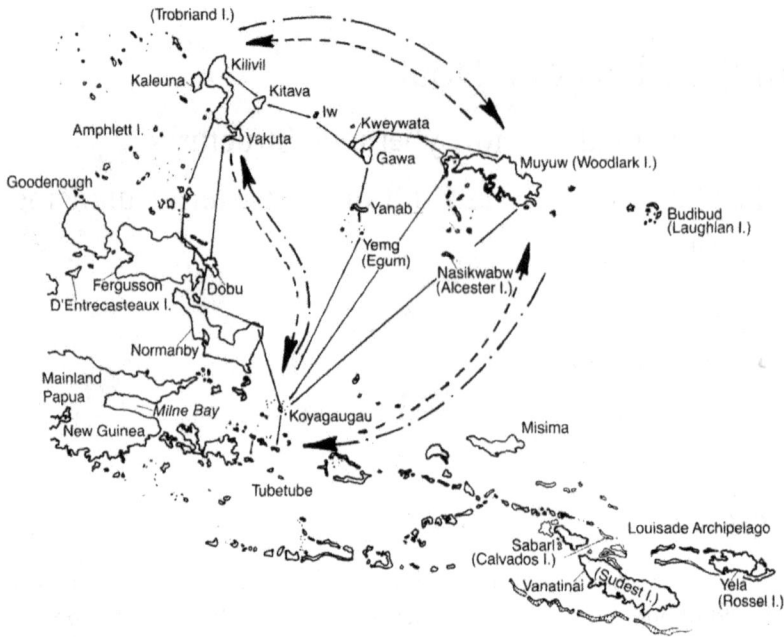

particular, refer to *anageg* by the term *kemurua*. *Murua* is their name for Muyuw. For them this concept includes Muyuw, or Woodlark Island, as well as Gawa and Kweywata islands to the immediate west of Muyuw where the boats are in fact made; the production of these boats is in fact localized. *Ke* appears to be the noun classifier for wooden things. The sense of this boat's "nickname" is 'Wooden thing from Muyuw.' The name expresses the fact that these boats are made in Muyuw. As we shall see, this place of making is no idle reference.

So, a fundamental meaning of these boat names is that while the boats are for elsewhere, that "for elsewhere" is fixed in the consciousness of "this" place. These boats bring other relations, sometimes distant and discordant, to these peoples as well. What I attempt in this contribution is to look more closely at this process of bringing relations to these societies. What are the ideas these boats carry?

A complete analysis of these craft is beyond the scope afforded me here. I make my case, therefore, by describing the significance of the species of the genus Calophyllum that are used to make these boats. Four different Calophyllum go into making the *anageg* class of boats. Discussing them leads to a brief consideration of a fifth kind, which, while not used for *anageg*, is the basis of the *masawa* class of sailing craft. There is a sixth species in the region. It is not used in boat construction for at least one very technical reason. Yet contiguous with the fifth species, it figures in the *el niño* dominated environment that governs many organizational features of this area.

There are several reasons for focusing on these trees. Among these are that at least one of these species, *Calophyllum inophyllum*, is commonly employed for boats across the Indo-Pacific region. I will assert, therefore, that while I am illustrating a specific case in a specific corner of that region, I believe that I am dealing with a problem and solution that are also common throughout the region and very likely part of its founding condition. This follows, we shall see, because of the very complexity of these technologies. All sailing technologies are complex. Yet, I was drawn to this topic as I slowly began to understand two things about the trees that went into these boats. One of these was the extraordinary amount of technical knowledge that seemed to be relevant to the selection of trees going into specific parts. The other was that everybody seemed to know much about this aspect of these boats. In some Indo-Pacific sailing traditions, knowledge of boat construction is a very restricted discourse. While that does not mean it did not also carry great cultural significance, what continually impressed me about the situation across the eastern side of the Kula Ring was the widespread nature of this information. Experienced sailors know far more about boats than the people who sail little. Nevertheless, a lot of knowledge – for example, detailed knowledge about the subtleties of certain design features –was, and is, broadly known. These are social facts of paramount significance. I argue here about what this knowledge is and why it is so pertinent to the people who maintain it.

Examining the boats that plied and ply the eastern side of the Kula Ring, it becomes evident that these craft are complex communication technologies in at least three ways. First, as sailing vessels they were and remain a principal means for the communication of words, products (primary shell wealth and secondary wealth in the form of pigs, pots, mats, vegetable foods and other products) and people. Second, by virtue of their conditions of production and reproduction, they constitute a moving model for complementary relations amongst the islands that produce and sail them. There are other items that also model interisland dependencies, foremost of which are customs pertaining to firewood. I have noted these elsewhere (Damon 1998, 2005b). But many of these other models do not move, and movement, as we shall see, is fundamental for the ideas, and problems, that boats express. Although nominally produced in two of many specialized production places, Gawa and Kweywata Islands, as *anageg* are traded throughout the system, people refine and replace many critical parts. This is not done with most other products, nor is it the case with the boats that course the western side of the Kula Ring. Hence the boats consciously reflect the totality of interdependent relations in which the individual island-cultures participate. Although I shall partly illustrate how this is so here, my major concern is the third way in which these boats move their movers. "Enchant" is not too strong a word here (Gell 1999: 169). By their forms and operation, I argue that these craft communicate the fundamental condition of existence in this region.

This condition may be simply stated: How to attend to life processes amidst conditions best characterized as chaotic. Exactly what I mean by "chaotic" will become clear through the course of this paper. For the moment, however, I shall invoke the literature on the greater environment of this region, perhaps most forcefully expressed by Tim Flannery's creative synthesis of its geology, climate and human history in *The Future Eaters* (1994). And it is now clear that across the arc of the South Pacific a feature that differentiates it like no other is the phenomenon of *el niño*, unpredictable but recurring alterations in wind, sun and rain that radically challenge many aspects of organized life in the area.[2] In this contribution I begin an argument to suggest that these boats operate like a mathematical equation specifying a necessary order among things, i.e. a set of relations among concepts; and that the problem this form, this "equation," attends to is that of the chaotic conditions of existence in this region.

It has recently been suggested that the idea of relationship is the paramount value amongst many Melanesian societies (Robbins 2004). This idea could certainly be sustained by a review of the dominant collective representations among the Kula Ring societies, even if what these relations are varies radically among them. As I have noted elsewhere (Damon 1990; 2005), the hierarchical forms that configure much of Trobriand life are replaced by images of reciprocal exchange relations among equivalent clans in Muyuw's finely expressed garden order. Ideas about relationships differ still across the southern Kula Ring societies. But what is interesting across these forms, and pertinent to the argument of this paper, is that ideas about sailing craft exist as motivating symbols or metaphors in all these societies. This is the case virtually everywhere else in the Indo-Pacific region as an increasing amount of literature is making clear.[3]

In the case of Muyuw, people can and do liken the whole island to a boat, gardens are built and discussed as if they were *anageg*, villages were turned into an image of one in the most important mortuary ritual, and behavior towards these craft is used to exemplify appropriate behavior toward people, especially spouses and children. The symbolic usage is pervasive. But I do not think this is a matter of just symbolism. Boats are good to think because they are syntheses of very complex relationships, and it is to a partial description of these relationships that this paper is devoted.

I shall now proceed to the description of the way the species of Calophyllum are worked into the remarkable structure of these boats. Although this analysis will show how dealing with principles of chaos fits into the design of these boats, only in my conclusion will I turn more formally to how *el niño* events are worked into other aspects of the social organization of this regional system.

The trees and their ecologies

I orient my descriptions to the table of Calophyllum shown here. It provides indigenous names (without taking into account dialect variations), the species listing, prime quality of the different trees' grains, their major

---

2   For a more recent review of relevant dynamics in this region, see Dewar 2003.

3   Among other places where this issue is discussed see Manguin (1986). For Polynesian examples see Raymond Firth (1959: 116); Oliver (1974: 653-654). Southon (1995) contains the richest discussion of these relations in the recent literature. Many essays in Feinberg 1995 also touch on these issues.

Calophyllum species of the northeastern Kula Ring, Milne Bay Province, Papua New Guinea

Indigenous Name	Determination	Grains	Uses	Location	Size in High Forest
Kakam	*inophyllum*	Very interlocked	Occasional keel; curved parts. Leaves as sail models. Maintains beach.	Shoreline	Not found: Small to large on shoreline
Kausilay	*leleanii*	Interlocked	Primary for keels & strakes	Coral outcrops/ garden edges in well-drained forests	Large only
Apul Siptupwat	*apul peekelii*	Modest interlocking	Negligible in Muyuw; *Masawa* keel	High "wet" soil forests	Large only
Dan	*vexans*	Too wobbly	Wild Pig food	Freshwater Swamps	Small to large
Aynikoy	*soulattri*	Straight heavier	Masts & poles Thinner	Higher/dryer "mountainous" areas	Small to large
Ayniyan	*goniocarpum*	Straight lighter	Masts & poles Thicker	Lower/wetter "mountain" areas	Small to large

uses, locations and a comment on the observed nature of the trees in high forest situations. Since Peter Stevens is the authority on the genus, I use his determinations alone; he is aware that I received different identifications from other systematists who worked from his key to the genus. He is reasonably confident of all of the trees with the exception of the one Muyuw call *dan*. In 1996 I collected a tree I was told was identical to *apul* on Iwa Island but there several of my informants called it *siptupwat*. Stevens thinks it was a different and better-known species, one he has called *C. peekelii*. I reported that to my Muyuw informants in 1998. Although I did not show them the 1996 voucher specimen, they told me Iwa people do not know trees as well as they do, the Iwa name means "big leaves," which *apul* has, and that the tree must be *apul*; and, they think, Stevens must be mistaken in calling it a different species, a fact I reported to him; he has not changed his mind. There is no generic term for the group of trees which we class as Calophyllum; all six, however, are understood to be a 'group,' *bod*.[4]

---

4   In Melanesia several Calophyllum species are in high demand for the international timber market, and four species, including *kausilay*, were cut from Muyuw during the highwater mark in that market, 1982–1995.

From kausilay *to* apul*:*
extreme sensitivity to initial conditions and transformations

The tree eastern Muyuw people call *kausilay* (*Calophyllum leleanni* p.f. stevens) – its pronunciations shift systematically moving towards the Trobriands — is the most important tree for building outrigger sailing craft in the eastern half of the Kula Ring.[5] Ideally it forms the keel and three strakes for the highest ranked, largest and most important boat in the region, the form called *anageg*. It is the standard. It is also frequently used as the keel for the second-ranked boat, which will have two strakes added to it from a different tree (which is not Calophyllum, rather one Muyuw call *antunat* [Sapotaceae, *Palaquium* sp.]). And in villages where one tends not to find either of these kinds of craft, the simpler dugouts are often cut from *kausilay*.

When I was first learning about the set of Calophyllum, my teachers often spoke as if this tree were the prototype for the set, with the other five being marked versions of this one (sometimes *kakam* was used in the same way). As time passed, however, I began to suspect this was an accommodation to my ignorance rather than a formal feature of their thought.

If asked why the tree is so important for keels, the first answer is immediate — the tree's grain is so 'interlocked,' *kasileu*. This quality is held to be critical for the desired shape and function of keels. The boats need the strength the interlocking supplies.

A unique set of beliefs and distinctive ecology mark the tree. Throughout much of this area the tree is considered to be a female person. I have specified the reasons for this elsewhere (Damon 1998). They may be summed briefly. Although many people in this region know one or two myths which explain why the tree is a female person, the features that make the association particularly salient include the facts that the tree tends to grow in groves or in nearly grove-like conditions,[6] has wood which is extraordinarily red in color, "like blood,"[7] and dies when cut – i.e. a new tree will not grow up from its stump. The fact of its growing in grove-like associations is explicitly related to an aspect of Muyuw's matrilineal identity. Because of that structure, Muyuw associate women with larger, collected numbers, in ways that distinguish them from men. For men, there is a tree that corresponds to their distinctive feature of being more solitary; that tree is not personified.

Although I was first told that the blood-red color was like the color of the

---

5   I collected voucher specimens for this tree in 1995, 1996, 1998 and 2002. The 1995 specimens went to the PNG Herbarium at Lae where the determination was *C. streimannii*, the systematist working from a key created by Stevens (See Stevens 1980). All specimens from 1996 on were sent to both Lae and Stevens. Stevens consistently identifies the specimens which Muyuw call *kausilay* as *C. leleanni*. p. f. stevens.

6   With an associated "mother" tree; as such, it contrasts with another which is conceived to grow singly and nowhere for any good reason, i.e. *aunutau*.

7   As the wood from this tree sits in the open as a keel or strake, it turns from deep red to a whiter and whiter color. Turning something from red to white, e.g. fishing nets and women, is a major practice in this region, the purpose being to enhance the object's productivity.

Tasim, *clumps of high forest interspersed among lower, regularly cut garden lands.*

flesh in one's thigh, the bloody appearance of the tree is also connected to the ways blood is associated with women.

Since many trees do sprout when cut, it is the last point that clinches the human character of the tree. I often felt bad cutting down other kinds of large trees to acquire a voucher specimen. But whenever I expressed that regret, people told me not to worry because it would grow back. By contrast, *kausilay* stumps start rotting fairly quickly.

At least two of these three features are related to the tree's ecology. With the exception of a patch of the trees along Muyuw's north central coast, the tree's ecology may be specified precisely: it grows almost exclusively on well-drained limestone soils, and is particularly common amidst patches of coral outcrops found in the well-drained uplifts forming the island.[8] Such areas are called *sasek*. The tree's root structure seems particularly well adapted to this location. The roots crisscross and curl around and through the coral hunks that form these outcrop-like structures. I believe this is why the tree is also found in some other areas which do not quite meet these conditions, especially steep slopes where other trees quickly fall down because their root structures cannot support them. This makes these slopes much more open than most uncut rainforest areas.

In eastern Muyuw *sasek*, slightly uplifted concentrations of coral limestone are the prime locations around which gardens are cut and within which patches of high forest are left to mature. These areas are called *tasim*, a word composed of the verb 'to cut' and the word for 'island.' Gardens – which are metaphorically likened to boats – are supposed to weave around *tasim* like boats weave around islands and reefs. The higher forests in *tasim* are thought to keep surrounding soils cooler and wetter, and by blocking the sun make crops and early fallow trees grow faster, both of which are

8 Nasikwabw, Alcester Is. on older maps, is a raised portion of Muyuw's barrier reef and so is nothing but well-drained limestone. The tree is particularly common there and that is one reason why the human community on that island is basically a sailing community.

Mature arcing kausilay *amidst a* sasek *that was once the edge of a garden area.*

perceived to be beneficial for the soils and eventually the crops that will be planted in them. They also provide the environment for *kausilay* to grow in the way that makes them so important for their function as keels and strakes. It is part of the indigenous understanding of the tree – and consistent with all my observations – that the tree will not transform from a seedling to a sapling and beyond in a high forest, only on edges created by *tasim* or *tasim*-like forms. The tree needs the liminal intersection of a high forest and a much lower area regularly gardened. As the tree matures it

Keel line, which must conform to the arc of a mature kausilay.

then grows out towards the sun. Keels and strakes have to be cut employing the tree's heartwood. Consequently the arcs that form as the trees grow on *tasim* edges become the forms around which a keel's "rock" (the technical term) is designed.[9]

Muyuw people class these arcs by means of the binary distinction between *amwagan* and *esol*. The former refers to a keel that is 'arced' (*kaydodo*), the latter to one that is 'straight' (*idumwal*).[10] As in a number of other cases where variation was expressed in binary contrasts, I was left with the sense that the point was describing a ratio of differences rather than stipulating a preference morally (i.e. aesthetically) or technically determined. Both forms can be said to be good, but every other feature of the boat must conform to the initial arc.

These boats, then, begin by being extremely sensitive to their initial condition, the arc of a growing *kausilay*. This point is worth noting, first because extreme sensitivity to initial conditions is one of the principles of chaos theory (Mosko 2005). Second, this kind of conditioning redounds through much of the practice of sailing these craft. Nighttime is the preferred time for leaving on many voyages because it is the only way to reliably order navigation given its basic form, which is, of course, by dead reckoning; the only firm knowledge one can have is where one was from. Trips to Budibud

9   Gawa people, who are the prime builders of the *anageg* class of boat, told me that they set aside straighter-growing *kausilay* for the strakes, the more curved for keels.
10   The latter, straighter shape is appreciated because when the 'front' (*dabwen*) and 'back' (*wowun*) ends of the boat crash into waves, they create great splashes of water, referred to as 'smoke' (*museo*). Dozens of cowry shells tied to the structures that generate the fronts and backs of the boat enhance this visual effect. The more arced type of the two contrasting styles has its prow and bow pieces much higher so they tend not to go as deeply into the waves. This contrast was explained to me in 1998 and when I first heard it I presumed the straighter version was then preferred. However, the boat I was examining and sailing in 2002 was considered more towards the *amwagan*, 'arced,' end of the continuum, and I was told it was "very good."

131

from Muyuw's southeastern shoreline involve an exception to the nighttime departure preference because a unique backsight sets the course. It is constructed from a line figured by means of a tall *kiyal* or *yal* tree (*Casurina littorale*) on a sand spit of an island ten or so miles southeast of Muyuw called Nubal. The navigator aligns the top of that tree with one of the mountains seen over its top in the center of Muyuw (In 1996 a prime objection to gold mining in that region was that mining activity would remove the mountain, and hence the means for configuring the route). Once set, the problem is holding that course until Budibud comes into view. Just as a boat's final structure must follow from the arc of the *kausilay* from which its keel is cut, so are boat courses set by an initial fixed setting.

The sensitivity to initial conditions exhibited in a keel's curvature is also found in expressions concerned with the keel's length because all of the remaining structures of the boat are fit to it. Outrigger floats, masts and sails are roughly calculated to fit to the keel; a sail, for example, runs the distance between the boat's two prow boards. But what is at issue here is a kind of proportion, not an exactly defined unit. So keel lengths are figured in terms of a unit called *ovatan*, which means one unit of outstretched arms, from the fingertips of one hand to those of the other.[11] *Anageg* come in three sizes, "three plus one" (very small), "four plus one," and "five plus one" (very big). I was told that the "plus one" unit did not mean another full length of one's outstretched arms. Instead, it referred to an indeterminate addition: So, five and some added amount. Rather than a fixed element conceived to be an atom which is then added to others, the unit of measurement is ad hoc and very approximate. However, what becomes fixed, by means of fine determinations formed in the process of production and then use, are the relations among the parts of the craft as a whole.

After learning about the way of calculating keel lengths, I asked why not "six plus one." My informant immediately told me that was impossible because the boat would be too hard to rig. The expression is *angineol singaya kikay*, where *singaya* means 'very' or 'extremely,' *kikay* translates to 'hard' or 'difficult,' and *angineol* is its 'tying' or 'rigging.' This expression refers in general to all of the tying that goes into the boat. Relations among the parts are managed, of course, by such tying. Yet in particular this expression pertains to the specific ways in which the sail is braced with respect to given wind conditions and directions. Because mast and sail sizes roughly correspond to the length of the keel, "six plus one" would call for a total size that is beyond the limits of what can be managed by existing materials and the human strength used to control them. This issue, of course, comes to the fore powerfully when the craft is being propelled by wind. "Six plus one" is the definition of the form's destruction.

This kind of proportionate thinking leading to a phase change may be seen in another of these boat's critical dimensions, one which will bring our discussion of *kausilay* to a conclusion and allow us to bring up another

---

11   This term is a noun classifier obeying the conventions by which this kind of lexical unit operates. Two such units are called *ovey*, three *oveytoun*, four *oveyvas*, etc.

Outrigger float ⟷ Keel distances
Variation to Phase Change

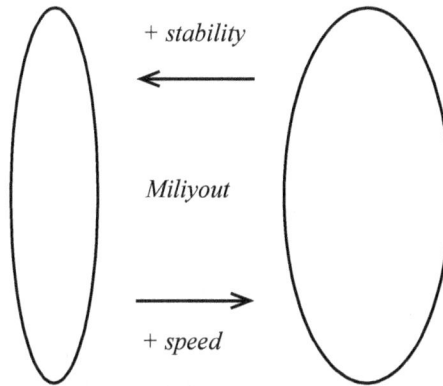

+ *stability*

Miliyout

+ *speed*

Kausilay: ananeg:: apul: tadob (masawa)

Calophyllum species in the region. The dimension concerns the distance between the main part of the craft and the outrigger float, a part of the boat's structure known as the *miliyout*. This distance is large enough for platforms on which people can walk, cook, and store a fair bit of material. The craft is also steered by someone crouching on the trailing portion of the structure, systematically raising and lowering a kind of rudder. Although nobody could ever tell me how wide the platform should be — I would guess an *ovatan* or more, hence upwards of two meters – their proportionate understanding reflects a trade-off between stability and speed. The greater the distance, the more stable the craft; the smaller the distance, the faster it can go.

One of the times this was explained to me my informant spontaneously brought up the outrigger form *masawa/tadob* that is built, paddled, and sailed in the western half of the Kula Ring. The man, from the sailing community of Yemga and an experienced mender and sailor of *anageg*, told me he refused to go on these other craft. They violated his sense of proportion and order. His point, and fear, was that the distance between the outrigger float and the main part of the boat was so small it was dangerous to the point of acute unsteadiness. By applying the same proportional principles for *anageg* to this form, he anticipated such extreme instability that he could say he would refuse to board such a boat. This is of interest because these boats have a very different design. Prototypically they are constructed from the kind of Calophyllum Muyuw call *apul*.[12] Although they have a strake or two added to them, their girth, and the boat's design, allows them to be much more of a dugout than is the case with the anageg form. Built from *C. apul* which do not arc like *kausilay*, *tadob/masawa* are longer, straighter craft that can be both paddled, and sailed efficiently (*anageg* are designed only for sailing and

---

12   This appears to be a new species; Stevens made the Muyuw name the scientific name, hence *C. apul p .f. stevens.*

can hardly be poled, much less paddled with any dexterity). While the tree apul is nearly insignificant in Muyuw, its wood is important to the people to the west. It is the prime building block for a form structurally very different from the Muyuw *anageg*. By projecting an *anageg's* principles onto this boat, my informant generated in his mind the chaos of a phase change; in fact the design represents the order of a different set.

A closing word on the ecology of these trees is necessary here because it demonstrates the intentional density of interwoven relations, relations for which these boats are stunning representations.

While Muyuw people know the tree *apul* well, they pay very little attention to it. Like *kausilay*, when mature, *apul* are tall trees that spread at the canopy top (40 m.); unlike *kausilay* they do not arc.[13] They need light like *kausilay* to grow, so will not be found in old high-forested areas; in younger forests they will go to the canopy top but saplings and intermediate sized *apul* are never found. The tree needs relatively wet rather than dry, well-drained areas where *kausilay* flourish. For some reason north central Muyuw is much wetter than the southeastern sector so *apul* are often found in the *tasim* there. Many stand around meadows that pockmark south-central Muyuw, an area of swampy conditions otherwise ideal for sago orchards. These meadows are inverted *tasim*. Found in high-forested areas, for long I thought they were natural creations generated from peculiar soil conditions. On the contrary, they are caused by intentional human responses to the *el niño* circumstances that periodically visit the island. Every time there is a long *el niño* drought, people go through these areas to burn the meadows. Without that irregular burning, forests would infill the meadows. People do not want that because the meadows provide critical components for sailing craft – vines mostly; some items for self-decoration; and, most importantly, havens for wild pigs. Two problems face these pigs. Humans are one of their dangers. The flora of the meadows is so entangled and scratchy that people – and their dogs – refuse to go into them. The pigs know that so they drop their litters there and use the meadows as safety zones when people and their dogs come after them, which they do frequently. All these meadows are also on slight rises, and these provide protection for the pigs when prolonged wet phases – the inverse of the *el niño* stage, the so-called *la niña* – flood the surrounding swamps. As noted, sago orchards thrive in the surrounding swamps, and every time a sago tree is downed, a meter or so of its top and bottom must be left for the "wild" pigs. Moreover, these swamps provide the critical conditions for another Calophyllum, one Muyuw call *dan*.[14] Like *kausilay*

---

13   As is the case with several other Calophyllum in PNG/Melanesia, they are large trees of moderately high quality that became very important in the international timber industry. On Muyuw these two were/are the only ones that grow predictably larger than 50cm dbh and do not have rot or other disease that would destroy their commercial value.

14   Peter Stevens identified most, but not all, of my *dan* voucher specimens as *C. vexans* although he suggested that the seed structure resembles a poorly understood form called *C. acutiputamen*. From further examination of Stevens' work I suggest the tree resembles *C. piluliferum* (Stevens 1974: 388 & 1980: 613). He doubts that (personal communication, 2006).

and *apul*, this third tree is a canopy-top tree. It is shaped, however, more like a Christmas tree so it doesn't spread. And unlike either of these other two it will rise to the top unimpeded by the surrounding canopy, so *dan* stands tend to have trees of varying sizes. Unlike these others, and unlike the remaining Calophyllum to which I turn next, it is not used in any boat construction. Its wood is considered too "wobbly" to be good for anything concerned with boats. It is not worthless, however, for its nuts are the only Calophyllum nuts wild pigs in this area devour. And when the nuts fall, their consumption changes the taste of the pigs, so much so that people make extra attempts to hunt and eat them.

Kakam: *from events to structures*

Reyava or *leyvava* from Iwa to the west, *kakam* from Gawa to Muyuw, and the obvious variant, *kwakwam* on Koyagaugau and Ole to Muyuw's south, these are the indigenous names for the most widely distributed of the Calophyllum species, *C. inophyllum*.[15] The trees are common. Very occasionally they will be found back from the shoreline and growing, therefore, more or less vertically into large, spreading trees with modest boles. However, most times they are found along the rocky or sandy shoreline reaching out to the sun by sending boles or enormous limbs first out over the water before secondary and tertiary branches bend upwards to the sun. Their positioning on beaches, people in this region claim, is thought to maintain a beach's coherence.

The tree's sap is sticky enough to be used as glue, and mixed with water, provides a ready cure for "red eyes," presumably a version of conjunctivitis. One of the ways locals rank the set of Calophyllum is by the degree to which the different species exhibit interlocked grains. As such, *kakam* ranks the highest; it is the most interlocked. And occasionally, therefore, the primary *anageg* makers use the tree's main bole as the keel for outriggers.[16]

But the really significant, and very well understood, use of *kakam* is different, and twofold. Wood from this tree is used for two primary and critical boat parts.[17] One of these concerns what are called in the European boat-building tradition the boat "ribs." These forms are tied to the keel in asymmetrically-shaped pairs against which the strakes are tied and sewn together. Each pair – prototypically 10/boat – is of slightly different shape and angle than the others. The basic form is that of a hockey stick. The short sides of the stick are tied together at the bottom of the boat resting across the

---

15   In Iwa I was told that the tree's flowers are called *kakam* so for some time I tried to investigate a possibility of some formal meaning in the name change across these islands. Does an Iwa-Trobriand part, the flower, become a whole in Muyuw?

16   On Budibud, to Muyuw's southeast, where other species of Calophyllum do not grow, *kakam* provides the standard keel for their version of the model. There, I was told, boles are trained to arc in the preferred way.

17   And a third and fourth, far less primary and critical: One of these is a bailer usually cut from at least a thigh-sized *kakam* root; the other an intricate, chicken-shaped and named device used in a ball and socket joint to act as a pulley for raising the sail up the mast.

top of the keel. The longer sides arc up, providing a structure for the strakes. The shapes should be asymmetrical, with the outrigger float side of the pair a larger angle, more obtuse, than the opposite side. This has to do with the dynamics of the outrigger float. It is always facing into the wind and waves. Waves suck it down, thus pulling down the whole boat. The more slanted side facing that float functions as a lever which first absorbs the force of the wave – its strakes should be, therefore, slightly thicker than those on the opposite side – and then pushes the boat and float back up. With each wave there is a rocking of the boat more or less perpendicular to its primary course. In any case, the ribs have to be especially strong because, first, they have to be at an angle, and second, they will have a series of holes drilled into them to facilitate tying of the strakes. The interlocked character of *kakam* grain provides the strength needed in the latter case; the natural arcing of secondary and tertiary branches coursing out over the water's edge and up to the sun provides the needed shapes in the former case.

Calophyllum Inophyllum (Kakam) *overhanging beach on Gawa Island just after being pruned to make a* tadob *bound of Iwa (1996).*

That arcing and interlocked strength go into the next piece I discuss, one of the most important in the boat. The piece is taken from a single *kakam* branch of sufficient girth, length and shape so that a socket for holding the mast is at one end, and the other end bends up along the outrigger side of the boat leading out over the outrigger platform. Altogether the piece will be about three meters long. The socket is a mast-mount resting in the bottom center of the boat tied to what is considered the most important structure in the boat, a complex spring tied to the boat's keel, ribs and strakes. The

Mast-mount in center, two pairs of ribs to left and right.

spring is composed of eight pieces of wood drawn from two different tree types, neither of which may be Calophyllum, for no Calophyllum species has the qualities requisite for this function. Tied to the part of this structure that swings over the outrigger float platform are four pieces from a different tree (one of the two used to make the spring) that serve to hold the outrigger float in its place. These pieces are likened to tensed leg muscles that keep a leg straight; the outrigger float is considered a boat's leg.

This piece of *kakam* thus receives the two most powerful forces to which the boat is subjected; on the one hand, the force of the wind on the sail and mast,[18] on the other hand, the first push of oncoming waves as the boat moves forward. Although I do not have space to detail them here, it is no accident that this piece has tied to it, rests on, and holds, three different springs, one of which, of course, is the mast. To briefly testify to the point that these pieces become a finely coordinated whole by means of the proportional relations of one part to another, let me note that a boat will be sailed, and then exchanged, only after the spring upon which this piece of *kakam* rests is finally considered to be of the correct proportions. The two primary pieces in the spring are then trimmed further with 'pumice' (*gimut*) which, clearly, is

18 When I asked an informant what would happen if there were not a mast-mount structure like the one depicted, he had to think a moment to conjure up an answer to this ridiculous question. He then recalled somebody who tried to make a short trip with a quickly rigged-up sail and mast and no mast-mount: The force of the wind on the mast drove it through the keel, splitting it and swamping the boat.

137

being used like a fine sandpaper. That trimming work is considered finished according to the way the boat feels when sailed.

Mast-mount extension over outrigger platform.

Lévi-Strauss writes that

the characteristic feature of mythical thought, as of 'bricolage' on the practical plane, is that it builds up structured sets, not directly with other structured sets,* but by using the remains and debris of events (Lévi-Strauss 1966: 21–22).[19]

Given the use of both *kausilay* and *kakam*, these craft are most certainly examples of a bricolage on the practical plane. An engineer with whom I have discussed these boats has kept reminding me that the sea is unforgiving: These complicated structures have to work. But they are built from determinations figured elsewhere or not at all. Out of the unconnected and natural growth patterns of the *kakam* tree, finely conceived structures are generated.

I suggest, however, that these boats are also myths, and by asserting this I draw upon two aspects of their forms. First, people obtain tremendous pleasure out of just watching them. They pore over all their details in ways that combine considerable aesthetic and technical interest. And it is according

---

19 The asterisk points out that the "events" from which myth-making draws, language, of course, have their own structures, and the same may be said with respect to the generation of arcing *kausilay* and *kakam*.

to this aesthetic and technical interest that people define a form that is used as a model for considering the appropriateness of other forms and relations.

Second, these boats should be considered a form that undergoes systematic transformation. These transformations are conditioned by the materials used to compose them and circumstances in which they must operate. Within any one locale, one form provides the dominant model for reality. So the proportion *kausilay: anageg :: apul : masawa (tadob) ::* eastern side of the Kula Ring :: western side of the Kula Ring. One day I was discussing the three known types of outrigger craft in Milne Bay Province with one of my best informants, Dibolel. I said there were three boats, the aforementioned *tadob*, the Muyuw *anageg*, and the *lakatoi* craft that was the main form sailed from the southeast end of the mainland of New Guinea (e.g. the Maylu) down the south coast towards Port Moresby. *Lakatoi* sail with a sail type often called a "Crab-claw sprit sail" which is the characteristic sail type in Polynesia (Horridge 1987: 141–147). Immediately Dibolel disagreed and told me *tadob*, whose sail type was the standard for Muyuw's second highest sailing craft, and *lakatoi* were the same. With his fingers he showed how the sail position of the former is turned into the latter by moving the sail from the prow to the center of the boat and then changing its angle by 90°. As two trees facilitate the transformation of one form into another, a sail shift transforms the latter into a third (*lakatoi*).

Ayniyan *and* aynikoy: *exterior and interior boundaries*

> … resilience focuses on the size and form of the domain of attraction, on behavior of the variables near its boundary, and on the susceptibility of the domain to contract under differing ecological or management conditions. It emphasizes nonequilibrium events and processes, variability, and adaptive flexibility. From resilience perspective, incremental change may not reliably signal its effect. If a boundary is reached, the effect will be abrupt, unpredicted, and disproportionate to the cause – a surprise (Winterhalder 1994: 37).

Prototypically, *anageg* are produced in Gawa and Kweywata, two islands to Muyuw's west. Occasionally the people of Yalab, south of these two islands, produce them. And the people of Budibud, to Muyuw's southeast, also produce a variant of them, though these boats, unlike those from Gawa and Kweywata (and Yalab), are not produced for exchange. My Muyuw informants said the Gawa and Kweywata boats come equipped with masts made from, they supposed, the Calophyllum they call *apul*. When I asked some Gawa people, they told me *kausilay*. Whatever the case, about the first thing that the first new owner of a boat will do is head for Muyuw's Sulog region to find a mast replacement. Everybody knows this, and while I was told that the same species might be found in the southeastern corner of the Kula Ring, it is a conceit of the region as a whole that the trees obtained from Sulog furnish the best mast material.[20] There, large numbers of two more Calophyllum species grow, and either may be selected for the best mast. They are called *ayniyan* and *aynikoy* and eventually were identified to be *C. goniocarpum p.f. stevens* and *C. soulattri*, respectively. I conclude my discussion of these species and boats by describing some of the factors that go into choosing between the two.

I categorize this material in terms of "exterior" and "interior" boundaries, drawing on the quote from Winterhalder. The "exterior" boundaries in this case refer to the 'tell-tales' (*bis*) tied onto and fluttering on the pandanus sail in the accompanying picture. These were made from yellow plastic; traditionally and often still to be seen, they are cut from another pandanus tree's leaves. In addition to the sails, people tie these streamers on the prow and stern pieces of these boats, and, along with the spray generated by a boat crashing into swells and waves, they are watched with great interest. They are part of what makes the sight of these craft truly beautiful. People liken the streamers to the flickering of stars, which are also said to have their own streamers (*bis*). And big men, those successful in the Kula, also wear them when dressed for the Kula. Associations are made among these forms, boats, stars and big men partly on the basis of these streamers. On all three forms the streamers are associated with power. When either stars or big men disappear (by setting or dying), periods of abrupt power are witnessed, often with sudden winds and squalls, and in extreme cases, cyclones. The normal setting of stars, and the consequent alternation of rain and sun that they model, are taken as models for appropriate periodicities in the slash and burn agricultural cycle practiced on Muyuw. A late 1996 cyclone that hit Muyuw and the ensuing 1997–1998 *el niño* were thought to follow from the death of one of my best Wabunun teachers. So the ties to power are important. And these streamers, especially on the boats, are not just for aesthetic appreciation. A steersman watches them carefully for minor changes in wind direction and, far more importantly, for eddies and curls that unpredictably accompany all wind streams and gusts. This phenomenon might not be minor. There is a delicate balancing act between the sail and outrigger float (mediated with every wave by the steersman's operation, another topic I cannot discuss here). Hence, a reversal of wind could swamp these boats in seconds. On the longest voyage I took on one of these boats, we twice deflected our course 60° and 120° in course changing that I experienced as wild, sudden rushes and adjustments of all lines aboard.

At night the steersman cannot see the streamers well and therefore must sense wind currents with his shoulders rather than his eyes; and so it is forbidden to wear a shirt if you are in the steersman position.

As the streamers define the exterior boundaries of this structure, the quality of wood in the mast composes its interior boundary. The critical condition for the mast is its ability to bend, virtually to swing back and forth. This enables the wind to spill out of the top of the sail lest, again, forces transcend the limits of the materials used for these constructions. And everybody

---

20 Although hardly anyone lives in the Sulog area, it is a gigantic resource area.

140

knows that what makes the best mast is a straight and straight-grained tree. These *ayniyan* and *aynikoy* both fulfill this function, partly because, unlike *kausilay* and *apul*, they regularly grow up under a canopy. Although both trees spread from the Sulog region in diminishing numbers, in that region itself they are very common, and on some ridges numerically the dominant species, some short saplings, others mid-sized trees, still others occupying the canopy top.

Sulog is the mountainous, igneous core of a geological structure that is a mixed classic coral atoll. While the raised coral platform around this center is very flat, as one approaches the region the land begins to roll until eroded mountains – or a caldera – are met. The two kinds of mast trees are found in increasing numbers as one approaches the higher igneous ridges. And they reflect the extremes of ecological variation in the region itself. While both have the desired straight grain property deemed best for a mast, one grows in lower, swampier regions, the other (*aynikoy*) on higher, drier ridges (*koy* translated means 'mountain,' 'hill,' or 'rise'). One (*ayniyan*) is slightly lighter than the other, and that means that it can have a larger diameter. Although one informant told me he only used *ayniyan*, my best and closest instructors refused to say one was better than the other. One manipulates the weight and diameter of the mast in order to facilitate swinging appropriate for the total conditions of the boat. In this context, the best tree depends upon many other factors and relationships. The choice of *ayniyan* or *aynikoy*, and the exact diameter each might afford, is one of many determinations where it is understood minute differences lead to critical variation. A mast's density and diameter, both of which determine how it will vibrate in the conditions generated by wind variation, end up being proportionate to every other feature of the boat. Along with the lines – halyards, sheets and shrouds in Western parlance – that visibly anchor its position in the boat, the mast forms an internal boundary condition for a boat's dynamics.

Sometimes, of course, that limit is reached. The *anageg* on which I sailed from Ole/Koyagaugau (Daboyin or Dawson Island) north towards Muyuw in 2002 had a mast made from *kausilay* (Once the captain agreed to sail me to Muyuw, his prime motive for the trip was to replace the mast). We were sailing under winds coming from behind us that were just under gale force, of a speed and direction that was dangerous. On the first leg of our voyage the boat captain recognized that conditions were less than ideal so he added a brace to the mast. On the second leg the winds were stronger and he made a decision that resulted in the mast snapping. That mast was replaced by another made from *kausilay* when we reached Nasikwabw, a portion of Muyuw's barrier reef that has been raised by further faulting and which, because it is entirely limestone, has no *ayniyan* or *aynikoy* available. The new mast was fit with exceeding care. Yet we were not two hours out of Nasikwabw towards our final destination before the captain realized it was not good. A few days after arriving in Muyuw we headed for Sulog for an *aynikoy* replacement.

Conclusion "...a meaningful synthesis." (Lévi-Strauss 1966: 131)

Jukka Siikala's work has been an important exponent of those parts of the recent anthropological tradition that kept together the analysis of form, time and history. It will be long, if ever, before we know all of the historical dimensions that went into the creation of the outrigger forms I have partially described in this chapter. Yet we can be sure that these craft were created out of the experiences time brought to the inhabitants of this region. The same holds for our understandings that enable perspectives like I argue for here. A casual acquaintance with Indo-Pacific ethnography tells us that boat references are critical; as early as 1973, within weeks of my first arrival on Muyuw, I was taken with these vessels, and with the aesthetic interest people had for them. But it was a long time before I had the background to fathom the technical understanding that went into their appreciation. And it was just as long before I could appreciate the problematic socio-ecological conditions that make these craft such a compelling image.

The founding myth of Wabunun, the village in southeastern Muyuw where I have spent much of my forty months on the island, concerns a *teleil* tree (*Terminalia catappa*) of a special kind grown only on the island of Iwa. Iwa people take extraordinary pride in their variety of the tree; its nuts have soft shells that, once cooked, can be broken easily with one's teeth in order to extract the edible material. Everywhere else in the region, the stories universally go, the variety of *T. catappa* has hard shells for which a heavy stone or hammer is needed. In any case, at Wabunun's founding, the story goes, a boatload of Iwa people sailed in, planted their kind of tree, and said "Do not forget us." I was frequently told this tale, but often puzzled over it because most of the time the only other things I heard about Iwa and its people from my Muyuw friends were extremely invidious comments. This was the case even though anytime anyone from around the northern side of the Kula Ring, including me, stopped in Iwa, they were often overwhelmed with gifts of *teleil* nuts, and often other tree products.

My understanding of this story changed dramatically when I returned to Muyuw in mid-1998 just after the 1997–1998 *el niño*. That event was the most severe in anyone living's memory, and virtually all of the indigenous safety nets for such events collapsed, at least inside the period. By the time I returned to the region, however, the rains had started and the recovery was proceeding apace. It was then that I learned what "Do not forget us" meant. Iwa, like Gawa and Kweywata, is a column of coral limestone shooting straight up out of the sea. It is only a couple of square kilometers, far too small to sustain an underground water lens capable of supporting anything but trees after a month or more of drought. Consequently, the people had lost all of their yam and taro stocks. When I heard about this I asked my Wabunun informants what they were doing. The strongest of them could report exactly how many yams they had shipped to Iwa, far out of sight, and only by a stretch of the imagination within two degrees of connection by means of Kula exchange. Yet that tree stood there like a beacon alerting people to what they could not forget.

In a recent review devoted to Norbert Weiner, Freeman Dyson wrote that Weiner's "Cybernetics was a theory of messiness, a theory that allowed people to find an optimum way to deal with a world full of poorly known agents and unpredictable events. The word 'cybernetics' comes from the Greek word for steersman, the man who steers a frail ship through stormy seas between treacherous rocks" (Dyson 2005). Time has passed since Weiner invented cybernetics. And with sufficient time we know the "agents" in the case described here are known, and known well. The trees and their ecologies are matters of selected understanding. The craft built from the individual histories of each of those trees conform to an articulated model of stunning beauty and considerable resilience. Yet the problem Weiner tried to broach at the dawn of our current epoch is exactly that which the peoples of the Indo-Pacific have been dealing with, for the most part successfully, for more than two millennia. This region imposed a major challenge to survival. The challenge was not just connecting the islands, which these boats assuredly did, and do. It was also how to create and manage the connections among the islands and the peoples on them. These boats served, I suggest, as a solution to the chaotic and capricious circumstances that are part of the region's very order. They provide a model of precarious dependencies that must be finely conceived, expertly crafted, and continuously observed. That these boats are cybernetic systems is more than a happy pun. For us, they will, perhaps, be more than objects of a curious and exotic sight. In time they may become forms from which we may yet learn much.

REFERENCES

Damon, Frederick H. 1998. Selective anthropomorphization: trees in the northeast Kula Ring. *Social Analysis* 42(3): 67–99.

Damon, Frederick H. 2005. "Pity" and "ecstasy": the problem of order and differentiated difference across Kula societies. In: Mark Mosko and Frederick H. Damon (eds.) *On the Order of Chaos. Social Anthropology and the Science of Chaos*. New York: Berghahn Books. Pp. 79–107.

Dewar, Robert E. 2003. Rainfall variability and subsistence systems in Southeast Asia and the Western Pacific. *Current Anthropology* 44(3): 369–388.

Dyson, Freeman 2005. The tragic tale of a genius. A review of Flo Conway and Jim Siegelmann: *Dark Hero of the Information Age: In Search of Norbert Weiner, the Father of Cybernetics. The New York Review of Books 52(12)*, 14th July 2005.

Feinberg, R (ed.) 1995. *Seafaring in the Contemporary Pacific Islands*. DeKalb, Illinois: Northern Illinois University Press.

Firth, Raymond 1959. *Economics of the New Zealand Maori*. Preface by R. H. Tawney. Being the 2nd ed. of *Primitive economics the New Zealand Maori*. Wellington, N.Z.: R. E. Owen, Govt. Printer.

Flannery, Timothy F. 1994 [1995]. *The Future Eaters*. New York: George Braziller.

Gell, Alfred 1999. The technology of enchantment, Chapter 5 in *The Art of Anthropology: Essays and Diagrams*. London and New Brunswick, N.J.: The Athlone Press.

Horridge, Adrian 1987. *Outrigger Canoes of Bali and Madura, Indonesia*. Honolulu: Bernice Pauahi Bishop Museum.

Lévi-Strauss, Claude 1966 [1962]. *The Savage Mind*. Chicago: University of Chicago Press.

Manguin, Pierre-Yves 1986. Shipshape societies: boat symbolism and political systems in insular Southeast Asia. In: David G. Marr and A.C. Milner (eds.) *Southeast Asia in the 9th to 14th Centuries*. Singapore: Institute of Southeast Asian Studies & Canberra: Research School of Pacific Studies, Australian National University. Pp. 187–215.

Mosko, Mark 2005. Introduction: a (re)turn to chaos. Chaos theory, the sciences, and social anthropological theory. In: M. Mosko and F. Damon (eds.) *On the Order of Chaos: Social Anthropology and the Science of Chaos*. New York and Oxford: Berghahn Books. Pp. 1–46.

Oliver, Douglas 1974. *Ancient Tahitian Society, vol. 1: Ethnography*. Honolulu: University of Hawaii Press.

Robbins, Joel 2004. *Becoming Sinners: Christianity and Moral Torment in a Papua New Guinea Society*. Berkeley: University of California Press.

Southon, Michael 1995. *The Navel of the Perahu: Meaning and Values in the Maritime Trading Economy of a Butonese village*. Canberra: Research School of Pacific and Asian Studies, Australian National University.

Stevens, Peter. F. 1974. A review of Calophyllum L. (*Guttiferae*) in Papuasia. *Australian Journal of Botany* 22: 349

Stevens, Peter. F. 1980. Revision of the Old World species of Calophyllum (*Guttiferae*). *Journal of the Arnold Arboretum* 61(2): 117–424.

Winterhalder, Bruce 1994. Concepts in historical ecology. In: Carole Crumley (ed.) *Historical Ecology. Cultural Knowledge and Changing Landscapes*. Santa Fe: School of American Research Press. Pp. 17–41.

Sun, Moon and the Tides

Cosmological Foundations for the Ideas of Order and Perfection among the Rotinese of Eastern Indonesia

James J. Fox

Introduction

Throughout the writings of Jukka Siikala, there is a central concern with the social implications of cosmologies that define cycles of time and processes of growth. Thus, for example, in his notable exegesis of the Cook Island cosmology, Jukka traces the procreation of the land and coming into being of the defining rhythms of day and night through the emergence of the sun and moon. In this cosmology, the sun and moon are the "eyes" of Vatea and are associated with male and female. Thus, in this conception: "The eyes of Vatea continue their journey around this hollow and symmetric universe, so that every morning is a new creation of day" (Siikala 1991: 53).

As a personal tribute to the work of Jukka Siikala, who as an ethnographer and a scholar has been engaged in advancing comparisons among populations of the Austronesian-speaking world, I would like to explore the nexus of various cosmological ideas concerning the sun, moon and sea in another Austronesian society, that of the island of Roti in eastern Indonesia. In this paper, I would like to consider how these ideas are linked to some of the most fundamental Rotinese understandings of growth, fertility and order in the world and how they were once ritually celebrated.

The discussion in this paper is part of a larger continuing endeavor intended to document and provide exegesis on Rotinese ideas of "origin." The origins of all important cultural goods and processes are recounted in a canon of ritual texts that details the deeds of two opposing "families:" those of the Sun and Moon (*Ledo do Bulan*) and those of the Lords of the Sea and Ocean (*Liun do Sain*). In this cosmology of opposing "spheres," the earth (*Dae Bafok do Batu Poi*) becomes the meeting place that benefits from the consequences of a series of encounters. According to this complex of accounts, the Sea and Ocean exchanged knowledge, women and wealth with the Sun and Moon. Ultimately, thereafter, ancestors of the Rotinese derived the benefits of these exchanges through separate encounters with creatures from the Ocean and Sea at specific sites along the shoreline and tidal flats of the island. Thus the origin of the knowledge of fire and cooking, of house building, of weaving and of planting, the prototypes of a variety of tools and implements, as well as the first seeds of rice and millet and the first generation of water buffalo all come from the Sea. Hence in ritual, the Sun and Moon are invoked to bestow fertility and bring forth wealth from the Sea. (For further discussion of various relevant Rotinese origin narratives, see Fox 1975: 102–109, 1980, 1993, 1997a, 1997b.)

Sun and moon as male and female

The Rotinese are clear in assigning gender associations to the sun and moon: the sun is "male" and "father," the moon "female" and "mother." A short Rotinese poem draws this analogy explicitly:

Au amang leo ledo	My father is like the sun
Au inang leo bulak	My mother is like the moon
Ti tuda leo ledo	Rising and falling like the sun
Moli mopo leo bulak	Growing and disappearing like the moon.

The parallelism in this poem is critical and indeed essential to understand the Rotinese conceptualization of the relationship between the sun and moon. The particular verbs – 'rising//falling' (*ti*//*tuda*) and 'growing//disappearing' (*moli*//*mopo*), which are used to characterize the sun and moon – identify a cycle that is both physical and symbolic. The cycle of the sun and moon provides the template for a complex set of philosophical ideas associated with the Rotinese concepts of *tetu*//*tema* that may be variously translated as 'order and perfection' or 'rectitude and wholeness.' Exegesis of these concepts begins, appropriately, with an understanding of the cycle of the sun and moon that defines the "heavenly sphere" as opposed to the "earthly sphere" of human endeavor.

The cycle of the sun and moon

In the heavenly sphere, the goal of the sun is *tetu*; the goal of the moon is *tema*. During the course of each day, the sun rises to the 'zenith' (*ledo-tetuk*) and then falls into the sea; while during the course of each month, the moon grows to 'fullness' (*bula temak* or *bula-tema-inak*) and then slowly sinks and disappears. For the Rotinese, the growth of the moon provides (in fact, governs) the pattern for all growth on the island. The verb *moli*, 'to grow,' refers to the waxing of the moon, the growth of plants and human life.

The Rotinese reckon a month of thirty days but, since the final days of the month are subject to readjustment, a month, in practice, need not have thirty days. To be more exact, the Rotinese consider a month to be divided into two cycles of fifteen days each. For fifteen days the moon waxes and during this time, days are counted using the word for 'day,' *faik*: *fai esak*, *fai duak*, *fai teluk*... After the full moon, as the moon begins to wane, the Rotinese say that the moon sinks (*nasa-bolo*) and days are counted using the root of the verb 'to sink,' *bolo*: *bolo esak, bolo duak, bolo teluk...*[1] When the moon is no longer visible, she has disappeared (*mopo*). If the new moon (*bula-moli-beuk*) appears before the fifteenth day of the "sinking" *bolo*-cycle, this presents no problem. Counting according to the old cycle is discontinued and days are reckoned in the *faik*-cycle again. Similarly if the moon begins to wane before the fifteenth day of the *faik*-cycle, counting is begun according to the *bolo*-cycle.

The Rotinese always regard the moon in its relation to the sun. The moon is at its fullest when, at about six in the evening, the moon rises in the east just as the red sun sets in the west. The red sun illuminates the white of the moon, turning it to pink. Of this the Rotinese say idiomatically: *bula pila la-nda*: 'The red moon, they meet [each other]' or simply, *pila la-nda*: 'Red, they meet [each other].' Similarly in the early morning, the dawning sun appears in the east as the moon sinks in the west and the two together are red. During the waxing of the moon, the Rotinese *faik*-cycle, the sun and the moon are not to be seen occupying the sky together, but gradually the sun gains upon the moon. At the end of the *faik*-cycle when the moon is full, the setting sun appears together with the rising moon. Thereafter, during the *bolo*-cycle, the sun and the moon occupy the daytime sky together for an increasing length of time until finally, when the moon disappears, the Rotinese say: *ledo no bulak-a so*: 'The sun has led the moon away.' The same verb, *no*, may be used to refer to a girl who is escorted to her husband's house.

The progress of the sun and moon is seen as a cycle. When the sun sets, it circles beneath the sea and reappears in the east. The moon, too, circles beneath the sea but its cycle around the earth is also a cycle of growth and decline. This waxing and waning of the moon consists of two distinct trajectories. During the *faik*-cycle, the moon goes through three named phases. The new moon is *bula-moli-beuk*, 'the new growing moon.' The second phase of the moon is the half moon. The half moon occupies a position in the zenith and for the Rotinese, during this phase the moon has assumed the proper position of the sun. For this the Rotinese say: *bula namatetu*: 'The moon becomes erect.' Finally the moon reaches its goal and becomes the 'full moon,' *bula temak*. The trajectory of the *bolo*-cycle is toward disappearance. The moon wanes from a full moon to a half moon (*bula namatetu*), when again it assumes the position of the sun, and finally disappears (*mopo*).

The cycle of the tides

The Rotinese recognize the moon's effect on the tides but for them it is the moon in conjunction with the sun that is responsible for this effect. The Rotinese name the tides according to their ebb, for only as the sea recedes can they fish their fish weirs constructed along the shoreline. Each named tide occupies an interval of two to three days. The succession of the tides is fixed but the duration of each tide allows some flexibility. The tides of the

---

1   One can also say of the moon, *ana ke*, 'it cuts.'

faik-cycle are the *meti molik*, 'the growing tides;' the tides of the *bolo*-cycle are the *meti daek*, 'the under or outer tides.'

The cycle of the tides is as follows:

Meti molik:

1. *Tasi ledo sulu*: 'The sea of the shaded sun.' The tide recedes just as the sun has set. (Approx. 6 p.m.).
2. *Tasi pepele leodae*: 'The sea of the evening torch.' The tide recedes in the early evening and fishing is by torchlight. This is a time of excellent fishing. (Approx. 7 or 8 p.m.).
3. *(Tasi) mamok*: During the two or three days of *mamok*, the recession of the sea is so insignificant that the Rotinese claim there is no tide: *meti ta*.
4. *Meti nituk*: 'The spirit tide.' The tide recedes in the middle of the night and fishing is by torchlight. (Approx. 12 p.m.).
5. *(Tasi) pepe lole balaha*:[2] 'The sea of the dawn torch.' The tide recedes in the early hours of the morning but fishing is still by torchlight. (Approx. 3 or 4 a.m.).
6. *Meti beuk*: 'New tide.' The tide recedes at about dawn. (Approx. 5 a.m.). After this begin the *meti daek*, the tides of the *bolo*-cycle:

Meti daek:

1. *Seko koa kako*: 'Scoopnet fishing [when] the *koa*-bird sings.' The tide recedes quickly. (Approx. 5.30 a.m.).
2. *Seko ledo todak*: 'Scoopnet fishing [as] the sun appears.'
3. *Tasi ledo hanak*: 'The sea of the hot sun.' The tide recedes very slowly as the sun moves toward the zenith. At this time, according to the Rotinese, there occurs the best fishing of the month.
4. *(Tasi) mamok*: Again, during *mamok*, there is said to be no tide.
5. *Tasi ledo laik*: 'The sea of the sun above.' The tide recedes in the early afternoon. (Approx. 3 p.m.).
6. *Tasi ledo nosok*: 'The sea of the afternoon sun.' The tide recedes in the late afternoon (Approx. 4 to 5 p.m.). During this time, it is also possible to fish the shore weirs in the morning.

Thus, in the course of a month, there are two periods of excellent fishing: *tasi pepele leodae* and *tasi ledo hanak*. These the Rotinese call *meti ina*: 'the great tides' or 'the mother or female tides' and they are each followed by a period of *mamok*, when there is no appreciable tide at all. All fishing activity ceases.

The Rotinese are insistent that *mamok* occurs when the feminine moon assumes the position of the masculine sun. When the half moon is in the

---

2   In Ba'a, the domain that neighbors Termanu to the west, this tide is referred to as *mbele lole mbilak.*

tetu position, at the zenith, the tides cease and neither women nor female animals are capable of giving birth. During this period of cosmic reversal, there is a lull upon the earth – a suspension of normal growth – and only at the resumption of the tides can women and female animals once more give birth.[3] There is a corollary of this notion, on which the Rotinese are equally emphatic. When the moon is 'full' (*tema*), this is the time for planting coconut trees, banana trees, and *pinang* trees.

Order and perfection as ideal and as reality

The word *tetu* may refer to objects (usually long and slender objects) that stand erect or in vertical position in relation to the ground. Thus the Rotinese say (cf. Jonker 1908: 627): *di-a napadeik na-tetu*: 'The pole stands erect' or *pelak-ala latetu-la ao-n so*: 'The maize holds itself erect.' The word *tetu* also means 'to be precisely balanced' and hence 'even.' Thus, for example, the Rotinese say: *mei-a ta napadeik na-tetu fa*: 'The table does not stand straight (i.e. is uneven)' or *dae-a natetu*: 'The earth is even (flat).' The word *tema*, on the other hand, refers to anything that is 'whole,' 'full,' 'undamaged' or 'unopened.' In its most common usage, *tema* is applied to whole pieces of cloth. In fact, the word *tema* as a noun means a broad uncut piece of cloth. Thus the Rotinese can say (cf. Jonker 1908: 616): *boa ka-temak*, 'the whole fruit'; *lafa ka-temak*: 'a full man's cloth'; *teu ka-temak*: 'a full year' or *tema pilas*: 'the red cloth.' As a verb (*naka-tema*) the word *tema* means 'to close,' 'complete' or 'make whole,' and by extension of this idea, *temak* may refer to a 'thicket' or a 'dense wood,' *nula makatemak*. Another use of the words *tetu//tema* is this: One erects a house (*naka-tetu uma*), but the feast and sacrifices to consecrate the house are referred to as: *naka-tema uma*: 'to complete the house, to make the house whole.' The union of flag and flagpole, the ancient symbol of legitimate rule, is also a union of *tetu// tema* objects.

   In reference to the cycle of the sun and moon, the terms *tetu//tema* define the ideals of order and perfection, rectitude and completeness. In the heavenly sphere, these ideals are achieved as the sun and the moon progress along their established courses. On earth, these ideals, in Rotinese conception, remain elusive and are never fully achievable. Thus despite the quest for order and perfection, the most frequent refrain in Rotinese ritual chants is simply:

Tetu ta nai batu poi	Order is not of this world
Tema ta nai dae bafak.	Perfection is not of this earth.

When the terms *tetu//tema* are applied to a man and a woman, they have a special sense. A virgin girl is called *ina-ana ao-temak*, a 'girl whose body is intact.' More commonly, a virgin is referred to as *mata-temak*, a girl with

---

3   By the logic of this thought, one could assume that most births should occur during the periods of *meti ina* but I have never had any Rotinese confirmation of this idea.

'whole (or intact) eyes.' In Rotinese, *mata*, 'eye,' is a euphemism for the genitals and the expression *ko'o mata*, 'to cup the eyes' means 'to cover the genitals' (cf. Jonker 1908: 151). Similarly, a young boy may be spoken of as *mata matetuk*, a boy with 'upright eyes.' This expression has definite sexual connotations but it may be used widely as a term of approbation for any "upright young man." When, as can happen on Roti, a boy and a girl are discovered to have had intercourse, a marriage is usually arranged immediately. The boy's house is, however, obliged to make a payment to the parents of the girl to wash away their shame. One term for this payment is *nalou oek*: 'to wash [the face] with water.' Another – and in this case a more significant – term for this same payment is *matetu matak*: literally, 'to make right the eyes.'

In one of the best known Rotinese ritual chants, *Pau Balo ma Bola Lungi*, which consists of a long recitation of the loves of a young noble, the refrain, *Tetu ta nai batu poi // Tema ta nai dae bafak*, occurs after each seduction. In this context, the refrain carries a double meaning. At one level, the refrain refers to the lack of order and perfection in the world, but these lines can also be translated in an entirely literal but more suggestive sense:

Tetu ta nai batu poi	Erection is not of the pointed rock
Tema ta nai dae bafak.	Virginity is not of the earth's mouth.[4]

The origin feast and the invocation of the moon

Another representation of the union of *tetu*//*tema* for the Rotinese is that configuration of rock and tree known as a *tutus*. A *tutus* consists of a ring of smooth stones set upon a foundation of loose rock encircling the base of a large tree. This forms a broad stone seating-platform that serves as a monument to the dead, a representation erected to honor prominent individuals as the final optional stage in a succession of mortuary rituals. The most important of these *tutus* in commemoration of clan founders were the sites for the performance of the annual *Hus* or 'Origin Feast' rituals.

At the Origin Feast or Great *Hus* (*Hu-Ina*) of the clan (*Masa-Huk*) of

---

4   The Rotinese express a concern for the virginity of their women. This was particularly marked among Rotinese of noble status. Noble women were more closely watched and they themselves were supposed to maintain a strict rule of conduct in their associations. Their bridewealth was also far more costly. Of the three levels of marriage in Termanu, each requiring a greater exchange of wealth on both sides, more feasting, and more ceremony, the most costly and prestigious form of marriage was known as *sao elok*. This form of marriage demanded that the girl be conducted to her husband's house as a virgin and elaborate symbolic means were taken to emphasize this. Below her waist, the bride was bound tightly in a girdle of coarse black cord. This cord was tied, knotted (the daughter of a lord had the right to nine knots) and thickly smeared with beeswax. In the presence of an old woman, the groom was obliged to undo the waxed knots of his wife's girdle without either breaking the thread or forcing the knots with his teeth. To undo these knots, the groom was permitted to use only the thumb and index finger of his left hand. The process of untying his bride was reputed to have taken – not hours, but days!

the Lord of the Domain of Termanu on Roti, the officiating Lord of Heat (*Manehanas*) would wrap a long *patola*-cloth, known as a *hahalik,* around his waist. Dragging this cloth behind him, he would approach a central *nitas* tree[5] with a raised spear. Stabbing the tree three times, he would call upon the Moon saying:

Kona, bulan, kona	Descend, Moon, descend
Kona, bulan, kona	Descend, Moon, descend
Kona, bulan, kona	Descend, Moon, descend
Kona musik nitas-a boboa	Descend on the right side of the *nitas* tree
Muni meti ma-isi	Bring the abundance of the tide
Muni tua ma-oe	Bring the juice of the lontar palm
Muni bafi mana-bongi-siok	Bring the nine-farrowed sow
Muni manu tutu natuk	Bring hundred pecking chickens.

In the dance that accompanied the *Hus*, the chorus would renew this invocation, chanting:

Sio bafi latola	Pigs of the Feast of Nine appear
Ma hu kapa ladadi.	Buffalo of the *Hus* come forth.
Besak-a ala soku lala bulan ten	Now they lift the spear of the Moon
Ma ala ifa lala ledo tafan-a	And they carry the sword of the Sun
De lalo neu bulan	They call upon the Moon
Ma langgou neu ledo, lae:	And they address the Sun, saying:

"Kona, mai	"Come, descend
Fo muni dini oe manahaik	To bring sufficient moist dew
Ma aü oe mananoük	And ample dampening water
Fo tete dae bafak	To rain down upon the earth
Ma totoli batu poi	And pour down upon the world
Ma fe tua ma-oe	And give the juice of the lontar palm
Ma tasi ma-isi	And the abundance of the sea
Ma kale duak	And two grains
Ma pule teluk	And three seeds
Fo kalen-na didiu	That the grain heads might bend
Ma pulen-na loloso."	And the seed might shoot forth."

From these various chants, one might gain the impression that the *Hus* was carried out to initiate the agricultural cycle, whereas in fact, these ceremonies were conducted after the harvest in celebration of bounty received. To be successful, these ceremonies required a ritual link to the Sea. This link was encapsulated in a relatively simple ritual known as *peda poi//fua bafa*, which

---

5 The *nitas* tree is the Indonesian *kelumpang* (*Sterculia foetida*). In ritual language, it forms a pair with the *delas*, the Indonesian *dedap* (a kind of *Erythrina*). Whereas the *nitas* is associated with the Sun, the *delas* is associated with the Moon.

involved the placement of two relatively common reef fish (*tio holu*//*dusu lai*) on top of the harvest baskets of rice and millet.[6]

Searching the tidal flats for bounty from the sea

In numerous Rotinese origin narratives, there are frequent references to scoopnet fishing along the shoreline as the tide recedes. On Roti, scoopnet fishing is a regular, almost daily practice but in the chants, this activity is represented as significant because of the possibilities it offers for encounters with creatures from the sea and the bounty they provide. In the chants, a common occasion for scoopnet fishing is to provide the two reef fish needed for the proper celebration of the *Hus*. The women who search for these fish are the ones who encounter other creatures who become the personified objects of Rotinese culture. In a certain sense, the search for the ordinary yields the extraordinary.

The following is an illustrative excerpt from a long chant that recounts the origin of the sea shells (*suti*//*bina*) that become the implements for spinning and dyeing. In this chant, an origin feast cannot proceed until the *peda poi*// *fua bafa* ritual is carried out. Two women are designated to search for the *tio* and *dusu* fish that are required for the ritual. They prepare their scoopnet and then set off for a specific coastal site, Tena Lai// Mai Oe, where they begin to fish in dawn's ebbing tide. And it is at this point they fish forth Suti Solo//Bina Bane.

Boe ma Manupui Peda hun-na	Manupui Peda holds his origin feast
Hus ta lakadoto	The origin feast is not lively
Ma Kokolo Dulu sio-na	Kokolo Dulu holds his Feast of Nine
Sio ta lakase.	The Feast of Nine is not noisy.
Boe ma ala kani batu dodo	They divine by shaking the stone
Ma ala lea te ndanda.	They consider by measuring the spear.
Boe ma lae:	They [the diviners] say:
"O, peda poin bei ta	"You have not yet placed a fish on top of the rice
Ma fua bafa bei ta."	And not yet set a fish on the basket's mouth."
Boe ma ina Nggiti Seti	The woman Nggiti Seti
Ma fetok ka Pedu Hange	And the girl Pedu Hange
Bafo Ama Laik tun	Bafo Ama Laik's wife
Ma Holu Ama Daek saon	Holu Ama Daek's spouse
Ala kedi la mau don	They cut a *mau* plant's leaves
De Mau mana'a don	A *mau* with a mouthful of leaves
Ma ala pena-la pole aban	And they pluck a *pole* plant's cotton tufts
De pole masapena aban.	A *pole* bursting with cotton tufts.
De ala teli kokolo ndai	They string and wind a fishnet

6 These reef fish are locally known as the *tio* fish and *dusu* fish and are referred to in ritual language as *Tio Holu ma Dusu Lai*. *Tio* is the bar-tail goat fish (*Mullidae: Upeneus tragula*); *dusu* is the blue-spotted emperor (*Lethrinus liaticaudis*).

De ndai mahamu lilok	A fishnet with a gold-weighted bell
Ma ala ane seko bui seko	They braid and twine a scoopnet
De seko matei besik.	A scoopnet with iron-weighted insides.
De ana ndae ndai neu alun	She hangs the fishnet over her shoulder
Ma ana su'u seko neu langan	And she balances the scoopnet on her head
De leo Tena Lai neu	And goes to Tena Lai
Ma leo Mae Oe neu,	And goes to Mae Oe,
Neu nafa-nggao lutu limak	Goes to grope in the "arms" of the fish-wall
Ma neu nafa-dama dea eik,	Goes to probe in the "legs" of the stone-weir,
Dea ei ma-nalek	The "legs" of the stone-weir that hold good fortune
Ma lutu lima ma-uak.	The "arms" of the fish-wall that bear good luck.
Nafanggao dea eik	She gropes in the "legs" of the stone-weir
Ma nafadama lutu limak.	And probes the "arms" of the fish-wall.
Siluk bei ta dulu	Morning is not yet in the east
Ma hu'ak bei ta langa dei.	Dawn is not yet at the head.
Boe ma ana ndai ndano, ndai ndano	She fish-catches, fish-catches
Ma ana seko toko, seko toko.	And she scoop-throws, scoop-throws.
Boe ma ana seko nala Suti Solo	She scoops up Suti Solo
Ma ana ndai nala Bina Bane.	And she fishes up Bina Bane.

This encounter follows a pattern that defines the relationship with the Sea and links this relationship, via the tides, to the Celebrations of Origin addressed to the Sun and Moon. Other encounters follow a similar narrative pattern.[7]

Conclusion

In this paper, I have tried to examine a particular nexus of Rotinese ideas that links the sun, moon and the tides. These ideas combine conceptions of natural processes and of ordinary everyday activities with a rich and complex interpretative world of great imaginative creativity. All of these ideas coalesce in a coherent ideal conception of a heavenly order and of the unattainability of such order in the human realm.

Knowledge of daily activities and of the interpretation of cycles in nature enhances an understanding of the ritual chants; these chants, in turn, illuminate the acts and intentions of an underlying cosmic spirituality. This, as I have tried to show, is another instance of what Jukka Siikala has exemplified in the exegeses in his monograph *'Akatokamanāva* (1991), under the rubric: "Cosmology As Signified."

---

7   Thus, for example, the chant narrative that recounts the origin of rice and millet follows a remarkably similar pattern (see Fox 1997a: 95–99).

BIBLIOGRAPHY

Fox, James J. 1975. On binary categories and primary symbols: some Rotinese perspectives. In: R. Willis (ed.) *The Interpretation of Symbolism*. London: Malaby Press. Pp. 99–132.

Fox, James J. 1980. Figure shark and pattern crocodile: the foundations of the textile traditions of Roti and Ndao. In: M. Gittinger (ed.) *Indonesian Textiles*. Textile Museum, Washington, D.C. (Proceedings of the Irene Emery Roundtable on Museum Textiles held in 1979). Pp. 39–55.

Fox, James J. 1993. Memories of Ridgepoles and Crossbeams: The Categorical Foundations of a Rotinese Cultural Design. In: J. J. Fox (ed.) *Inside Austronesian Houses: Perspectives on Domestic Designs for Living*. Canberra: Department of Anthropology, Research School of Pacific and Asian Studies, Australian National University. Pp. 140–179.

Fox, James J. 1997a. Genealogy and Topogeny: Toward an Ethnography of Rotinese Ritual Place Names. In: J. J. Fox (ed.) *The Poetic Power of Place: Comparative Perspectives on Austronesian Ideas of Locality*. Canberra: Department of Anthropology, Research School of Pacific and Asian Studies, Australian National University. Pp. 91–102.

Fox, James J. 1997b. Genealogies of the Sun and Moon: Interpreting the Canon of Rotinese Ritual Chants. In: E. K. M. Masinambow (ed.) *Koentjaraningrat dan Antropologi di Indonesia*. Jakarta: Assosiasi Antropologi Indonesia/Yayasan Obor Indonesia. Pp. 321–330.

Jonker, J. C. G. 1908. *Rotinese-Hollandsch Woordenboek*. Leiden: E. J. Brill.

Siikala, Jukka 1991. '*Akatokamanāva: Myth, History and Society in the Southern Cook Islands*. Auckland: The Polynesian Society in Association with the Finnish Anthropological Society.

Mythical and Textual Perspectives on the Past

For What Purpose?

An Unusual Tokelau Vernacular Text
Written by Peato Tutu Perez

Judith Huntsman

Historians and anthropologists are increasingly using vernacular written texts as documentary sources. This, I think, is all to the good. But some scholars are understandably somewhat ill at ease with these documents, perhaps because they are uncertain how to interrogate them. Jukka Siikala drew upon such texts in his book *'Akatokamanāva* (1991) to elucidate the origins and transformations of the Ngāpūtoru polity (the islands of Mauke, Atiu and Mitiaro) in the Southern Cook Islands. His theoretically sophisticated and culturally informed handling of them was exemplary. For this volume in honor of Jukka, I have chosen to follow his example, on a very modest scale, by presenting and interrogating one unusual Tokelau vernacular text, recently composed as an eyewitness account of particular events over a period of four decades in Fakaofo atoll.

Vernacular written texts which authors or inheritors offer to scholars to consult or copy are quite different from the communal "oral traditions" that scholars and sojourners in Polynesia have noted and recorded over the years. This is because their authors have composed them for some specific purpose and they are not part of their society's repertoire, though the society may draw upon them. For example, "family books" record genealogies, family history, etc. to preserve and protect the interests of present and future generations by reference to the actions and dictates of past generations. An essential question for the scholar to ask is: "For what purpose was the text written?" The answer to this question lies as much in how the narrative is constructed as in the story the narrative tells. Where is the writer positioned, if positioned at all? What style or styles of storytelling does the writer employ? How are the episodes and events related to one another? These are some questions to be asked of the text itself. But the purpose or intent of the text cannot be broached unless the interrogator is familiar with the historical and socio-cultural milieu of which its author is a part and the author's position in it. Thus, to begin, I briefly portray the relevant socio-cultural milieu (see Huntsman and Hooper 1996: Ch.2 for a fuller exposition) and present a brief biography of the author of the "unusual text," including how it came to be written.

About Tokelau

The three Tokelau atolls lie some 500 km. north of Samoa in latitudes of 8° to 10° south and longitudes 171° to 173° west along a northwest to southeast axis of some 150 km. Atafu is the most northerly, Fakaofo the most southerly and Nukunonu is positioned in between, a bit closer to Fakaofo than Atafu.

From the latter half of the 19th century, the three Tokelau atolls, while sharing basic institutions and language, were virtually autonomous polities: each doing things its own way and each with its own history. Yet, Tokelauans recognized and celebrated the bonds of kinship and the common past that united them. Their ancient history relates how Fakaofo gained ascendancy after an indeterminate era of inconclusive and periodic conflicts between the atolls. Associated with Fakaofo's pre-eminence was the "great god of all Tokelau," Tui Tokelau, whose presence was beyond but was manifested by a huge stone that stood before the god-house in Fakaofo, and whose principal worshipper (on behalf of all Tokelau) was Fakaofo's reigning paramount *aliki*. Fakaofo exacted tribute and exploited the resources of the other two atolls, Atafu and Nukunonu, and unions of one sort or another resulted in links of kinship between the atolls.

Thus, in the early 1800s early visitors to the atolls wrote of the three atolls as one polity (see, in particular, Hale 1846 and Wilkes 1845). Fakaofo was dominant, home to the paramount *aliki*, host to the instantiation of Tui Tokelau and holder of the *pule* 'power/authority' over all Tokelau. Nukunonu and Atafu were subject to Fakaofo's tribute demands and *pule*. Western intrusions ended this empire, but not the relations between the atolls that had been forged by intermarriage.

The 1850s brought Christian proselytizers of the Protestant London Missionary Society (hereafter LMS) and the Catholic Marist Mission to Fakaofo, but they were turned away. Then, virtually simultaneously in 1861, Atafu was persuaded to seek a Protestant teacher by a resident Tokelau convert and the people of Nukunonu quickly committed themselves to the Catholic faith of a returned chiefly son. Fakaofo continued to resist conversion. This all, of course, makes political sense. By converting to Christian faiths, Atafu and Nukunonu rejected Tui Tokelau and thereby challenged Fakaofo's domination. Later, other foreign intruders provoked Fakaofo's eventual conversion, and that atoll ended up hosting the two contesting Christian faiths – Protestant and Catholic. The missions and later colonial powers treated the atolls as three equivalent and autonomous polities. Fakaofo made assertions to the contrary from time to time, but they were dismissed by these outsiders and effectively resisted by Atafu and Nukunonu.

In 1889 Tokelau was declared to be under the protection of the British Western Pacific High Commission. Subsequently the atolls were included in the Gilbert and Ellice Island Protectorate (1909) and then annexed as part of the Gilbert and Ellice Island Colony (1916). In 1925–1926, after some years of negotiation between Britain and New Zealand, New Zealand assumed responsibility for the atolls' administration on behalf of the British

Crown, and the atolls formally came under the delegated authority of the Governor General of New Zealand who then delegated certain powers to the Administrator of Western Samoa (see Huntsman and Hooper 1996: Ch.8). The colonial presence was both brief and sporadic, and Tokelauans by and large welcomed it, not perceiving it as compromising local *pule* 'rule,' but as *tauhi*, 'protecting and caring for' them. Following the Second World War, Tokelau's political status changed yet again. With the passage of the Tokelau Islands Act of 1948, Tokelau became a part of New Zealand and, later in the year, Tokelauans became New Zealand citizens. The Tokelau Islands Act of 1948 with subsequent amendments establishes Tokelau's political status as a dependency of New Zealand, a status that most Tokelauans cherish.

Through the 1950s and 60s Tokelau life remained much as it had been in the earlier decades of the century. The compact villages of thatched dwellings and cookhouses with spacious churches and meeting houses and modest hospitals and schoolrooms were each located on one islet at the western margin of each atoll. Outrigger canoes were beached at the lagoon shore between the vertical sides of coral reclamations upon which dwellings were built and from which latrines extended out over the lagoon. Men paddled and sailed their outrigger canoes to islets across the lagoon to harvest coconuts and other produce, swam in the lagoon and walked the reef to net or hook small fish, and passed over the reef and through the breaking waves by canoe to capture the larger fish of the surrounding ocean. To be a proficient fisherman was to be a man, and knowledge of fishing techniques and the expertise in using them were what made a man a 'master fisherman' (*tautai*). Women typically stayed in the village, looking after the young and elderly, plaiting the coconut and pandanus mats that covered the coral floors of their houses and cookhouses, allocating and cooking the fruits that the men harvested and the fish that they caught. However important these daily routines were, things communal took precedence and communal activities were a part of weekly, if not daily, activities. People attended meetings, engaged in communal tasks and played games together. The council of elderly men met in council at least once a week. All women met under the aegis of the elderly matrons at least once a week. The able-bodied men either joined the elders or met on their own to organize communal projects and activities. The competing 'sides' (*fāitū*) of the village met to plan their play or a project, and clubs met irregularly in pursuit of their special interests. The churches too called meetings of elders or women or other sectors of the congregation. Life in a Tokelau village was busy, at times tirelessly so, with communal feasts and cricket matches and evening dance festivities. All this activity, and indeed much of the fishing and harvesting, was carefully programmed and ultimately approved by the Elders' Council.

A person's position was determined primarily by age. *Toeaina*, 'elderly men', and *lōmatua*, 'elderly women/matrons,' each collectively held *pule*, 'authority,' in directing and admonishing the younger generations of men and women, respectively. The authority of age was acknowledged in every

159

activity; the senior person was properly in charge and deferred to, and even when just two people were engaged in a task, the elder one would direct the younger. This pervasive age hierarchy was, however, a collective hierarchy and a person gradually became more authoritative and less subject to authority of others over time.

In short, through the 1960s and for many decades before, Tokelau village life was dominated by communal activities. Weekly meetings and days designated for certain activities structured the normal week, ending with hours of church services and activities on Sunday. The arrival of the supply ship, bearing visitors and officials, meant another routine, but this only happened every three months or so. Occasionally, the ship might bring a party of visitors from one or both of the other atolls to celebrate an event, such as a church opening, or a team and its supporters to compete in cricket. On these rare occasions when Tokelau got together, some tension prevailed. On the one hand, people were reconnecting with kin from other villages, eating together and gifting one another. On the other hand, people were representing their village, intent on outdoing the other (or others) in whatever activity had brought them together. While in a sense they were all Tokelau together, they were also three villages in competition.

About the author

The author of the "unusual text," and of a number of other ones, was the late Peato Tutu Perez (1904–1980), elsewhere characterized as "undoubtedly one of the most knowledgeable and articulate Tokelau traditionalists we have ever had the pleasure of working with" (Hooper and Huntsman 1992:250).

I knew Peato well. He was my first real mentor during my initial fieldwork in Tokelau, summoning me to his house one Sunday after church for my first lesson. He patiently taught me, wisely counseled me and firmly supported me for six months, then he left Tokelau to live the rest of his life (12 years) in New Zealand where I visited him frequently. Though he valued and espoused the verities of Tokelau life, he was not an uncritical "traditionalist," and he saw the future of his children and grandchildren in New Zealand. The whole family, his six children and their children, as well as Peato and his wife, "chain-migrated" to the Wellington area over a period of five years or so. All this, however, was close to the end of a very interesting life, some of which needs to be told.

Peato was the son of a half-caste Portuguese trader and his Tokelau wife who lived in the 100 percent Catholic village of Nukunonu. However, Peato was brought up in Fakaofo with his mother's parents (his maternal grandfather could recall the years before Christian conversion) and the Tokelau catechist, who was a surrogate "father" to him and shepherd of the minority Catholic congregation there. Peato was destined to succeed this "father" and in 1928, after a period of religious training in Samoa, took his place as the spokesman and leader of Fakaofo's sometimes beleaguered Catholic minority. He was, as well, a renowned 'master fisherman' (tautai), one of the few who had hooked more than 100 skipjack (in his case 107) in one 'stand' (tulaga), that is, one continuous period of casting from the stern of the canoe.

In late 1949, Peato moved to Nukunonu where he assisted the newly resident *pāpalagi* priests in building the mission premises and establishing the mission school. He never really learned English, but he quickly took up writing Tokelauan in an orthography devised by the priest who founded the school.[1] This same priest gave Peato the typewriter that he was still using in New Zealand in the 1970s to compose and refine his texts on Tokelau history and traditions.

I had glimpsed and listened to many of these texts when he was my mentor in Nukunonu, and again in New Zealand. What struck me was how original and exploratory they were. Take, for example, the matter of the nights of the moon, and sequence of moon/months with their associated stars and fishing. Tokelau men write down these sorts of things again and again in exercise books, and they endlessly debate different counts, and particularly how Tokelau counts equate with Gregorian months. Peato laid it all out, and methodically worked out the inconsistencies in the two calendars. Peato was a man of principle, and also a man with well-established antipathies: he thoroughly disliked pomposity and had an abiding suspicion of Samoans.[2]

In the later 1970s, I arranged for Peato to spend some time in Auckland consulting on several projects. He brought with him some manuscripts he had been working on for me to photocopy. They were in essence two texts that were quite distinct in subject matter, despite some duplication, and together amounted to over 50 closely-typed pages. One dwelt on knowledge related to fishing – moons, stars, fishing methods and etiquette; the other was primarily a description of customary social relations. During this visit Peato composed and tape-recorded a spirited exposition on fishing especially for my colleague, Antony Hooper (see Hooper and Huntsman 1992), and regaled us again with stories of his years as catechist in Fakaofo. It was then that we suggested that he set down these stories in writing. He did so with alacrity and three months later presented the text to me to do with as I wished.

Over the years Hooper and I have dipped into Peato's texts, plucking out what was particularly relevant to our own projects. The text written at our suggestion has been of particular value for the insider view it gives of events otherwise reported by visitors. However, that text as a whole has always intrigued me – both in what it said and how it was constructed.

It is, in essence, a semi-autobiographical account of events in Fakaofo

---

1 I note for the record, because the matter is contentious in Tokelau, that Peato modified the priest's original orthography to conform with the more widely preferred orthography of the language.
2 Fanaafi Mai'a'i wrote (1957: 159) "The Tokelau people in no way admire the Samoans," leading me to suspect that she might have been speaking to Peato who took pride in 'speaking straight' (*tautala hako*).

from just after the turn of the century to the 1940s. The text is at the same time historical and thematic, and in the end chronology is abandoned to the message.

I approach it here by first setting out the structure of the text, and reproducing in translation a key part. Then, I discuss the message of the text and how the structure underpins the message. The primary divisions of the text are mine, indicated by square brackets; the secondary ones are marked, in one way or another, in the text. My interjections also are enclosed in square brackets. Close translations of the Tokelau text are marked by single quotes, as are my glosses of some key words with the Tokelau in parentheses.

The Structure of the Text

[**Preamble**: The tenure of Peato's "father" as catechist (1907–1928) and the relations between the Protestants and Catholics during the 'reigns' (*nofoakiga*) of three Protestant pastors.]

- During the long 'reign' of a Tuvalu LMS pastor, 'not a single thing disturbed the relations between the congregations,' but in the end 'difficulties arose between the pastor and his congregation' and he departed.
- During the 'reign' of the succeeding Samoan LMS pastor, some 'thoughtless recklessness' (*fakahētonuga*) acts by impetuous boys resulted in 'misunderstanding' between the congregations....[3] They challenged one another and told exaggerated or false stories about what each had done [primarily conveyed through dialogue]. Intervention by the catechist and pastor ended the disturbance 'without further words being said to make matters worse.'
- A Tuvalu LMS pastor replaced the Samoan pastor and a relationship of 'mutual respect' (*mafutaga fealofani*) prevailed between the congregations and nothing untoward occurred.

[**PART I**: Peato's interactions with several LMS pastors and events in Fakaofo during the first 12 years of his tenure as catechist (1928–1940).]

- Peato replaced his "father" as catechist, during the above Tuvalu pastor's 'reign.' Unspecified 'troubles' (*fakalavelave*) arose between the pastor and his congregation, and he and his family went to live on an islet across the lagoon.[4] Peato and his wife visited them, and reconciled the pastor and

---

3 An account of the "Great Cyclone" of January 1914 interrupts the story of the "disturbance" at this point.

4 Only people who are sick or outcasts reside outside the village confines.

his congregation. Thereafter, all was well in Fakaofo and peace continued to prevail between the congregations.

• An elderly Samoan LMS pastor replaced the Tuvalu pastor and 'the mutual respect and consideration between the Fakaofo congregations increased still further.' He and Peato together instigated many projects beneficial to all Fakaofo, e.g., the extension of swamp taro cultivations that 'firmly established the mutual respect between the Fakaofo congregations.'

• During the 'reign' of the subsequent Samoan LMS pastor, numerous clubs and then the Aumaga sprang up,[5] both to serve the village and to compete in cricket.[6] Both Catholics and Protestants joined the clubs, and when the elders engaged them for work projects, the work was quickly and well done, as they competed in work as they did in cricket. Then the Aumaga was formed to be at the service of the elders, and the Aumaga came to dominate the separate clubs, symbolically gaining control of the cricket ground. But with all able-bodied men in the Aumaga, work projects were carried out less effectively because there was no competition. This led Peato and the pastor to propose a major project, for which they organized the Aumaga into competing sides, one led by Peato and the Protestant *faipule* and the other by the pastor and the Catholic *pulenuku*.[7] Each side organized its half of the work, and competed to finish first. The feast at the project's completion celebrated 'the fine work for the benefit of all the people of Fakaofo.' Later, good relations between Peato and the pastor and their congregations were compromised in a dispute over the boundary between plots of land earlier granted to the two churches. In the end, Peato, having established that he was in the right, allowed the altered boundary to stand. An agreement was written and signed so that the matter of the boundary [which had been a source of periodic conflict for years] 'would not again arise to trouble the congregations, and would gradually vanish so that peace would prevail between them.' [This episode is largely conveyed by dialogue.]

---

5   The Aumaga was adapted from the Samoan *'Aumaga* and introduced to Fakaofo by a man who had spent many years in Samoa.

6   Exactly when and how cricket was introduced to Tokelau remains something of a mystery. It undoubtedly came from Samoa, probably in the early 1900s. Certainly by the 1930s it was Tokelau's national sport and still is today.

7   The *faipule* and *pulenuku* were administration appointees: the former was the local representative of the administration (or *malo* 'government') and the latter was usually referred to as the village mayor.

[**PART II**: The 1940–1942 'reign' of the subsequent Samoan LMS pastor, and contestation between this pastor and Peato. I give a slightly abridged close translation of the text.[8]]

[**Preamble.**] Within two weeks of his arrival the Pastor began his scheming by summoning the Faipule and Peato to explain to him the conduct and relationships of the congregations, village and government.[9] The Faipule set these out clearly. Firstly, the congregations were independent in the conduct of their services and their schools; the administration had no concern with them, and the village simply supported them. Secondly, the elder's council, on behalf of the village, supported what is best for all. But when each had its own work to do, LMS people worked for the good of the LMS and Catholics worked for the good of Catholics. And, thirdly, the administration worked for the good of everyone, whether LMS or Catholic…

Folau replied to the two of them, "You should fully understand my assignment in Fakaofo…. I have been given two assignments: first, to look into enhancing the standing of the LMS in Fakaofo, and, second, to rectify the position of the Fakaofo village authority and administration." He added that he anticipated difficulties between the congregations.

To this Peato responded, "Troubles between congregations can be traced to those who are in charge of them."

As the Faipule and Peato departed, the Faipule expressed anxiety about the encounter. Peato replied, "Why do you pay any attention to him, the good of Tokelau rests with the people of Tokelau."

The First Thing He 'Revealed' (*aliali mai*): He tried to dismantle Peato's cricket club, which many LMS men belonged to, by demanding that all LMS men who had joined leave it, saying that they must not associate with Peato who was an evil person.

When Peato heard about this, he immediately called a meeting. Peato said, "I did not found this club. What I did was play some games, my crew joined another crew to play cricket with another club simply because we wanted to play. Afterwards I heard about you starting our club and calling a meeting. The meeting was held but I did not attend, leaving the decision to you. You agreed to start a club and you named it. Will I be loyal to that name or will I abandon it?" The response was that the club would not be dissolved. Peato said, "Whoever wishes to leave, let him go, but to go is bad for the club if one leaves because of the Pastor's edict, yet he is free to go." Some men left but not many; most remained. The Pastor's house was close to the cricket ground and he was observing when the game began.

---

8   My translation of portions of this text draws upon an earlier translation by Antony Hooper.

9   "Government" means the NZ administration that the *faipule* represented in the village.

The Second Thing He 'Revealed': The Pastor ordered his congregation that during games, when Peato's Angelus bell rang, not to halt play but carry on, not to pay respect to false things.

For many years Fakaofo people had respected each other's religious practices. A persistent and strong belief of all Fakaofo people is that the cause of evil in Fakaofo is the pastors. So it was that LMS people were not happy with this…

The Third Thing He 'Revealed': When anything was apportioned throughout the village, the practice for many years was for the portions allotted to the pastor and catechist to be exactly equal.[10]

The Pastor demanded, "When the special portions are made, do not make Peato's portion equal to mine. Make mine larger and make his smaller, make mine twice the size of his." This new departure caused discord in Fakaofo.

In those days Peato had two canoes: Peato captained one and the medical dresser the other. On days of communal fishing, the catch from both canoes was taken to the village distribution place. After that instruction was given, Peato told the medical dresser to continue taking his catch to the village distribution place, while he took his canoe's catch to his house.

When the council of elders realized that Peato's catch was not being taken to the village distribution place, an outcry arose. This was because for the past 30 years, when the pastor's canoe went out to fish on communal fishing days, the catch was never taken to the village distribution place, and not a single person objected. However, when Peato did this, there was an outcry. But Peato had not done this without purpose; he was making a point.

The Fakaofo Council did not know about the pastor's assertion to the Faipule and Peato that he had been sent to Fakaofo to enhance the position of the LMS within the village and administration. He had 'revealed' these things, but not who had so instructed him.

The Fourth Thing He 'Revealed': A local government decision regarding Sabbath rules prohibiting lighting fires or cooking food on Sunday had provoked a major rift between the congregations. Many meetings were held that divided the congregations, many arguments resulted, but no resolution was reached.

One thing that provoked the Pastor's hostility towards Peato was that Peato did not bring his congregation to the meetings; Peato attended alone. Peato said, "No, this is not a matter for congregations so I will not bring my congregation to the meeting." The problem was that the Faipule was afraid of the Pastor and the two assignments he had received in coming to Fakaofo.

Peato had instructed his congregation to hold off lighting fires until a decision was reached, and they did this. At the meeting, Peato asked the

---

10   The reference here is to the *inati* system whereby food and other things are absolutely equally allocated to or levied from village members. When allocations are made, special portions are set aside for the pastor and catechist.

Faipule to spell out the administration rules regarding the Sabbath. The Faipule proclaimed these rules: (i) cooking fires are prohibited on Sunday, (ii) cooking is prohibited on Sunday, (iii) fishing is prohibited on Sunday, and (iv) any play is prohibited on Sunday. Then Peato asked the Faipule, "Are these new rules or longstanding rules?" The Faipule replied, "These are longstanding rules from the time when Australia looked after Tokelau."[11]

Peato responded, "When my 'father' was catechist, choir practice was held every Sunday and when it was over the women and men would play cards and other quiet games, but not a single objection was raised. Where was the rule in those days?"

A Protestant man who referred to the late magistrate as his "father" interjected, "My 'father,' during the many years he was magistrate, started enforcing the Sabbath rules."

Peato rejoined, "Let me describe things that I myself have witnessed. First, the Deputy Commissioner resided in Fakaofo for several months… his servant lit a cooking fire every day including Sunday. Where was your 'father' and his rule when the Commissioner's cooking fire was lit? Second, the next Deputy Commissioner resided in Fakaofo for several months, lighting his cooking fire every Sunday, and even going fishing every Sunday. Where had your 'father' hidden his rules when he transgressed your 'father's' rules? Third, the present *faipule* had replaced your 'father' as magistrate when another officer resided here for several months, and he went fishing every single Sunday. Was the *faipule* blind to the rules those days, did he not see him abuse the law?"

The Faipule replied, "Is this rule abided by in Australia, by the commissioners coming from Australia? It is not something I hear of, it is not something I see. You know that sometimes we must look the other way."

The pastor spoke to Peato, "Oh, white chiefs, they are exempt from these laws."

Peato answered, "Oh! It is no wonder then! The administration discriminates against people and religions, this is racial discrimination (*fakailoga lanu*)!" Peato continued, "I and my congregation do not light fires on Sunday, because of that rule, even though we compromise our well-being. This is what I say to the Faipule, to his statement of the rules, it gives me access to the administration. I know that if we do not obey these rules, I have no access for we have transgressed them. I have not hidden anything from you all. I shall send my appeal against these rules that constrain me and my congregation to the government in Samoa."

I sent two long telegrams to the head of the Catholic church in Samoa to transmit to the Administrator in Samoa and I signed my name. I told the Administrator the reason for these difficulties was that the pastor ruled the

---

11   The period (c. 1909–1925) when Tokelau was a Protectorate and then Colony loosely attached to the Gilbert and Ellice Islands Administration is usually referred to in Tokelau as the time of Australian oversight. I have yet to fathom why.

village and the government in Fakaofo. The wireless operator was reluctant to sign for the message, but Peato persuaded him, arguing that he could not be certain that the telegrams had been sent unless they were signed for, and that he [Peato] might well end up in jail if the telegrams were not sent. Also the pastor might try to prevent the message being sent in light of his assertion that he had authority over the village and the government. Anyway, the message got through and an inquiry was sent from Samoa by the administration, bringing McKay to Fakaofo.[12]

Day of the inquiry

McKay questioned the *faipule* about the matter at issue, and the *faipule* explained: "It is not, not a regulation but a custom that has been followed in Fakaofo to respect the Sabbath under the authority of the elders."

McKay asked, "The Sunday Sabbath is based upon Tokelau ancient custom?"

The Faipule replied, "Oh no. It was something done by the elders for the welfare of Fakaofo."

McKay responded, "Meaning that the elders would do something to repress one part of Fakaofo and to support the other part of Fakaofo – is that how the rule of the elders works in Fakaofo?" The Faipule did not respond.

The Pastor interrupted, "May the white chief be filled to overflowing with the will of the Almighty."

McKay countered, "Are you superior to me? You, Pastor, be still, you have no business in this matter."

McKay asked Peato to give his explanation of the matter at issue. Peato said, "I just learned this very day that there is no government rule concerning the Sabbath, but it is a rule of the Fakaofo elders. I am amazed – I am hearing utterly new statements about this. The Faipule and Pastor took a determined stand that these were government rules, that these four Sabbath rules were imposed when Australia looked after Tokelau and Ellice."

The Pastor and Faipule had instructed that on the day of the inquiry the congregations would sit separately so that McKay might see the majority were LMS and the minority Catholic.

McKay spoke, "Upon receiving Peato's message I set to reading the laws for Tokelau – the law book from the Australian administration of Tokelau and Ellice. These laws still apply to Tokelau. There is absolutely no law like the four stated concerning the Sabbath among those laws, just as Peato says. The laws allow eating places and coffee shops to be open on the Sabbath because people want to eat on Sunday – they cannot stop up their mouths. Other shops are closed by law." He added, "I have come often to Fakaofo, and

12   C. G. R. McKay was Secretary of Samoan Affairs in the New Zealand Administration of Western Samoa, whose responsibilities included Tokelau.

for the first time encountered this arrangement [of the congregations seated separately]. Why did not someone tell me so I would know? The LMS there, the Catholics there." Then he gave his judgment, "There is no government law like those stated concerning the Sabbath. It is not a government day, but a day of the churches and it is up to them to honor their day. Under the NZ flag there is freedom of religion, all may choose their religion. It is prohibited for one religion to curtail the freedoms of another." Then McKay told Peato that he would go and speak with the head of the Catholic church in Apia, and also with the head of the LMS.

After McKay left, the Pastor did not in the least desist in what he was doing in Fakaofo.

The Fifth Thing 'Revealed': He tried to get Peato to sign a paper on which he had written a list of things for the advancement of the LMS in Fakaofo, but Peato was not tricked.

He summoned Peato to come over so they might talk about matters for the betterment of the congregations. Peato went over and there was the Pastor with eight members of his congregation. The Pastor spoke – devious and round about were his words – of his wish for peace between the congregations and within the village (how expansive and righteous his words sounded!) but Peato just sat there, knowing full well the pastor's intentions. He said that it was their wish to improve relations between the congregations, that what had passed should not be recalled but relegated to the past. Then he came to the point: "There is a document already written by the LMS officers for you to sign along with them."

Peato responded that he was all for reconciliation but was not going to sign anything he had not inspected – for it is difficult for one to trust another. The document had ten items written on it – on a large piece of paper – but all the writing was on the lower part of the page leaving the upper part blank. Peato said: "This is the first time I have seen a document like this – with space above rather than below – and I am not signing it unless I know why the document is written this way. Give me the document to take away and make a proper copy, exactly the same, but from the top for signing. For Peato is not going to bind himself and his successors to what might later be written above. I am not blind."

Again, the Pastor did not succeed; Peato did not sign his name.

The Sixth Thing 'Revealed': The Pastor summoned Peato by letter to come with his congregation to discuss a matter concerning the welfare of Fakaofo. The subject of the meeting was not mentioned.

Peato told his congregation about the Pastor's letter, and they talked about it. Peato told them he was not happy with the letter since it did not state the subject for the meeting. "How could they go to the meeting and within the space of a single minute either say 'Yes' to a proposal that would divide Fakaofo, or 'No' to something which might be good for all Fakaofo.

The matter is hidden from us, and I suspect that there is something evil at the bottom of it. My thoughts are that the elders should stay behind while I go with some younger men to learn what the matter at issue is." The elders agreed to this, and Peato went with two younger representatives of the Catholic church. We found gathered all the elders of the Protestant church – all 28 of them.

First, the meeting sought a chairman. The Pastor said that Peato was chairman, but Peato refused. An elder then replied to Peato "You are chairman," and Peato said, "How shall I be chairman if I do not know the matter under discussion? I am not chairman."

The Pastor then revealed the purpose of the meeting. "The matter we wish to address is this: To constitute Fakaofo so that it has the status it had in the past; to recognize the *aliki* (*tupu* 'king') so that if some disturbance occurs, it will be dealt with as in Samoa where whenever there is disagreement in a village, the *aliki* pronounces upon it and that is the end of it."

When this proposal was revealed, two elders seized the opportunity to declare: "Yes! Fakaofo is ruled by *tuafenua* ('rough side of the land,' i.e., commoners). The king and *aliki* have been set aside and commoners have come to rule Fakaofo! Fakaofo is ruled by commoners!" These phrases were repeated perhaps five to eight times before they were stopped, but were passionately reiterated, with dramatic gestures, throughout the meeting. Those assembled sat with bowed heads. Peato noticed that none of the elders muttered among themselves, but just sat with bowed heads. Peato decided then that the elders of the Protestant church supported the proposal, that it was the Pastor's proposal and he had already discussed it with his congregation. Peato said that he and his congregation would not join the discussion, but they could do as they wished.

A long time passed and nobody spoke. Although Peato felt that the Pastor had incited the pair of elders, he just sat and did not speak. The Pastor told Peato to speak, but Peato just sat. Nobody said anything. Peato realized that the Pastor was intent on deceiving the Catholic church about traditional authority, and that the Pastor and these two elders planned to be kings of Fakaofo, because the Catholic church opposed the things being done in Fakaofo. Time went by and nobody spoke. Peato said: "How is it that no elder speaks?" and went on to say: "Those things these two elders said to you – what shall be done? It is right that you should talk about the matter, but not appropriate that I, a child, should talk while you do not. However, I shall speak."

Peato spoke thus, "First of all, my respects to the elders. I presume to speak since, as I think you know, I listened to my grandfather who was raised in the heathen days. There were days and enough that we were together and he told me about Fakaofo. When he had finished one of his tales, these were his concluding words, 'We are just talking so that you can hear about the ancient history of Fakaofo. But let these be because these things were abandoned by Fakaofo Aliki long departed.' Those were the words he spoke to me."

"I ask forgiveness of you if my words are mistaken and abhorrent to you, but I shall speak of the things that I have heard. I will not talk of things from very long time ago, because I am wary of you elders, but will confine my words to the period of Taupe the King. Taupe was the instrument of God's profound purpose. It was Taupe who made these arrangements. The *Latupou* were recognized as high *aliki* of Fakaofo, and it was they who succeeded one another as the reigning *vainiu*. There was contention (*feteke akiga*) over who should be installed as the *vainiu*. The title *vainiu* referred to the king, he who guided Fakaofo – with respect to you elders from this child who speaks before you. The *Lafalala* were also *aliki* of Fakaofo, a little below the *aliki* of the *Latupou*, and it was they who consulted together about Fakaofo, and when they had come to a decision, the *faipule* joined them. The majority of Fakaofo belonged to the *faipule* group, and they ruled together with the *aliki* of Fakaofo, and when they had all reached a decision they arranged a meeting of the whole land, held at the *malae* of Fakafotu."

"The meetings of *aliki* and *faipule* were held at Hakavā. It was *aliki* and *faipule* who made this decision, 'All men of Fakaofo shall be equal in accordance with the will of God that all people be equal (*tutuha ia tagata uma*).' And another decision which they made was this, 'As soon as a man is grey-haired he joins in the governing (*pulega*) of Fakaofo, without regard to his rank (*tulaga*) in Fakaofo.' And another decision which they made was this, 'The oldest man of Fakaofo, without regard to his rank, will be made the embodiment of the dignity and honor (*mamalu*) of Fakaofo.' Given to him was our title, '*aliki*.' You are a Christian and I too am Christian, my *aliki* name, one I am proud of to this day, is conferred upon the elders." Thus spoke Peato.[13]

Then Peato spoke again to the elders: "I turn now to these two who are kings of Fakaofo. Don't think that I am a child who is not aware of our relationship. I know it well. And I say to you, this system which you propose for Fakaofo is an invitation to trouble." Speaking to the eldest elder, "If I speak and you are forbidden to speak, is it good? You may think it is good, but I would be ashamed. If the *aliki* of Fakaofo go to a place to consult about Fakaofo, it would be I who went while you stayed outside. Would that be good? You may think it good, but I would be ashamed – because of the decision made by our forebears that you should represent us because you are the elder while I remain outside because I am the younger." Then speaking to all, "Do not remove the stone set in place by your parents, because that brings only conceit and vanity. Do you want to sit on high, while the *aliki* of Fakaofo sit below? Leave your pride to *aliki* and the elders."

As soon as Peato's speech ended the Pastor asked that the subject be put to rest, and they take a break. The Pastor's scheme was not raised again.

---

13   For a detailed exposition of these arrangements and transformations, see Hooper 1994.

The Seventh Thing 'Revealed': One afternoon when Peato was holding a service, the Pastor incited boys from his school to make a racket in order to disrupt the service and thereafter to sit on the LMS compound wall and mock those leaving it.

No one paid any attention to the boys after the service. Shortly thereafter a man came to Peato's house but did not say what he had come about until there was shouting and a fire burning on the *malae* for some reason unknown to Peato. Only then did he tell Peato why he had come. A boy from the Pastor's school had run over to their house to tell the LMS people to prepare because the Catholics were hatching a fight over the disruption of their afternoon service.

The visitor had investigated but discovered no meeting so looked around for Peato and found him in his house. Peato told him, "I have already told my congregation to ignore what the Pastor does, because anger only brings disrepute on the person and his faith."

Not long after, rain fell and put out the fire. Those [LMS] people who had gathered retreated to talk about things and soon they began to argue. Among them were those that had kin who were Catholics and they were scolded by the others. They argued back and forth, and it all ended without resolution.

The Eighth Thing 'Revealed': Some weeks after that incident, a canoe of boys from the Pastor's school went off to cut coconut fronds.

Upon their return, lightning struck the boys' canoe. One boy died, the same boy who had made the racket to disrupt Peato's service. Others were injured but got better. The story went around that Peato had taken revenge on the dead boy for what he had done.

The Trouble: Suddenly one day Peato was summoned by the policeman to come to where the court was convened. Peato arrived to find the Faipule, Pulenuku and Pastor there, along with a committee convened to judge Peato.

The Faipule questioned Peato, "Is it true that you uttered words to kill the boy?" Peato asked, "I am being tried?"

The Faipule replied, "No," but the Pastor responded "Yes, you are being tried."

Peato turned to the Faipule: "I am to believe that I am being tried? You tell me no, but the other Faipule, the Pastor, tells me yes I am being tried. Which of the two of you is trying me? My reply is that I know not any words that I said. Though I might have thought that way, nothing like that issued from my mouth. Make your judgment from my two replies."

The Faipule responded, "Excuse please this is not a trial. You were only summoned to be asked and reply. It is over."

Not long thereafter a ship came, and that ship brought a letter instructing the Pastor to return to Samoa. He had not even been there a full year before being removed. He told his congregation that he would return, but he never again came to Tokelau.

[**PART III**: Three unrelated incidents.]

• [c.1943] Local dispute over succession to the position of Pulenuku escalated with the hostile factions seated separately and violence threatened. The local acting pastor, the Faipule and Peato effectively intervened – and Fakaofo was again at peace.

• [1921] A widely supported local coup d'état deposed officials appointed by the colonial administration. A fine of five tons of copra was imposed for this illegal act. The villagers collectively, competitively and quickly made the copra required – 'the work was enjoyable because everyone was of one mind.' Thereafter, the deposed officials were legally replaced.[14]

• [1931 & c.1940] The first inter-atoll cricket competition was between Fakaofo and Atafu. The elders halted play after each had achieved a victory. 'Fakaofo could remain with its victory, Atafu could go with its victory, and peace would continue to prevail between the islands.'[15] Later, a Fakaofo side traveled to Nukunonu to compete. Though they lost, they returned telling of the wonderful time they had had and praising the hospitality of their hosts.

Discussion

Structure and style

The three sections of the text are differently constructed. In Part I (including the Preamble), Peato has followed an established Tokelau convention of Protestant historical accounts by segmenting his chronological history by the "reigns" of Protestant pastors, but with a difference. Unlike the usual Protestant narratives, which dwell on the "good works" of their pastors, his narrative incorporates significant local events and initiatives. The brief Preamble, covering the "reigns" of three pastors when his "father" was catechist, depicts three situations: discord between an LMS pastor and his congregation, "disturbance" or "misunderstanding" between the congregations, and "mutual respect" between the congregations. These situations provide a template for Part I in which Peato interacts with three pastors. With the first he resolves the "discord" between the pastor and his congregation.

With the second, he joins in good works that "firmly established the mutual respect between the Fakaofo congregations." With the third, he again collaborates in "good works" further cementing "mutual respect" until this is compromised by "difficulties" that are amicably resolved "so that peace would prevail between them."

The core of Peato's text is Part II composed as a series of reports of eight

14   See Huntsman and Hooper 1996: 280–282, for a full account of this episode based on Peato's account and the report of the district commissioner who set matters straight.
15   See Huntsman and Hooper 1996: 314–315 for an Atafu account of this test series.

skirmishes between Peato and the pastor bracketed by their initial meeting and the pastor's abrupt departure – "never to return." The pastor "reveals" something and Peato counters it in this extended account of "disturbances" between the congregations.

The events related in Part III appear at first reading to be afterthoughts, a postscript peripheral to the structure of the text that might have ended with the departure of Peato's 'enemy' (*fili*). But on closer examination each incident reinforces and extends themes alluded to earlier. Notably, none of the three stories involve church congregations, and Peato himself plays no role in the last two and a minor role in the other.

Two overall stylistic features of the text are the selective use of dialogue and the author's presentation of himself in the third person. Dialogue is used exclusively in confrontational situations, most effectively and with ironic humor, in Part II. That Peato has written of himself in the third person serves to distance Peato as author from Peato the protagonist. Only once, when Peato is under extreme duress, does "I" appear outside dialogue. First, the narrative is not one of high seriousness; many passages of dialogue are humorous – the kind of ironic humor in which Tokelau people delight. Peato makes particularly good use of dialogue in relating his major confrontations with Pastor Folau.

Messages

'Mutual Respect.' The abiding and repetitive message in Part I is a positive one of pervasive 'mutual respect' and 'peace' (*fealofani*) within and between the congregations, and is foreshadowed in the Preamble, set in the era of Peato's "father." Yet there are incidents of 'difficulties within the LMS congregation' during the 'reign' of the first pastor in his predecessor's era, just as there are at the beginning of Peato's era, and of 'troubles between the congregations' at his "father's" time and in his own, harking back to unmentioned antipathies of the late 19th century between Fakaofo's Protestants and Catholics (see Huntsman and Hooper 1996: 236–252). In emphasizing the 'mutual respect' between the congregations and between the catechist and pastor, Peato is depicted as not opposed to Protestantism or to Protestant pastors, even Samoan ones; rather he is opposed to anything that compromises the welfare of Fakaofo. He is a peacemaker between the congregations and a mediator between the Protestant congregation and their foreign pastor. When 'troubles' or 'misunderstandings' arose, Peato, as a "native" of the place, was better placed than his "foreign" counterpart.[16] He had a wide social network, intimate knowledge of his fellow villagers and a deep understanding of Tokelau culture. Furthermore, he was a *tautai*

---

16 A rule of the Samoan-based LMS was that a pastor must be an outsider to the congregation he served. The reasoning was that he would be neutral and uninvolved in local politics, having no kin loyalties. In Tokelau this meant that all LMS pastors were foreigners (until the 1970s), because the kin network of virtually every Tokelauan is Tokelau-wide.

'master fisherman.' All these advantages he calls upon when, in Part II, he is confronted by the LMS pastor, a stark contrast to his predecessors of Part I, who places the congregations in opposition by his actions or 'revelations.'

The message of 'mutual respect' is extended in the first incident recounted in Part III where the 'difficulties' are political, not religious, yet it has the same scenario of escalating hostility and intervention with 'peace' as the outcome.

Competing in Work and Play for the Benefit of All. The accounts of the second and especially third pastors' 'reigns' in Part I dwell in some detail on how Fakaofo men came together to competitively work and play, irrespective of their religious denomination, for the benefit of all Fakaofo. Here Peato, as author, is propounding another, related message. Controlled competition enlivens both work and play; more particularly, when work is undertaken without a competition people are lackadaisical, but when in competition they work quickly and well.

The most telling incident is of 'the fine work for the benefit of all the people of Fakaofo' completed expeditiously by competing teams, one under the leadership of the senior Protestant village official and the Catholic catechist, and the other under the leadership of the senior Catholic village official and the Protestant pastor. Distinctions of position and religion are nicely confounded as all are both joined and divided. What is celebrated in this story is the communal euphoria created by good-natured, controlled competition, and the 'benefits for all Fakaofo' that result. It is this theme to which the text returns in the last part, with the story of how all Fakaofo, again divided into competing teams, quickly paid the penalty for an illegal act that had ousted the colony-appointed village authority, resulting in the legal replacement of the overturned regime. But there are negative divisions too, as when the pastor insists that the Protestant and Catholic congregations be seated separately, reiterated in the first incident of Part III when the opposing parties seat themselves on opposite sides and the larger stands forth, threatening violence on the smaller. Again and again Peato celebrates intermingling. A recurrent Tokelau strategy for promoting village unity and peace is to mix people together in different ways. If sides threaten to become combative, they are replaced by a different configuration of sides.

Tokelau Values and Character. While Part II, where 'mutual respect' does not prevail, is obviously the counterpart of Part I, its embedded message is about Tokelau character, with the pastor's character as its antithesis. Here is the outsider, the intruder, the usurper par excellence, his manner and behavior the antithesis of Tokelau propriety: arrogant (vs. humble), aggressive (vs. mild mannered), demanding (vs. accommodating), devious (vs. straight), etc. But it is not just about the evils of this Samoan pastor, it is also about Tokelau people being duped or led astray, about Tokelau people being too accommodating to an outsider, being reluctant or afraid to stand up to arrogance and aggressiveness, and being mystified and led astray. All these characteristics various other Fakaofo actors exhibit, but not Peato, who from the first is alert to the pastor's intentions, and fearless and clever in standing up to him. Does Peato, as author, present Peato, the protagonist, as "heroic?" I suppose he does in a sense, but in a very Tokelau sense. In many respects the whole episode is a Tokelau trickster tale, which could plausibly be transferred to East Africa with the pastor as the "scheming and calculating" hyena "ultimately doomed to failure because of its clumsiness and short-sightedness" and Peato as the clever and shrewd hare (Beidelman 1980: 29).[17] But I would argue that Peato saw it as a story of Tokelau triumph, overcoming dissension and conflict. Part III supports this argument. Each incident is a confrontation of some kind and none of them involve congregations and Peato only has a minor role in one of them.

The accounts of the two inter-atoll cricket tests combine the messages of 'mutual respect,' controlled 'competition' and Tokelau values/character, and on a Tokelau-wide scale as the atolls begin to compete in what had become the national sport and obsession of Tokelau. Here inter-atoll antipathies (a matter that Peato does not otherwise address in the text) are mediated by controlled competition and 'mutual respect.'[18]

At a first reading, this text is a chronological firsthand account of the 'difficulties' and 'troubles' between Protestants and Catholics that beset Fakaofo in the early decades of the 20th century told by a major protagonist. A closer and culturally informed reading not only corrects this simpler characterization but highlights the messages of the text. These are messages conveyed in Peato's other texts, and ones that pervaded his conversation. Peace and prosperity, good works for the benefit of all are achieved through common purpose; common purpose is created by 'mutual respect,' intermingling and controlled competition.

---

17 Tokelau has its own trickster tales with negative "ogre" hyena-like tricksters and positive clubfooted/youngest/smart child hare-like tricksters (Macdonald 1977).
18 See Huntsman and Hooper 1996: 252–256, 313–315.

REFERENCES

Beidelman, T.O. 1980. The moral imagination of the Kaguru: some thoughts on tricksters, translation and comparative analysis. *American Ethnologist* 7: 27–42.

Hale, Horatio 1846. *United States Exploring Expedition...: Ethnography and Philology.* Philadelphia: Lea and Blanchard.

Hooper, Antony 1994. Ghosts of hierarchy I: the transformation of chiefly authority on Fakaofo, Tokelau. In: M. Jolly & M. Mosko (eds.) *Transformations of Hierarchy: Structure, History and Horizon in the Austronesian World.* Special issue of *History and Anthropology* 7: 307–320.

Hooper, Antony and Judith Huntsman 1992. Aspects of skipjack fishing: some Tokelau 'words of the sea.' In: A. Pawley (ed.) *Man and a Half: Essays in Pacific Anthropology and Ethnobiology in Honour of Ralph Bulmer.* Polynesian Society Memoir 48. Auckland: The Polynesian Society. Pp. 249–256.

Huntsman, Judith and Antony Hooper 1996. *Tokelau: A Historical Ethnography.* Auckland: Auckland University Press.

Macdonald, Judith 1977. Trickster and Hero: A Study of Their Universal Character and Their Reflection in Tokelau Tales. Unpublished M.A. thesis in Anthropology, University of Auckland.

Ma'ia'i, Fanafi 1957. A Study of the Developing Pattern of Education and the Factors Influencing that Development in New Zealand's Pacific Dependencies. M.A. thesis in Education, Victoria University of Wellington. New Zealand: Islands Division of the Department of Education.

Maude, H. E. 1981. *Slavers in Paradise: The Peruvian Labour Trade in Polynesia, 1862–1864.* Canberra: ANU Press.

Siikala, Jukka 1991. *'Akatokamanāva: Myth, History and Society in the Southern Cook Islands.* Polynesian Society Memoir 47. Auckland: The Polynesian Society, in cooperation with the Finnish Anthropological Society.

Wilkes, Charles 1845. *Narrative of the United States Exploring Expedition during the Years 1838, 1839, 1840, 1841, 1842.* Vol. 5. Philadelphia: Lea and Blanchard.

A Bird is a Woman is a Dancer

Meaning in the Lyrics and Performance of Kiribati Dance

Petra Autio

Introduction[1]

"This song was made because of a tree so that [it is] not because of a tree but because of a woman." This is how Tokitebwa Iakoba, a dance teacher and a song and dance composer, living on the Kiribati island of Tabiteuea Meang, explained one dance song. During fieldwork I took his explanations at what seemed to me face value; words as labels for things in the world. Later, when attempting to translate the songs, I ran into difficulties. Not only can the word for "tree" stand for a number of other things, many of which could be relevant in this context (like "choreography of a dance," "skill," "weapon,"[2] "a person from a place") there was the whole context of the performance to be considered as well, including the movements, structure, and pattern of the performance and its social organization.

I had come to this southern Kiribati village to study something else, but ended up studying dance because dancing simply imposed itself upon me. I arrived in the village during the preparation for a big dance event, and dance/dancing had a privileged place in the community. While at other times, other things filled the agenda, I could not help but wonder about (from my Western perspective) the significance of traditional dancing in the society.

1   This paper is based on the research I have conducted for my Ph.D. dissertation, supervised by Professor Jukka Siikala. The main part of the research, including fieldwork, was funded by the Academy of Finland as part of the research project *Departures: Constructing community in a diasporic world*, led by Professor Siikala. At different stages my research has been funded by the Sasakawa Young Leaders' Fellowship Fund of the University of Helsinki, The Finnish Cultural Foundation, Emil Aaltonen Foundation and the University of Helsinki Chancellor.

I would like to thank Clifford Sather, Louise Klemperer Sather and Timo Kaartinen for their valuable comments and help in focusing the argument in this paper. As in any fieldwork-based study, I am indebted to the Kiribati people who helped me, Arebonto Katangitang and his family in particular, but the inspiration for this paper in particular I owe to my dance teacher Tokitebwa Iakoba, for his patient explanations as well as for his kindness.

2   While there is no space to elaborate on it in this paper, there is a relatively obvious metaphoric connection between dancing and fighting or warfare.

What did dancing mean?

The sung poetry was a place to start the quest for meaning, as it plays an essential role in Kiribati dancing, like it does in Micronesia and Polynesia in general (see Kaeppler 1976). A particular dance choreography is always made for a particular song; a song may have more than one choreography, but a choreography can only belong to one song. A dance song might tell the tale of the heroic deeds of ancestors or demigods, praise the beauty of a meetinghouse (*maneaba*), make a confession of love to a beautiful woman, or proclaim the supremacy of one's song/dance. The following is one example of a dance song which was performed in Tabiteuea Meang in 1999 and 2000:

E kiba te man te taake	it / fly / [article][a] / bird / Te Taake
mai iaon Bwebweriki	from / above / Bwebweriki
E na umakina kai ni katikuna	it / will / hurry-up / stick (or tree) / to / cause-to-stay
ma kakan ni kana	with / want [repeatedly] / to / eat
Ngke e a kaitibo	when [past tense] / it / [auxiliary][b] / meet
ma Te Korouangutungutu	with / Te Korouangutungutu
ni kaitara ngaia te nnen ni motirawa	to / cause-to-face / it [object] / [article] / place-its / to / rest
Bwa e aonga n reke iai	for / it / so-that[c] / to / be found / there [affirmative]
te baronga	[article] kin group
Manoku raran te kai	bay / leaning-its / [article] / stick (or tree)
Te bike Nei Tei	[article] beach / Ms. Tei

[a] The Kiribati article *te* does not indicate definitiveness or indefinitiveness.
[b] Auxiliary indicating a sense of immediacy or incompleteness.
[c] Idiomatic.

A free translation might be

The bird, *Te Taake*, flies from above Bwebweriki
It will hurry up to its perch
It wants to eat

When it met with Te Korouangutungutu,
just facing it in the resting place
so that its kin group may be found there
A bight, the leaning of a tree
the beach, Miss Tei

Kiribati song texts, or poems, may not make much sense at first to the unaccustomed eye. Even Kiribati people without expertise in song-making will readily admit that often they do not understand what a song means. Kiribati composers skillfully use various literary and sound devices to create meanings in poems: metaphor and allusion, word play and innovation, assonance and rhyme (Luomala 1976: 348; Uriam 1992: 112). Persons and tenses can be used in unexpected ways, and things can be expressed through their opposites. Despite its impressionistic appearance, even a short poem may tell a story by way of intertextual references and allusions (cf. Kaeppler 1985 on Tongan songs).

Studies of Kiribati dance have emphasized the role of the song composer (sing. *tia kainikamaen*, pl. *taani kainikamaen*)[3] and his knowledge (*kainikamaen*), and rightly so (see Kempf 2003; Lawson 1989; Whincup & Whincup 2001). Composers possess valuable, carefully guarded expert knowledge about making songs. The traditional composition process involved spirits and the use of magic, though there appears to be variation among composers as to whether they still employ these methods. Kiribati dancing is inherently competitive, and songs frequently make reference to the skills of the composer and the supremacy of the song or the dance, and contain degrading remarks about the achievements of the opponents. *Kainikamaen* includes, for example, knowledge about certain codified or conventional meanings of words in the context of songs, and words which, inserted into the song, are powerful in themselves (e.g. dangerous, protective, or insulting) (see Lawson 1989: 304–308).

Meanings might not be widely circulated, but they are nonetheless public. The meaning(s) intended by the composer can probably be decoded by another composer. Even when a song composer comes up with a new expression, its meaning is not totally idiosyncratic, because in the last analysis, it is meant to be understood by other people, if only – and crucially – by one's rival composer.

However, on the basis of my data, I feel composer-centered explanations of meaning are incomplete. One reason is that in the dance events I observed in Tabiteuea Meang, the composers were not necessarily on the scene at all. Tokitebwa, who taught *E kiba te man*, did not know who had composed it, only that it came from the north (Butaritari or Makin) because of the dance style. Some of the songs danced in Tabiteuea in 1999–2000 were made by local composers, but many were not, and it was not unusual that people – even those teaching or dancing a song – did not know who had composed it. Yet dancing was thoroughly competitive, even giving rise to extra-dance arguments. Songs and choreographies travel between islands, probably many through the capital island of South Tarawa where there are people from all of the islands. In my study it was the dance teachers (*tia katei*; pl. *taani katei*) who emerged as the significant personae. Generally speaking, a dance performance is given meaning by reference to the particular, local social relations at stake (Autio n.d.).

A Kiribati dance performance consists of an aggregate of several elements of verbal, musical, and bodily expression. The I-Kiribati make certain distinctions which can be used to take apart the dance analytically, even if the elements are inseparable in an actual performance. On the one hand, certain body positions and movements are named and have codified meanings. On

3   Another, more modern designation for a composer is *tia ototo* (pl. *taani ototo*). It does not have the connotation of spirits and magic, and is preferred by composers who want to disassociate themselves from the old spirit beliefs.

the other hand, the structure and patterning of the performance as a whole also "means" something – not necessarily in the sense of denoting or representing, but rather in the sense of producing or causing, that is, they have meaning in the sense that they have, or aim to have, social consequences.

Here, I make use of the insight that language, in addition to having – in most cases – sense or meaning, may also have consequences. Words not only describe the world, but form it, change it, and are used as conscious tools in attempts to do so. For example, John Austin 1975 [1962] argues that in addition to having sense and reference, a speech act may have a certain force *in* saying something or may achieve certain effects *by* saying something (1975 [1962]: 121). In this paper I propose to pay attention to both "the said" and "the saying," as well as to "the dance" and "the dancing." Although I base my argument on theories of spoken language, in what follows, "saying" is to be understood in a more general, metaphorical sense, extended to include purposeful as well as unintentional non-verbal communication practice. How the world is and how it should be are not only said but also done, implied, gestured, and danced.

On an ethnographic level, the purpose of this paper is to examine the meaning(s) of one dance song and its performance, *E kiba te man Te Taake*. On a more general level, I want to contemplate the meaning(s) of Kiribati dancing more generally. Here, I first discuss one approach to meaning, namely that of Gregory Bateson's idea of frames of play and ritual action. In the case of Kiribati dance there are two relevant contexts: the overall ethnographic and historical context and the context, or frame, of a dance performance. I briefly introduce the general ethnographic setting and describe traditional Kiribati dance, paying attention to the performance context. I then proceed to analyze Kiribati dance performance by looking at its constituent parts or aspects.

Framed metaphors:
A twofold relationship between the word and the world

In his essay, "A theory of play and fantasy," Gregory Bateson (2000 [1972]) discusses certain kinds of frames of action in which the messages exchanged are both true and untrue at the same time. Bateson (2000 [1972]) defines the frame as metacommunicative discourse about the relationship between speakers. This discourse includes more or less conscious messages telling what kind of a message is involved and how it should be interpreted. In so doing, the metadiscourse partly defines the meaning of signs within a given frame.

According to Bateson, frames of "play," "ritual" and the like are characterized by paradoxes: a sign does not denote what the signified would denote in other contexts and the signified is non-existent. In everyday communication it is agreed, for example, that in *some* respects a tree is like a woman but it is not so in *all* respects, i.e., a tree is not the same as a woman. Bateson argues that in play-like frames this discrimination is both done and not done. In play/ritual/art it is understood that a tree is *like* a woman, but simultaneously, that a tree *is* a woman. In ritual-like frames, then, there are two kinds of relationships between the sign and the signified (as Roman Jakobson [1981: 19] put it, "the word and the world"). In one, a sign is distinguished from what it denotes; in the other, the two are equated. It is as Tokitebwa said: "This song was made because of a tree so that it is not because of a tree but because of a woman."

While Bateson discusses frames as a psychological phenomenon – how people use frames to make sense of the world and their interactions with each other – my data concern social action and publicly accessible signs. I take the psychological fact of framing as given and use Bateson's ideas as an interpretative device in order to make sense of Kiribati dancing against a background of Kiribati culture. I argue that it is instructive to view Kiribati dancing/dance performance[4] as a particular frame of ritual-like action. Dance performances are restricted in time and place and there is a particular mode and pattern of using language and the body. Both the language of dance poetry and the movements (signifying action) display features associated with ritual language, such as formality, parallelism and the use of metaphors (cf. Bloch 1974; Du Bois 1986).

Ritual language is frequently seen as performative, but the social consequences of the formalization of ritual language continue to be debated. Maurice Bloch (1974) has argued that because of the formalization of language, ritual speech and songs communicate very little meaning but instead have a capacity to influence people, making the message appear self-evident. For Bloch, formalization of language becomes a form of authority (1974: 64). Critics of Bloch, like Robert Paine (1981b: 2; see Paine 1981a), have seen formality as a vehicle of persuasion rather than coercion. What is more, John Du Bois (1986) has shown that self-evidence and authority accredited to ritual speech depend on the relationship between the ritual speech form and the social constitution of the speech event. This last point will figure prominently in my conclusion.

Kiribati introduced:
Social system and the dance

Kiribati is a Micronesian, central Pacific state consisting of 33 islands scattered across 3.5 million square kilometers of ocean. There is an Austronesian-speaking population of about 100,000, inhabiting 21 of these islands. Formerly known as the Gilbert and Ellice Islands Colony, the people of this state are called Gilbertese, or today, I-Kiribati. From the 1920s on, the Gilbert Islands became known from the writings of Sir Arthur Grimble (1957,

---

4   While I make use of some of the insights of performance theory (cf. Bauman 1984; Bauman & Briggs 1990), I use "performance" and "to perform" in this paper in a concrete sense, not as an analytic concept. For example, a dance performance is understood here as the actualization or instantiation of a particular song and its choreography.

1969 [1952], 1989) and Father Ernest Sabatier (1977 [1938]); then, later, Henry Maude (1968, 1991 [1963]). More recent anthropological research on aspects of the social organization has been done by, for example, Peder Lundsgaarde (1970, 1974, 1978) and Jean-Paul Latouche (1984) in southern Kiribati, and Bernd Lambert (1966, 1978, 1981) among others in the northern islands. Kiribati is part of the Austronesian culture area, and its socio-political organization has much in common with the rest of the Austronesian world (cf. Goodenough 1955; Lundsgaarde & Silverman 1972).

In terms of the traditional socio-political system, Kiribati is divided into three groups: the southern, central, and northern Gilberts. On the whole, Kiribati society is democratic, which is manifest in meetinghouse (*maneaba*) governance by elders as the leaders of their kin groups or districts. There are hierarchical structures as well, becoming stronger as one moves from south to north. In the north, some of the islands were ruled in the past by high chiefs (*uea*) (see Lambert 1978). By contrast, the socio-political systems of southern Kiribati, Tabiteuea Meang included, have been described as "true democracies" (Grimble 1989: 151; Uriam 1995: 4). On all islands certain hierarchical structures related to seniority and gender are taken for granted. The meaning of democracy is roughly the same as it was for the ancient Greeks: the equality of all free men.

However, considering power as perceived value rather than in political terms, one may in fact perceive a system of precedence brought to Kiribati by migrants-*cum*-invaders from Samoa, comprising ranked clans (see Grimble 1989: 219–230; Maude 1991 [1963]), with special value given to 'the first thing' (*moanibwai*) and genealogical seniority. On the other hand, authority has a dual character: power resides both with the stranger-king and the autochthon, with the guest (*iruwa*) arriving from the sea and the landowner welcoming him. Furthermore, on the island of Tabiteuea, the rule became 'chiefs are forbidden' (*tabu-te-uea*), that is, the chief-to-be is bound by *tabu* to the extent that his power cannot be realized, or turned into temporal power. As I will argue in my dissertation (Autio n.d.), in Tabiteuea there is a strong predisposition to decentralize power. Thus, initial hierarchical structures are transformed into egalitarian ones.

On a different level, yet in a way analogous to the decentralization of power, there is a general disapproval of drawing attention to oneself, for example, by boasting or by other attempts to differentiate oneself from others. However, balancing this normative evenness, uniformity and harmony (*boraoi*, lit. 'to meet well'), there are contexts in which competition is not only permissible but expected. The foremost of these is dancing.

Kiribati dance (*ruoia, mwaie, bwatere*) has thrilled outside observers at least since Robert Louis Stevenson, and there are a number of scholarly descriptions as well. Early on, P.B. Laxton and Te Kautu Kamouriki (1953) produced a movement-by-movement, line-by-line analysis of a dance and a song. Song texts have been analyzed also by P.B. Laxton (1953), Katharine Luomala (1976), and Mary Lawson Burke (Lawson 1989).

Tony and Joan Whincup (2001) have recently documented dancing as well as people's experience and interpretations of it by both photography and interviews (see also T. Whincup 2005). An ethnomusicological study, with descriptions of several types of dance and concomitant music, was conducted in the 1980s by Mary Lawson Burke (Lawson 1989; Burke 2001).While recognizing the significance of dance groups, the studies by the Whincups and Lawson approach the subject more, though by no means wholly, from the individual actor's point of view. Generally speaking I employ a more structural approach, and have considered dancing as part of the local social organization as a whole.

The social relations of dancing

Dancing is a group activity in two senses of the term. First, dancing is practiced in groups, which are always in implicit or explicit competition. Sometimes groups are founded for a particular competitive event, and in the capital island of South Tarawa, there are a few semi-professional performance groups (see Lawson 1989). Competition, however, is built into the activity itself. As Mary Lawson (1989: 351) notes, if there are no opposing groups, the I-Kiribati will invent them, as the Gilbertese resettlers did in Titiana, Solomon Islands (see Knudson 1964: 222).

A dance group consists of dancers (dance students) and performance specialists, possibly with assistants. Not only is song composition a skill practiced by experts, so is the composition of dance movements and the teaching of dance. An individual may have knowledge in one or several areas of expertise.

In the local context of Tabiteua Meang, it was the people called *tia katei*, 'the one who makes stand,' who were the central personae. Competition was perceived to be chiefly between such persons and the dance groups that formed around them, the latter consisting of students and assistant teachers. While the dancers want to *niko*, 'be beautiful and good in form,' in the end it is the honor of the *tia katei*, or teacher, which is at stake.[5]

It appears from other accounts that composers are often the core of the group. However, the difference between composers and teachers or other performance specialists is not necessarily a great one (there might also be local variation in the appellations). Some of the people called *tia katei* also compose songs or make dances, and many dance-related specialists possess some *kainikamaen* knowledge. Nevertheless, since it happened that in Tabiteuea the composer was not around at all, nor even known, the "meaning"

---

5   The Whincups report that traditionally competition was more between individuals and that there has been a shift of emphasis to competition between groups (T. Whincup & J. Whincup 2001: 118; T.Whincup 2005: 125). However, this seems to apply on the level of an individual dance: the subject of evaluation used to be more the skill of the individual (*niko*) than the skill of the whole row of dancers. In the latter case an important criterion is *booraoi*ness, uniformity of the row. During my research though, this proved to be problematic in some of the cases. The problem concerned the relationship between the dance groups and the village community as whole. Nonetheless, even when the individual dancer is evaluated, the evaluation reflects on her group and teacher.

of a dance song, let alone the whole performance, could not be exhausted by interviewing the author. Dance is more than *kainikamaen* knowledge put into practice; it necessarily includes many actors and the social relations between them.

The second way dancing is a group activity lies in performance. Traditional Kiribati dance is danced to singing or chanting and clapping by a group of people. Moreover, the performance always needs an audience. A dance performance proper is always a public affair, in explicit contrast to dance training, which is regarded as secret[6]. Most traditional Kiribati dancing takes place in public events, where dancing is performed in a *maneaba* in front of an audience which consists of guests of honor (*iruwa*) and members of the community. Traditional dancing can be an item among others when entertaining *iruwa*, or dancing itself can be the motivation/reason for the event; the line between these two is thin.

During a dance performance in the meetinghouse, people fall into four partly overlapping categories: dancers, singer-clappers, honored guests and 'people' (*aomata*), i.e., everyone else. Each has a defined role *vis a vis* the dancing. The honored guests sit in the front row, while the general public remains on the sidelines. A variety of activities occurs on the sidelines: for example, dressing up dancers, eating, sleeping, and nursing babies. *Iruwa* are the ones who are entertained, 'are made to watch' (*kamatakuaki*), and so, in this sense, are the official audience. Yet the guests of honor seem strangely irrelevant at times. The real audience for whom the dancers are performing is the local community, the people, *aomata*, who in the last analysis judge the performance. Even in formal contests with a panel of evaluators, 'people think' (*a taku aomata)* is a powerful judgment (cf. Burke 2001: 11; Siikala 1991: 73).

The people who sing and clap either sit or stand behind the dancers in a particular formation; the configuration of the dancers and singer-clappers varies from one dance type to another (see Lawson 1989: 37–52; Whincup and Whincup 2001: 117–118). In the dances (ca 180) I observed in 1999 and 2000 in Tabiteuea Meang, most dancers were teenagers or young adults, and 80 per cent of them were female, though there are no age restrictions and dance as an activity has no connotation of femininity. The number of dancers in most dances varied between one and ten. The number of accompanying people also varies, but in an event involving a whole village or several villages, it will be dozens, a crowd consisting of all able and willing villagers.

Considering that dancers and other performance actors are organized into competing groups, one would expect that one group would perform at a time, and that in performing a dance, the dancers and singer-clappers would belong to the same dance group. This is indeed often the case, certainly in formal competitions. However, in Tabiteuea Meang there were also occasions on which this was not the case, making the social organization of performance

---

6   A dancer performing a particular dance for the first time in public is said to 'come out' (*otinako*). Dance practices, by contrast, are regarded as private – one cannot freely go to watch a group's practices, unless one is affiliated with the group.

more complex. On these occasions, members of different dance groups might perform together as well as with people who did not belong to any group. Dancers from different dance groups might even dance together in the same row. More typically, singing groups could consist of inhabitants of one or more villages. I observed some events with this kind of social configuration, and they were hardly less competitive than the formal competitions I saw.

Tokitebwa once said, "When a song is sung, it is the same as if people (*aomata*) talk." Interpreting the two kinds of social configuration of performance in the light of what he said, when a dance group is performing by itself (i.e., all dancers and singers belong to the same group) one part of the community is making a statement *as if it were* the whole. In the logic of ritual, obfuscating the distinction between all and some, they momentarily become the community.

When there were members of more than one dance group as well as others participating in the singing, the singers were in fact the same people (*aomata*) as those on the sidelines, blurring the two categories. In this case it *is* the community which speaks in singing. However, this makes for an ambiguous situation, because some of the singer-clappers were also members of dance groups, in which case they accompanied dancers of their own group as well as those from other groups. Thereby some of the singer-clappers end up speaking *for* their opponents.

Considering these events of Kiribati dancing as a frame of action, metacommunication concerns the relationships existing between dancers, teachers, singers, and the two kinds of audience, the guests of honor and the local community. There is, on the one hand, a relationship of opposition and competition between dancers and between teachers, and a relationship of authority represented by the people (*aomata*) over the performers.[7] On the other hand, there are instances where these relationships become confused, because people may stand on both sides of the fence.

Elements of dance

Excluding the context just described, it is possible to take a dance performance apart according to indigenous notions which distinguish some of its elements. These are:

- The song (*kuna*) [incl. melody] and the song text or lyrics (*mwanewe*),
- The dance movements or choreography (*kai*) which are specific to the song and follow the song's reiteration pattern,
- The clapping of the song (*uboana*) – each song is accompanied by clapping in a particular configuration, and

---

7   Although it will not be discussed in this paper, one can also postulate a relationship between the local people and the *iruwa*. Despite the privileged role of the guests, in the last analysis it is the locals who make the calls.

- The returns of the song (*okina*) – each song is sung (*e aneneaki te kuna*) in a particular way in which strophes can be repeated in complex patterns.

*The song and its lyrics (*kuna *and* mwanewe*)*

Kiribati song lyrics, or rather, poems, can be discussed in many ways. Here I have chosen to discuss the lyrics of *E kiba te man Te Taake* with regard to three issues: the position of the song within the corpus of Kiribati oral tradition, its root metaphors, and their "self-referentiality." In terms of metaphors, I have analyzed 24 dance song texts and found the most common topics to be (a) mythico-historical persons or events, (b) love, and (c) song and dance.[8] These are not mutually exclusive; for example the song *E kiba te man Te Taake* describes the journey of a mythical/ancestral creature but is at the same time a tribute to a beautiful woman. Furthermore, songs frequently contain some reference back to themselves or to dance.

Regarding *E kiba te man Te Taake,* Tokitebwa told me:

> There was a bird, Te Taake. Its skin was white and its body was handsome. It flew in the heavens, in a place where there were no people. The name of that place was Bwebweriki. But it was not a true land, since it was a land of spirits. […] Te Taake flew from Bwebweriki to its true place, where it would stay. It wanted to eat. That place was indeed its true place. When it [Te Taake] flew, it met with someone, with Korouangutungutu, in the place of resting. Te Taake was not concerned with him, they just met and Te Taake went on. The name of its true place was Bikeuea, a beach of a bight [*manoku*]. This song has been made because of a woman. Her name is Te Taake, but her body is that of a woman. (From fieldnotes 24.1. 2000)

The song tells about a bird/mythical ancestor, Te Taake, who is looking for a place to dwell, a true place. "He wants to eat," in other words, produce food. On the way, Te Taake meets another character, Te Korouangungutu. Te Taake is not concerned with him, does not engage in either fighting or friendly interaction, because he has something more important to do: he refrains from interaction in order that his kin group (*baronga*) could be found. Te Taake finds his true place at a place called Bikeua, on the beach of a bay, and there becomes (in my interpretation Te Taake is simultaneously a woman and a man but its femininity becomes apparent on the beach – the Kiribati third person singular pronoun is not gendered) a woman, Nei Tei. The song is related to Kiribati oral tradition. The names in the song connect it to the whole narrative corpus of Kiribati mythology, folklore, and history. The mention of a personal or a place name is often a reference to a particular story or a

---

8 In Tabiteuea Meang I collected the lyrics of 56 songs of various kinds, of which 24 were dance songs I saw performed as well (many of them more than once, and a few of them dozens of times during practices). Of the dance songs, one had a Christian message (generally speaking, there are an infinite number of Christian songs). In a larger collection, religious songs might form a group of their own.

historical event. In this song, the names Te Taake and Korouangungutu are intertextual references to a story told by way of poetic references.

A significant part of the oral history of Kiribati describes the migration of Gilbertese people from Samoa to the Gilbert Islands. There was a historical migration from Samoa, which is estimated to have taken place in the 13th century A.D. (Maude 1991 [1963]: 7; 1994: 137; Uriam 1995: 168; Grimble 1989: 268–294). Archaeological and linguistic evidence, and some oral history sources all point to the fact that there was an earlier migration from the Gilberts to Samoa, and that the epochal migration was "a return." In the narratives, the time spent in Samoa and the departure from Samoa are described in metaphorical terms by reference to a tree called *Kai-n-tiku-aba*, 'Tree of staying-land' (Maude 1994: xvi–xvii, 109–111, 135–137*)*. The tree here is a metaphor for the community and its unity (Maude 1994: xvi–xvii).

The tree *Kai-n-tiku-aba* grew in Samoa, and people and beings lived in that tree. Eventually, there were disagreements and the tree was burned down (an event called the Breaking of the Tree of Lands, *uruakin Kaintikuaba*), broken, and people were dispersed. Versions from different islands or families vary as to who they describe as living in the tree, what the reason was for the breakup (usually misbehavior of those who lived on the top of the tree) and who burned the tree. Several versions mention Te Taake and Te Koroangutungutu as inhabitants of the tree, and agree on where they migrated to after the breakup. Te Taake has even been mentioned as the culprit, causing the breakup (see Latouche 1984, *The Story of Karongoa*, 72).[9] A version from Tarawa, told by Tem Mautake, runs as follows:

> When Nareau [the creator being] had done those things (i.e. separated Heaven from Earth), he planted a tree on Samoa. The name of the tree was Te Ieiretia, and some call it Kaintikuaba. That was a marvelous tree, a Tree of many branches, and spirits (*anti*) grew from the branches – as if they were the fruit of the tree. Those who grew among the branches of the north were Nakaa, and Te Take (Tropic Bird) and Tekoroangutungutu (Yellow-billed Tropic Bird) [...]
>
> But the Tree was broken. The man Teuribaba was the breaker of the Tree, for he was angered when the people of the branches insulted his head. They sat in the branches of the Tree and dropped excrement upon the head of Teuribaba. So Teuribaba arose and broke the Tree of Tamoa [Samoa], and the people of it were scattered. When the Tree fell, Te Take and Tekoroangutungutu flew north to Beberiki [Bwebweriki] (Butaritari) and Tetoronga (Makin), and Taburimai with Tituabine, and Riiki, and Taburitongoun went in the canoe called Kabangaki to Nikunau [one of the southern Gilbert Islands] (*An Anthology of Gilbertese Oral Tradition*, 115).

---

9 Another story presented by Latouche (1984: 197) tells that Te Taake "would not stop defecating [repeatedly] from above, and for that the people below were constantly complaining." There is a more detailed narrative about Kaintikuaba as well as a narrative about the journey of Te Taake in Latouche (1984), but their thorough analyses would require much more space than is available in this paper.

In an account from Butaritari, there were three creatures: Te Take (the Tropic Bird), Te Ngutu (the Yellow-billed Tropic Bird) and Te Koro (the White-tailed Tropic Bird). In this account too, after the tree was burned, "Te Take flew with Te Ngutu and Te Koro to Beberiki (Butaritari) and Tetoronga (Makin)" (*An Anthology of Gilbertese Oral Tradition*, 115: 125–126).

The beings on the *Kaintikuaba* tree are the ancestors and the founders of the various clans (*boti*). Te Taake, who is also known by the name of Keaki, is the ancestor of the Keaki *boti*. The red-tailed tropic bird (*te taake*) is the totem of this clan (Grimble 1989: 229; Uriam 1995: 127 fn. 40). In some contexts Te Taake stands for the clan as a whole; "Taake people" (see e.g. Uriam 1995: 127).

Moving on to the level of vocabulary of the 24 songs, I analyzed the ways in which positive images are created when praising (*kamoamoa*) something. I found that the majority can be traced[10] to a few key words/ root metaphors. Four categories emerge formed around the words *te kai* (stick or tree), *wa* (canoe), *man* (bird) and *ang* (wind). The last one, *ang*, differs from the others by being the force behind the others.

All of these root words refer to dance in some way. *Kai* is the term for the series of movements of a dance, its choreography; in some contexts *kai* refers to a weapon (cane of hitting), which again is a metaphor for dance. *Kai* as a tree can be used as a metaphor for composition knowledge (*kainikamaen*), a dancer, or a woman. "Bird," similarly, can be an image of a dancer or a woman. The formation of the dancers is called a canoe, and the progression of the canoe is likened to the dance. *Ang*, 'wind,' is also *angin te mwaie*, 'the spirit of dancing'. Like the wind bends and tosses the branches of the tree and speeds the canoe racing over the waves, so does the spirit of dancing move the dancer.

There are also whole songs, which I have called "self-referential songs," that are devoted to the topic of competition, or are songs about song and dance. In the particular song referred to above, the reference to dancing is in one sense in the song as a whole: as the bird flies, the dancer dances.[11] This meaning is enhanced by some of the arm and head movements which are said to imitate a frigate bird. Such movements are characteristic of the dance style from the northern Gilbert Islands (called *kateitei*, from *te eitei*,

---

10 I considered two kinds of basic relationships between words: metonymy and exemplar/instantiation. In the songs the key words are used themselves or are represented metonymically by a part (e.g. leaves of a tree, sail of a canoe) or by named exemplars or species of a larger category denoted by the key word (e.g. *te buka*, a species of tree [*Pisonia grandis*]; *te taake*, a species of bird [*Phaethon rubricauda melanorhynchos*]).

11 Speculatively, "Miss Tei" could refer to a dancer. *Tei* means standing, and dancing is frequently talked about as standing. Another allusion could be in the word "tree" (in "leaning of the tree"), which can metaphorically be "dancer" or "woman," as in the song Tokitebwa referred to in the first quote. The word for tree, *kai*, also means 'dance movements,' or 'choreography. ' *Kai,* however, has numerous meanings and is also used as an auxiliary word in all manner of expressions, and in this way has dozens of potential meanings. Even if the meanings are, of course, context-bound, there are perhaps too many to draw conclusions.

'frigate bird;' see Whincup & Whincup 2001, or, for a different etymology, see Lawson 1989: 446).

Dance movements

The most striking visual characteristics of Kiribati traditional dance are the air of extreme restraint and the almost angular movements. Movements of the upper torso and the head are emphasized; some dances are performed in a sitting position. Rather than moving continuously, the dancer moves from one position to another (even if this takes place rapidly as the tempo accelerates). The transitory pauses are timed by the clapped rhythm. Mary Lawson (1989: 37) describes Kiribati dancing as consisting of "poses, slow movements between poses, and abrupt movements leading directly into them." The correct execution of the choreography is paramount; the dancer never improvises. Ideal dance is 'hard' (*matoa*), which implies the positive attributes of strength, endurance and restraint.

In the poses, arms are typically held straight or in carefully prescribed angles. Movements of the head and eyes are an essential part of a dance. Carriage, the way the dancer stands (*tei*), is significant (cf. Hall 1996 on Ireland); in a sitting dance (*bino*) or a kneeling dance (*katorobubua*), changes in the angle of lean/recline (*ee*) of the upper body is part of the choreography. An exception to the use of clearly posed angles are certain women's dances, which use the movement of the hips and the behind (*iobuki* or *buki*). In *iobuki* the pelvis is moved in circular or swinging motions, whereas the upper part of the body conducts arm and head movements similar to those described above. The various kinds of hip movements, though rounded, require the same exactitude and control as angular movements. In *iobuki* it is imperative that movements of the pelvis be kept separate from those of the upper torso.

Pelvic movements notwithstanding, men and women dance similarly and also dance the same dances. In all dances the precise execution of positions and motifs is paramount and the dancer is controlled by the choreography (*kai*) down to her/his look, yet dancing must not appear jerky. Here some gender differences in style do come into play: as the dancer balances between gracefulness and the demonstration of force, men clearly display more strength, even aggression. On the one hand, there are named body postures and movements which have codified meanings. Some of their meanings are quite abstract, however (see Laxton and Kamouriki 1953).[12] Obscurity, allusiveness, and abstraction are, in fact, common and often valued characteristics of both poetry and movements in Oceanic dancing (cf. Kaeppler 1976, 1985; Smith and Kaeppler 2006a, 2006b). If dance movements were set along a continuum from the more descriptive and imitative to more ornamental and abstract, I would suggest Kiribati dancing stands at the abstract end, despite some imitative movements.

---

12   Movements in Kiribati dance have been described as decorating the text or enhancing its meanings (Lawson 1989: 439).

The basic directions of movements are in terms of right/left, up/down and forward/back. Movements in the right/left dimension are those of the arms, head and eyes, as well as rotation of the body. An implicit vertical central line dividing the body distinguishes the movements of the right from the left arm (see below). The forward-back dimension refers first to steps. Steps seemed mostly to be forward (*butirake*) and back (*kerikaki*), facing forward. Second, there is the lean (*ee*) of the upper body. The correct posture of the Kiribati dancer in standing dances is a slight forward bend of the upper body, from the waist up with the back straight. In sitting dances, choreographies can make use of leaning the torso in different directions and to varying extent.

In one of the basic positions, both arms are extended forward in a fairly wide angle, the fingers of the right hand on the same level as the eyes, and those of the left hand on the level of the breast. Vertical movement of the whole body is by bending and straightening the legs. In the basic posture the knees of the dancer are very slightly bent, just enough not to be "locked." In the dance, however, the dancer can be required to bend her/his knees more deeply (*titiku*), and there can be movement up and down. There is also aesthetic valuation based on how deep the dancer is able to *titiku* without showing fatigue or losing control, such as legs shaking.

*Clapping (*uboana*)*

Clapping (*uboana*) contributes centrally to the air of restraint and control in Kiribati dance. The pattern of claps in a particular dance song is an essential part of that song. Kiribati dance music has become more melodic since the introduction of Western music, but I would argue that rhythm, which the claps create, continues to be more important. A Kiribati dance song can be sung with different melodies, while still retaining the clapped rhythm, but to alter the clapping would mean to alter the choreography.

Claps structure choreography. Insofar as Kiribati traditional dancing is movement from one position to another, there is a pause, however transient, at the "extreme" of the movement, that is, at the moment when an arm or head is in the precisely correct position. This body position (and pause) usually coincides with, and is timed by, a clap. In this way claps mark the limits of movements and thus control the dancer/the dance. While the timing of the claps controls the time of holding and then changing positions, there are aesthetic rules which determine the dimensions of movements, i.e. how far back the arm can be extended. If the dancer extends her/his arm too far back, she/he is said to "fall into the ocean" (cf. Lawson 1989: 390).

Returns (okina)

Each dance poem or song is sung in a particular way, in which its parts are repeated in a prescribed manner. [13] A strophe has its returns (okina). While there are typical repetition patterns (e.g. a two-strophe song of standing dance is sung A-A-B-B), each dance song has its own "singing," i.e. the manner in which its parts are repeated. A dance song as a whole is often repeated three times, with the tempo accelerating[14] each time (A-A-B-B-A-A-B-B-A-A-B-B). And, the whole performance is usually carried out twice, with a small break in between allowing the dancer to assume the beginning position.

The potentially complex but symmetrical structure of a performance becomes evident when singing and movement are analyzed together. Choreography accompanies the lyrics: the reiteration of a part of a song usually means reiterating its choreography. Importantly, however, the motifs in the choreography of the second run of a strophe can also be mirror images of the first in terms of right and left. Along with the possible preparatory movements (katauraoi) and endings (motika), the repetitions of subparts and repetitions of complete parts of the song, as well as repetitions of the whole song, and the singing or form of a dance performance, may become increasingly complicated.

Structure of performance: symmetry

E kiba te man te taake has two strophes. In the performance of the song, the song leader first calls out "na–ko–e!" (ready–steady–go) followed by four claps (*) in the rhythm * * * | *. This is the standard way to begin certain kinds of dancing. In sync with the three claps in rapid succession, rest, followed by the fourth clap marking the beginning of a dance/song, the dancer may execute a series of movements called katauraoi, 'make prepared.' Katauraoi (as well as motika) movements are not obligatory and they are only done once, in the very beginning and the very end. The song/dance begins with part A, which is sung twice. The second time, the dancer performs the same movements as the first time but as mirror images in terms of right and left, and whereas in the first completion the dancer takes steps forward, during the second she retraces them. By way of an example, in the first round during the line E na umakina, the dancer's right hand moves beside her right side at waist level, and the left hand is extended forward so that the fingers are at eye level. In the second round, her left hand moves beside her left side and the right is extended forward. Part B is then sung twice, and the choreography is the same for both rounds.

After the last line of part B the accompanying singers clap their hands three times to mark the rhythm which the dancer follows in assuming the

---

13   For analyses of the musical structures of different dance types, see Lawson 1989: 463–466.
14   This practice was originally adopted from Tuvaluan *fatele* dancing.

beginning position; the whole song is then repeated three or even four times. If a *motika* (ending) is done, in this song it is done during the last three claps of the last round. It means that on the last round the motif pace of the three last claps is different from the earlier rounds. The dancer knows it is the last round by the whistle of the song leader. There are also songs in which a *motika* constitutes a part on its own, with the movement sequence executed to a short chant, a single word, or a clap pattern without lyrics. Representation of performance structures could further be refined by adding the clap pattern between strophes.

With choreographic references as sub-indexes, the structure of the *E kiba te man te Taake* performance can be represented as:

$$_{katauraoi}-A_{right}-A_{left}-B-B-A_{right}-A_{left}-B-B-A_{right}-A_{left}-B-B_{motika.}$$

In my material there were also some simple songs such as A-A-A. A more complicated example would be:

$$_{katauraoi}-A_{right}-A_{left}-B_{right}-B_{left}-A_{right}-A_{left}-B_{right-}B_{left-}A_{right}-A_{left}-B_{right}-B_{left-motika.}$$

An example of a more elaborate configuration of reiterations within each other was a sitting dance (*bino*), where the song tells about the village meetinghouse. The song/dance has five sections and can be represented like this:

$$A-B_{right}-B_{left}-C_{right}-D_{right}-D_{left}-C_{left}-D_{right}-D_{left}-E.$$

Two parallel reiterations of a verse where a movement which was executed with the right hand the first time is executed with the left on the second, and vice versa, seem a common, though not a universal feature of choreography. In the choreographies that contain such movement parallelism, it is typical that the first reiteration begins with a movement in which the right hand is more active, and is above the left and/or in an upright position. On the second singing, the order of the hands is reversed. Also movement motifs in the middle of a verse tend to begin with the right hand in the upper or more active position. In Kiribati dance the greatest significance seems to attach to the whole that the two sides comprise. The parallel but mirrored movement sequences strongly contribute to the impression of symmetry, which seems to be an important criterion for beauty for the I-Kiribati (see Grimble 1957: 202). In other words, form is beauty, and thus form has meaning, as opposed to the common Western idea that it is the content which is meaningful.

Ahistoricity, de-individualization and the power of performance

The performance of a Kiribati dance aims to be ahistorical and un-individual in the sense that it should be the correct execution of the choreography – individuality of style, let alone improvisation, is not the purpose. Another important factor is that because of the repetition patterns there is a recurring return to the beginning. A Kiribati dance song might refer to a (hi)story, but its performance has a synchronic form: time in performance is cyclical rather than linear.

Symmetry is another crucial feature of performance. The complex repetition patterns on several levels often aim at symmetry in the right-left axis (also sometimes backward-forward). Symmetry in the structure of a performance creates a sense of wholeness and of closure. This contributes to a sense of timelessness. Importantly, asymmetry of structure would leave an open ending, while symmetry leaves little room for counter-arguments.

Analogically with Maurice Bloch (1974: 62), I would argue that the signifying action in dancing purports to erase the historicity and individuality of the event, making it appear self-evident (cf. Du Bois 1986). Formalized language, movement and the performance structure as a whole indicate that the performance has force in saying something. Unlike in Bloch's argument, this does not automatically translate into authority, but there is a forceful effort to do something, to affect people, to have consequences. In other words, the performance makes a strong claim for the authority of the dancing group and its teacher.

Conclusion

One question in this paper has been: What does it mean when something is said to mean something? One can first look at meaning in what is said: what do the signs (lyrics of the song, perhaps movements) refer to and what message do they thereby convey? In *E kiba te man te Taake* there are several referents and messages to be found. "This [the dancer] is Te Taake, the ancestor," looking for home. "This is Te Taake, the bird," "the beautiful woman," "the skillful dancer." It has been suggested in this paper that these messages are true and untrue at the same time, constituting a particular relationship between the sign and the signified. The dancer is Te Taake, the ancestor, and is not.

Second, one can consider meaning in the saying: the performance. The crucial characteristics of a dance performance are symmetry, control, and reiteration. I have argued that the symmetrical structure of the song/dance, repetition, control and de-individualization all make for an effect of timelessness. Howard Morphy (1995) has discussed how, among the Yolngu of Australia, ancestral events are re-performed through ritual action – so that the ancestral events of Dreamtime take place (literally) again and again. Perhaps in a similar way, Te Taake flies, again and again, looking for a home, the dancers finding their true place each time the song is performed. By re-enacting the past, the ancestral migration continues on in the present. Put in other terms, the performance is saying "this is how it has always been." Therefore, it is indisputable.

But at the same time as it is reiterating an ancient pattern, dance is all about the present moment. Symmetry and the reiterative structure of performance lead to predictability, predictability to inevitability. Inasmuch as inevitability and predictability spell redundancy (cf. Bloch 1974), meanings become all the more dependent on the social constitution of the event, on the particular social relationship at stake. Hence, it is the social which makes the structure of the performance significant and vice versa. It is the competing groups, led by Tokitebwa or someone else, that proclaim: "this is the most beautiful woman," "this is the most skillful dancer," and finally, "this message is true." Still, truth cannot be forced on people. The burden rests upon the performer to convince people (*aomata*) of the truthfulness of his message.

However, the scenario can be more complicated than performance groups and ultimately their leaders taking turns to persuade the audience that their claim to be the best is true. When the singer-clappers all belong to the same group as the dancers, the situation remains one of relatively simple competition. Because singing is the same as people speaking, a unified performing group speaks as if they were the whole community. But, as has been described, there were cases in which it was the community speaking – in other words, part of the people participated in the performance – and what is more, not all the singers aligned themselves with the dancers. Thus there is a double paradox: people plead their cause to themselves, and on the other hand, they assert first one cause, then another. Truth shifts, preventing power/value from concentrating in one person or group. One could perhaps see here something of a paradigm of decentralization of power in this southern Kiribati society.

Finally, I have argued that one of the layers of meaning evinces what I have called the self-referential nature of Kiribati dance songs. While weapons and canoes point to the heroic voyages and battles of the past, at the same time they also refer to the dance which is in the present – the allusive descriptions of battles, sailing or flying are also metaphorical ways of talking about dance itself. Dance is a significant activity in itself, not just a reflection of the society. Could it be that not only does dance evoke mythology, but also, through those metaphors, mythology evokes dancing?

REFERENCES

An Anthology of Gilbertese Oral Tradition. From the Grimble papers and other collections edited by H.C. Maude and H.E. Maude. Translated by A.F. Grimble and Reid Cowell. Suva: Institute of Pacific Studies of the University of the South Pacific, 1994.

Austin, J.L. 1975 [1962]. *How to Do Things with Words.* The William James Lectures delivered at Harvard University in 1955. J.O. Urmson and Marina Sbisà (eds.). Second Edition. Oxford: Oxford University Press.

Autio, Petra n.d. *Social Organisation and Notions of Power in a North Tabiteuean Village.* Ph.D. dissertation manuscript.

Bateson, Gregory 2000. *Steps to an Ecology of Mind: Collected Essays on Anthropology, Psychiatry, Evolution and Epistemology.* With a new foreword by Mary Catherine Bateson. Chicago: University of Chicago Press (first published by Chandler 1972).

Bauman, Richard 1984. *Verbal Art as Performance.* With supplementary essays by Barbara A. Babcock, Gary H. Gossen, Roger D. Abrahams, Joel F. Sherzer. Prospect Heights: Waveland Press.

Bauman, Richard & Charles L. Briggs 1990. Poetics and performance as critical perspectives on language and social life. *Annual Review of Anthropology* 19: 59–88.

Bloch, Maurice 1974. Symbols, song, dance and features of articulation, or is religion an extreme form of traditional authority? *European Journal of Sociology* 15:55–81.

Burke, Mary Lawson E. 2001. The evolution of performance competition in Kiribati. In: Helen Reeves Lawrence and Don Niles (eds.) *Traditionalism and Modernity in the Music and Dance of Oceania: Essays in Honour of Barbara B. Smith*. Sydney: University of Sydney. Pp. 3–18.

Du Bois, John 1986. Self-evidence and ritual speech. In: Wallace Chafe and Johanna Nichols (eds.) *Evidentiality: The Linguistic Coding of Epistemology*. Norwood: Ablex. Pp. 313–336.

Goodenough, Ward H. 1955. A problem in Malayo-Polynesian social organization. *American Anthropologist* 57 (1): 71–83.

Grimble, Arthur Francis 1957. *Return to the Islands*. London: John Murray.

Grimble, Arthur Francis 1969 [1952]. *A Pattern of Islands*. London: John Murray (16th imprint).

Grimble, Arthur Francis 1989. *Tungaru Traditions: Writings on the Atoll Culture of the Gilbert Islands*. Edited by H.E. Maude. Honolulu: University of Hawaii Press.

Hall, Frank 1996. Posture in Irish dancing. *Visual Anthropology* 8: 251–266.

Jakobson, Roman 1981. Linguistics and poetics. *Selected Writings III: Poetry of Grammar and Grammar of Poetry*. Edited, with a preface, by Stephen Rudy. The Hague: Mouton.

Kaeppler, Adrienne L. 1976. Dance and the interpretation of Pacific traditional literature. In: Adrienne L. Kaeppler and H. Arlo Nimmo (eds.) *Directions in Pacific Traditional Literature: Essays in Honor of Katharine Luomala*. Honolulu: Bishop Museum Press. Pp. 195–216.

Kaeppler, Adrienne L. 1985. Structured movement systems in Tonga. In: Paul Spencer (ed.) *Society and the Dance: The Social Anthropology of Process and Performance*. Cambridge: Cambridge University Press. Pp. 92–118.

Kempf, Wolfgang 2003. "Songs cannot die": ritual composing and the politics of emplacement among the resettled Banabans on Rabi Island in Fiji. *The Journal of the Polynesian Society* 112(1): 33–64.

Knudson, Kenneth E. 1964. *Titiana: a Gilbertese community in the Solomon Islands (Gizo I.)*. Report on the results of a field study for the "Project for the Comparative Study of Cultural Change and Stability in Displaced Communities in the Pacific". Eugene, Oregon: Department of Anthropology, University of Oregon.

Lambert, Bernd 1966. Ambilineal descent groups in the Northern Gilberts. *American Anthropologist* 68(3): 641–664.

Lambert, Bernd 1978. Uean abara: the high chiefs of Butaritari and Makin as kinsmen and office-holders. In: Neil Gunson (ed.) *The Changing Pacific: Papers in Honour of H.E. Maude*. Oxford University Press, Melbourne. Pp. 80–93.

Lambert, Bernd 1981. Equivalence, authority, and complementarity in Butaritari-Makin sibling relationships (Northern Gilbert Islands). In: Mac Marshall (ed.) *Siblingship in Oceania: Studies in the Meaning of Kin Relations*. Ann Arbor: University of Michigan Press. Pp. 149–200.

Latouche, Jean-Paul 1984. *Mythistoire Tungaru: Cosmologies et Généalogies aux Iles Gilbert*. Paris: SELAF.

Lawson, Mary Elisabeth 1989. *Tradition, Change and Meaning in Kiribati Performance: An Ethnography of Music and Dance in a Micronesian Society*. Ph.D. thesis. Department of Music, Brown University.

Laxton, P. B. 1953. A Gilbertese song. *The Journal of the Polynesian Society* 62(4): 342–347.

Laxton, P.B. and Te Kautu Kamouriki 1953. *"Ruoia"*: A Gilbertese Dance. *The Journal of the Polynesian Society* 62 (1): 57–71.

Lundsgaarde, Henry Peder 1970. Law and politics on Nonouti Island. In: Thomas G. Harding and Ben J. Wallace (eds.) *Cultures of the Pacific*. NY: Free Press. Pp.

242–264.

Lundsgaarde, Henry Peder 1974. The Evolution of Tenure Principles on Tamana Island, GI. In: Henry Peder Lundsgaarde (ed.) *Land Tenure in Oceania*. Honolulu: University of Hawaii Press. Pp. 179–214.

Lundsgaarde, Henry Peder 1978. Post-contact Changes in Gilbertese Maneaba Organization. In: Neil Gunson (ed.) *The Changing Pacific: Papers in Honour of H.E. Maude*. Melbourne: Oxford University Press. Pp. 67–79.

Lundsgaarde, Henry Peder and Martin G. Silverman 1972. Category and Group in Gilbertese Kinship: An Updating of Goodenough's Analysis. *Ethnology* 11(2): 95–110.

Luomala, Katharine 1976. Five Songs from the Gilbert Islands. In: Linda Dégh, Henry Glassie and Felix J. Oinas (eds.) *Folklore Today: A Festschrift for Richard M. Dorson*. Bloomington: Indiana University. Pp. 347–356.

Maude, Henry Evans 1968. *Of Islands and Men: Studies in Pacific History*. Melbourne: Oxford University Press.

Maude, Henry Evans 1991 [1963]. The evolution of the Gilbertese *Boti*: An Ethnohistorical Interpretation. Reprinted from the *Journal of the Polynesian Society* 72(1), 1963. Wellington: The Polynesian Society, with permission by the Institute of Pacific Studies and Gilbert Islands Extension Centre of the University of the South Pacific.

Maude, Henry Evans 1994. Introduction to Chapter VII: Migration to the Gilbert Islands. *An Anthology of Gilbertese Oral Tradition*. From the Grimble papers and other collections edited by H.C. Maude and H.E. Maude. Translated by A.F. Grimble and Reid Cowell. Suva: Institute of Pacific Studies of the University of the South Pacific, 1994.

Morphy, Howard 1995. Landscape and the Reproduction of the Ancestral Past. In: E. Hirsch and M. O'Hanlon (eds.) *The Anthropology of Landscape: Perspectives of Place and Space*. Oxford: Clarendon. Pp. 184–209.

Paine, Robert 1981. Introduction. In: Robert Paine (ed.) *Politically Speaking: Cross-Cultural Studies of Rhetoric*. St. John's: Institute of Social and Economic Research, Memorial University of Newfoundland. Pp. 1–6.

Sabatier, Ernest 1977 [1938]. *Astride the Equator: An Account of the Gilbert Islands*. Translated by Ursula Nixon. Foreword, endnotes and bibliography by H. E. Maude. Melbourne: Oxford University Press.

Siikala, Jukka 1991. *'Akatokamanāva: Myth, History and Society in the Southern Cook Islands*. Auckland and Helsinki: The Polynesian Society in association with The Finnish Anthropological Society.

Smith, Barbara B. and Adrienne L. Kaeppler 2006a. 'Micronesia'. *Grove Music Online* ed. L. Macy. Available at <http://www.grovemusic.com> [www-document] Accessed 1.12.2006.

Smith, Barbara B. and Adrienne L. Kaeppler 2006b. 'Polynesia'. *Grove Music Online* ed. L. Macy. Available at <http://www.grovemusic.com> [www-document] Accessed 1.12.2006.

The Story of Karongoa. Narrated by an Unimane of the Boti of Karongoa n Uea on Nikunau in 1934, transcribed by Tione Baraka of Taboiaki on Beru. Translated by G.H. Eastman. Edited, annotated and revised by H.E. Maude. Suva: Institute of Pacific Studies of the University of the South Pacific, 1991.

Uriam, Kambati K. 1995. *In their Own Words. History and Society in Gilbertese Oral Tradition*. Canberra: The Journal of Pacific History and the Australian South Pacific Cultures Fund.

Whincup, Tony 2005. *Te Mwaie*. Traditional Dance in Kiribati. Refereed papers from the 1st international Small Island Cultures conference. Kagoshima University Centre for the Pacific Islands, February 7th–10th 2005. Available online at <http://www.sicri.org> [pdf-document].

Whincup, Tony and Joan Whincup 2001. *Akekeia: Traditional Dance in Kiribati*. Wellington: Tobaraoi Travel and Susan Barrie.

The Flower and the Ogre

Narrative Horizons and Symbolic Differentiation in the Kei Islands of Eastern Indonesia

Timo Kaartinen

Horizon in the most obvious sense is a view across the sea, such as the vast expanse of the Arafura Sea I stopped to gaze at several times each day of my fieldwork on the eastern coast of the Great Kei Island.[1] But this horizon was empty of visible islands and relatively absent from the talk of people living on its shores. Their interest lay with other places they knew to be populated by other people, generally up and down the coast (south being "up" for them), and the more distant homes of trade allies and a diversity of strangers in the north and west, blocked from view by the long, mountainous island on which they live. To my immediate hosts, whose ancestors had fled the colonization of the spice-producing Banda Islands in 1621, the unseen Banda Sea in the north and west was also a horizon for remembering and narrating their past.

In spite of its maritime setting, this social geography and the cosmological perspectives associated with it bear comparison with the forest-bound societies discussed in the first part of this book. In the Kei Islands, abstract spatial coordinates such as "up" and "down," or "sea" and "land," are used in reference to unmarked, daily movements and activities in the village setting. More distant relationships, on the other hand, tend to be defined in terms of place, not space. The reason for this is that the identities and hierarchical relations of groups which co-habit each coastal village are built on a plurality of ancestral origins, and alliances and marriages between these groups and various outsiders. Ultimately the islanders' reflexive, symbolic awareness of their differentiated social existence is focused on the incorporation of some aspects of a foreign, outside world into their self. This world of foreigners is the ontological horizon elaborated in origin myths.

These local perspectives on place and space raise a theoretical issue I want to address in this article: what explains the fact that people living in the same

---

1   The fieldwork on which this paper is based was conducted in Southeast Maluku, East Indonesia, over fifteen months during 1992 and 1994–1996, with the sponsorship of LIPI and the Gajah Mada University. I am grateful for the financial support of the Academy of Finland, the Nordic Institute of Asian Studies, and the Väinö Tanner Foundation.

place see different things in the horizon; at what level of experiences and practices are their horizons systematically related? Marshall Sahlins offers two possible answers by contrasting the practical mastery of perceptual points of view or *habitus* with certain people's ability to objectify their own acts and perceptions in mytho-poetic terms (Sahlins 1985: 53). *Habitus* refers to the integrative effect of relatively unreflected routines and practices objectified as "custom." In mytho-praxis, or collective action oriented by mythical categories, the constitutive categories of society are instantiated in actions and events and brought to the center of symbolic awareness. We should not expect the whole structure to come in view at such moments: the concrete contexts we can observe express local reversals of the value of its signs (1985: 103). What is true for actions and practices that follow the logic of myth is also true for the practice of narrating myths. While mythical perspectives are systematically related in terms of their evaluations of culturally valued agency, the value of categories is reversed in different contexts and perspectives of narration. In his Cook Islands ethnography Jukka Siikala (1991) has stressed the differing effects that different ways of narrating myths have on society. Narrations may focus on continuities or analogies; events may unfold either in space or time. This makes it possible to ask how "mental maps" and spatial memory make it possible to reproduce constitutive acts in narrating recent events (Siikala and Siikala 2005: 127) and how principles of social differentiation are crystallized in different chronotopic perspectives (2005: 130).

In this article I address these questions with reference to two Keiese myths in which the actions of ancestral heroes are placed in two contrasting chronotopic settings. In the first myth the dominant horizon of the story is the cape which separates the familiar, coastal seascape east of the island from the world of trade, outside contact, and historical forces west of the island. In the second myth the action takes place on land, against the background of the mountain which rises behind the coastal villages and blocks the sunset from their view. The context in which the two myths were told to me was a dispute about a love affair which was blown up into larger proportions because of a struggle for political authority. It is significant that the people involved actually had a choice between resolving the dispute in customary or in mytho-poetic terms. I argue that their impulse to frame it through mythical discourse derives ultimately from the notion in which the value of personhood, which is at stake in all sexual and marital disputes, derives from the world outside the local community. I will therefore begin by describing the significance of external relations for Kei society before proceeding to the case history and textual analysis at hand.

Piracy and the world of trade

The islands and archipelagoes spread over the vast maritime area between the Lesser Sunda Islands, New Guinea and the Philippines have for centuries been in contact with each other through trade. Until the late 19th century this area was only partially colonized by European powers, and the difficulties experienced by the Dutch East India Company to enforce its spice monopoly led it to label it a pirates' haven. This perception by outsiders obscured a more complex reality of long-distance alliances between island communities for which inter-island trade was a vital part of social reproduction. Food production in the larger islands was vital for maintaining the production of trade goods in certain strategic locations, and trade centers which were either colonized by the Dutch or politically subordinate to them were regularly visited by people who otherwise lived beyond the sway of centralized power.

While piracy referred to the appropriation of cargoes on the open sea, the Dutch distrust of outlying areas was fueled by a Keiese custom which allowed people to appropriate anything that drifted to the shore. Around 1860 a merchant ship was wrecked near the shore of the Great Kei Island and it was soon emptied of the goods it carried by local villagers. Complaints by its captain and owner led to an investigation during a rare visit to the area by the commanding colonial officer (Eijbergen 1866: 257). In the Keiese perception such events did not indicate the absence of law and order, but the fact that customary relations had not been established between the ship's captain and the chief or ruler who mediated the community's relationship to him.[2] A payment received by the chief would have made it possible for his people to recognize the trader as a party to regular exchanges. By the account of Hein Geurtjens, an early 20th century missionary, people would then have entered the ship and perused the goods; buyers would have tied a string around the object that caught their fancy and then visited their home for something of equal value in order to complete the purchase (Geurtjens 1921: 240).

Kei, Tanimbar and other more remote parts of Southeast Maluku did not have many outside visitors before the 19th century. John Townsend Farquhar, a British officer posted in Banda during the Napoleonic wars, suggests that the "blood-thirsty nature of natives" made traders disinclined to visit these areas (Miller 1980:50). This did not prevent the islanders from making yearly visits to the main Dutch port in Banda with their own boats. Written accounts of such trade connections exist from as early as the 1640s, a period during which parts of the archipelago continued to actively resist Dutch colonial power (Heeres 1896: 691). Historically the inter-island trade of peripheral islands was clearly an expression of antagonism rather than subordination to colonial order, a sign of defiance against the spice monopoly which the Dutch and their local allies sought to maintain by periodically destroying spice groves which lay outside the areas under their control. In many societies of the area this led to a peculiar reframing of trade as a kind of warfare. In Banda Eli, the village in which my fieldwork in Kei was focused, the objects acquired from ancestral trading trips were characterized as the spoils of war. Trade only counted as a kind of exchange if it took place locally; in faraway

---

2   A construction of similar rank between these authorities is suggested by the fact that *anakoda* and *kapitan*, which both mean 'captain,' are common chiefly titles in Kei.

places it was reconceptualized as the violent capture of outsiders' riches.

Such reframing of trade and political relations is not unique to Kei but appears in the ethnography of Raja Ampat, a group of islands off the Papuan coast. Raja Ampat paid annual tribute to Tidore, an island-sultanate which led the navies ordered by the Dutch Company to punish illegal cultivation of spices in distant islands. Even if the tributary visits were essentially an act of submission, homecoming islanders celebrated their voyage by rituals similar to those performed after a victorious pirate raid (Kamma 1982: 81). Developing Kamma's observation in reference to Biak, an island of West Papua, Danilyn Rutherford suggests that Biak people do not see the outside world as a social order, but rather as an eschatological horizon through which they project the thoughts and impulses that arise from their participation in national institutions and economies. Instead of becoming a point of reference for identity, traces of contact with the foreign are incorporated as an "alien body within the self" (Rutherford 2003: 28). In Rutherford's argument the foreign is fetishized as the source of valued surplus – a means for reproducing and extending debts instead of resolving them, or extending the value-creating potential of the brother-sister bond instead of replacing the sibling with the spouse – with the effect that the image of society's unity and vitality is projected to the future (2003: 64, 74). In a society structured by different contexts and sequences of exchange, relations to foreigners thus evoke what Roy Wagner (1981: 43) calls a "differentiating" mode of symbolization in which the conventional separation and order of these contexts collapses and actions and objects which symbolize the pursuit of value signify value itself. In Nancy Munn's (1986: 11) terms, the "alien body" incorporated in the self consists of spatiotemporal relations that go beyond the self or expand dimensions of the spatiotemporal control of an actor.

Even if Kei Islands society differs from Melanesia in the sense that exchanges coexist with a stable social morphology (Barraud et al. 1994: 13), Keiese ideology also contains a paradoxical affirmation of outside contact as a context for enhancing and reproducing the vitality of society. I have already mentioned the "capture" of trade goods and the appropriation of flotsam as examples of this perspective. At the same time, excessive vitality from the Kei Islands perspective is a threat to social order and calls for purifying rituals addressed to a spirit called *hukum* or 'law' (1994: 77). The Keiese ideology thus combines two fundamental values, the existence of society as a singular cosmological entity called *haratut* and society as a differentiated entity constituted by law (*lor*) (1994: 17). It should also be noted that exchanges in Kei society do not objectify relations between individual subjects but between larger social entities (1994: 105). The differentiating symbolism of myths and vitality-affirming rituals destabilizes and collapses these relations, revealing an underlying motivation whitc is something more complex than just individual "desire" repressed by the (conventional) symbolic order. A better concept for making the relevant distinctions is ontology which Bruce Kapferer (1988: 79) defines as "fundamental principles of being in the world and the orientation of such a being toward the horizons of its experience." Before discussing the different ontologies at play in Keiese myths and the mytho-poetic self-definitions and ideological constructs they make possible, I will describe the social and situational context in which I recorded them.

Myth as the interpretation of action

Just before the feast which ends Ramadan, the monthlong fast observed by Muslims throughout the world, a young Christian paramedic was caught together with his Muslim girlfriend in a house next to the government health clinic in Banda Eli, the village in which I was doing fieldwork. Before the paramedic was rescued by his superior, a doctor from Java, he was beaten up by the girl's brothers. Word of the event spread quickly to neighboring villages and to the boy's and girl's parents, all of whom resided in other coastal villages towards the north. By the next morning, people in the neighboring village called Renfaan had taken the side of the unlucky health worker and destroyed the gardens of people who lived in Tuburlai, the hamlet at the northern end of Banda Eli. I arrived to hear the tense arguments and waited in the house of Wandan, the old hamlet head, to join the meeting he had called to resolve the issue. But the girl's father, an old teacher working in another hamlet some kilometers further south, refused to attend. Instead, he sent a letter to his children, telling about the "shame" he suffered and threatening to denounce the girl if she went on with the relationship.

The dispute might appear as a minor event blown out of proportion by the effervescence surrounding the religious holiday. There were indeed alternative ways of handling it, but all of them involved diverse relations through which the parties were integrated as a society. The issue which had upset the parties was not so much the breach of the religious boundary but the fact that the boy came from a group called "four houses" and the girl from "seven houses" – two large, ancestral groups of common people divided between several villages. These groups are identified with two mountains, called Kar and Bo, from which their forefathers descended to present-day settlements on the shore. What Wandan was trying to arrange was a ritual reconciliation between the two groups. In the absence of an old coin, or some other token of recognition from the boy's family to the girl's, there was no meeting. Since each party was under the protection of chiefly groups it fell to higher authorities to restore the peace. But by that morning things were already complicated by the issue of the spoiled gardens. With little territory of its own, Banda Eli relied on the chiefs of neighboring villages for agricultural land. Far from regretting the damage to the gardens, the acting village head of the neighboring village asserted they were on his land. If the people of Tuburlai continued to defy him he would expel them from their present home. While certain chiefly groups in Banda Eli represented themselves as the "owners" or "protectors" of Tuburlai people, they were cautious to assume such a role in this case because their closest allies in Renfaan were competing with Bunga, the landowner, for the position of village headman. As later immigrants to the Kei Islands, the Bandanese chiefs depended on friendly relations with the neighboring village for their rights to garden land,

201

and the stakes of interfering openly in the political affairs of the other village were simply too high.

The political relations within each village were thus less important than the ancestral ties which cut across the social and linguistic boundary which separates Banda Eli from the larger society of Kei. The nature of these ties depends partly of the hierarchical position of the groups, and it needs to be pointed out that Banda Eli was founded by later immigrants from the islands of Banda in Central Maluku whose original home was colonized by the Dutch in 1621. During my fieldwork, somewhat over a third of Banda Eli's population consisted of descendants from the Bandanese immigrants who claimed the same rank as the chiefly class of Kei. Refusing to assimilate into the Kei society through intermarriage, these people define their relationship with allied Keiese groups as "stopping over" in each other's houses, which is essentially a commensal relationship of nurture and protection. Banda Eli people of common rank, on the other hand, acknowledge their origin in the Kei society, and in addition to their relations to each other, these groups may be variously subordinated to several chiefly groups in different villages at the same time.

The failure to handle the dispute I have described in customary terms is significant because it immediately changes the issue into one about ancestral history and myth. Nobody turned up to present a token to the girl's father in order to constitute him or his representative as a party in the settlement; instead, the spoiling of the gardens amounted to an affront similar to an illicit love affair, making it impossible to consider the issue as a conflict between two groups. An illicit love affair is a patent case of "excessive vitality," and the means of symbolic control which were mobilized in response to it cannot be reduced to political ambitions and strategies.

To clarify this point let me return briefly to the different articulations of trade and the internal exchanges of Kei society. Keiese views of overseas and local trade present a sharp contrast: the former involves a surplus of value whereas in the latter, exemplified by Geurtjens' account of trade visits, the trade object is simply replaced by a locally derived one of similar value. In this context, the other's regard for the local object's value is already established by the "custom" performed by the ship's captain and the chief. Overseas trade, on the other hand, does not aim at mutual recognition and a shared framework of value. Instead, the surplus of value represented by the supposedly contested object suggests a collapse of the relationship between self and other. Overseas trade is therefore not a case of negative reciprocity but a space of symbolic resistance to reciprocity. The most illuminative case of such resistance is the sense of *malu* which translates as 'shame,' or more precisely, 'vulnerability to public appraisal,' which is experienced by a young woman's male relatives after she has run away with a lover. The social relationships of nurturing vitality and of exchange which Kei society normally keeps distinct are assimilated to each other, concentrating symbolic awareness to the vitality they both represent. In the absence of a customarily established context for exchange, in which "replacing" one thing with another integrates it into the broader, ritual work of "return" (Barraud *et al.* 1994: 15–16), symbolic awareness is focused on a singular intentional field. In one possible rendering, *malu* results from loving a daughter who is also loved by a stranger whose love I do not want, though my daughter's love means I also love him. One part of the self is thus alienated by the absence of any mediation between these contexts of "loving."

Kei Islands myths present several different perspectives to such loss of the boundaries between the self and its intentional objects. The two narratives by which certain people illuminated to me their own position in the dispute context I have just described are far from trying to justify a particular action; instead, they represent two contrasting ontological views of self-differentiating events. I will first turn to the story told by Lahmudin, one of the common people of Tuburlai, whose clan belonged to the same category of ancestral groups as the health worker involved in the case. His story affirms a connection between Bunga and the autochthonous Keiese people. On the previous evening the narrator had discussed Bunga's threat to evict these people from the village with Maria Imaculata, an old lady allied to my Bandanese hosts, whose son was competing with Bunga for headmanship. "If Bunga makes good his threat," Lahmudin said to the lady, "tell him to send people to take apart our houses and move them to his backyard."

The background of this argument was that while Bunga's claim to the land was based on having conquered it in a war, the man who gave him the weapons to do so was Lahmudin's ancestor. It is significant that the myth also underlines the derivation of Bunga's name (which means 'flower') to obviate the outcome of the myth which in the end associates Bunga with vitality and life. The effect of this narrative focus is to make Bunga's posturing in the context of the dispute appear as a conventional and predictable aspect of his chiefly status. The next section presents an outline of the myth and comments on it in more detail.

Drifting wood and withering flower

In the beginning of Lahmudin's story

an old man called Metimur sets his fishtrap at the reef called Nam Howod on the west coast of Great Kei, but catches only two pieces of driftwood. He casts them away, only to find the same pieces of wood the next day. He complains to his wife who recognizes the driftwood as *nabi laut*, strange valuable objects which should be kept. On the third day the wood is back in Metimur's fishtrap, and he takes it and saves it under the rafters of his house. The old couple goes to tend their garden, and when they return the house has been cleaned and food made for them. The same thing happens on the following day, and the man and woman say to each other:

"Tomorrow let's wait behind the house and see who it is." While they hide behind the house, two brothers are already making noise preparing food. The old couple go back in and grab the two boys. They smell them.

After smelling, the old woman says: "Grandfather, let's not kill these two but raise them as our children. So that there will be four people in the house. So that there will be four people in this village of Nguerhir."

In the end the two grow up: they are skilled with bow and arrows at the age of fifteen and want to marry. Then the elder brother says: "Father, make me a bow and arrows. I want to shoot at Mount Kar."

The father answers: "Don't. A princess lives there with three or four hundred warriors. They will descend and attack us here in the coastal village of Nguerhir."

Then the elder brother says: "Grandmother, make me provisions. Seven bundles of cooked rice, seven boiled eggs." Then he shoots. The elder brother shoots his arrow. Then he says: "Grandfather, I want to follow the arrow to the mountain. Plant a flower. If the flower withers, I am dead. If the flower is blooming, I live."

Then he goes. He looks and looks for it and gets right in front of the house of the princess at her fortress. And he asks the princess: "Princess, have you my arrow, from this quiver?"

And the princess answers: "I have kept it here in the rafters." And the two stay in the house for a week, staying inside the whole time. In other words, they make love. They are a good match, so they make love. Then he begins to talk about provisions again: seven bundles of cooked rice, seven boiled eggs, in order to shoot his arrow to Fotun Kub. But the princess says:

"Don't shoot. In Foton Kub there is a seven-fathom ogre. At the north wind he goes to kill people in the south, and at the southern wind he kills people in the north."

He says: "Princess, I have already shot, so I have to look for the arrow." And he says: "Princess, plant another flower. I will look for my arrow in the cave of the seven-fathom ogre."

He goes to the cave, and facing the ogre, hears him say: "Who are you?"

He says: "Me. Looking for that which came from my quiver."

The ogre answers: "I eat your arrows whole." And the seven-fathom ogre says: "Just watch." The ogre opens his mouth and eats him whole, and he dies.

At once the flower in front of the princess's house withers. The flower in front of the house of his elders and younger brother withers too. Then the younger brother says: "Father, make me a bow and arrows, too. I will look for my brother. And Mother, provisions for me too: seven bundles of rice, seven boiled eggs. Father, plant a flower. If the flower withers, I and my brother are dead. If my flower does not wither, it means I live ..."

The younger brother follows the same trajectory as the elder brother, but when the princess welcomes him back from the ogre's den he says "No, I'm his brother." He manages to kill the ogre and cuts open its belly, finds his unconscious brother and revives him. When they face the princess she names the elder brother Bunga Omaratan and the younger, Bunga Belyanan, from *bunga* which means 'flower' in Malay. The island is divided between the two brothers, and the elder settles on the eastern coast with his people, four great houses which represent the autochthonous society.

The motif in which strange objects are collected from the seashore and turned into human beings through culturalizing actions is common in Keiese myths. In some, a shellfish found and cooked by an old woman turns into a child who grows up to be a great hero and king. The strange thing is clearly the object of actions by people who, because of their age, are no longer fertile. But the autochthonous society with its many people is a site of superfluous fertility. The first sign of this is that two dead pieces of wood turn into two live flowers which signify the personhood of the two brothers. At this point the boys become the main agents of the narrative; the elder brother's relationship to the princess is the first step towards realizing fertility as a value. Note, however, that the elder brother cannot accomplish this alone since he is devoured by the ogre which resembles the autochthonous, androgynous god Ubila'a in Susan McKinnon's (1991: 82) ethnography of Tanimbar. By abstaining from leviratic marriage the younger brother avoids this fate; the separate identity of the two brothers then becomes the basis for the differentiation of the island and its original society. By virtue of their different relationships to this being, the homologous relationship between the brothers is changed into an analogous one which implies a differentiation of their persons (and produces a diarchy of political functions).

Up until the events on the mountain, the myth follows an aesthetic which Marilyn Strathern (1988: 181) calls replication: rather than elaborating the difference between the two brothers, it underlines the form taken by the autochthonous society's relations to the exterior. The excessive fertility of the mountain means that someone marrying into the autochthonous society risks being devoured by it; the younger brother's battle with the ogre may suggest a rescue of his brother but also a struggle to exorcise an alienated part of himself. The only difference between the brothers' actions lies in the order in which they deal with the princess and the ogre. I would like to stress the importance of the names which the brothers receive from the princess. They convey both analogy and the difference between sexual love and the affection and recognition of in-laws. Such analogical awareness makes it possible to value different aspects of love as productive of society without losing the morally significant distinction between them (Wagner 1977). Lahmudin's subtle comment on the context in which he told me this myth implies that the elder brother – and his descendant, the current chief – owes love to his people even if he should be respected by outsiders.

To understand the different dimensions of the often-heard idiom of "having" or "owning" people, it is useful to look into another myth which I heard after services in the Protestant church of Bunga's village. My Muslim hosts made sure I attended this church because the congregation consisted of the subordinates of their closest allies in the neighboring village – the old Catholic couple whose son was contending with Bunga for the position of village head. In response to my question about the origin of the Protestant families, Johannes Renfofan told me the following story about Terngun, the first inhabitant of Tuburlai:

> The coconut oil of Terngun's daughter spilled on the ground because of a strong wind. Then Terngun asked his wife: "Why did this child's coconut oil get spilled?"
>
> His wife responded: "I do not know who arrived, but the northern wind..."
>
> Thus he said to his wife: "Make provisions. Maybe I should ask the northern wind."
>
> Thus she was going to make provisions, and she asked: "What provisions?"
>
> "I will climb a coconut tree and harvest some leaves for you to make bundled rice."
>
> Thus she cooked seven bundles of rice in coconut oil. Later he went to the shore in War Minahaar and got in his canoe, and a sea-eagle asked him: "Terngun, where are you going?" – "I'm going there." He asked and asked for a favorable wind.
>
> "Take me along," the sea-eagle said. He took him along.
>
> Later at the cape a sea urchin said: "Terngun, where are you going?"
> "I'm going there."
>
> "Take me along, let the three of us go."
>
> At another cape, where the shore is littered with logs, an octopus asked: "Where are the three of you going?"
>
> "I am going to make war over there."
>
> "Take me along." They went. But people did not know what Terngun was going for, they just went and nobody knew why. They just went on to the northern end of the island.
>
> On that night they stayed there. They took the provisions, the rice bundles, and went to the village chief. "Why are you going there?"
>
> "We are here to wage war against the North Wind. I will ask the North Wind why he spilled my ... her coconut oil. You three, think. Sea-eagle, can you lift this canoe or not?"
>
> The sea-eagle said: "I will try. Only worry if my two wings break. If not, I'll lift you."
>
> From the sea urchin he asked: "How about it, Urchin?"
>
> "When he raises the waves to sink our canoe I'll suck water and bilge it out."
>
> "What about you, Octopus?"
>
> "See my eight arms? These four will hold on to the canoe, and these four will anchor you to the stones."
>
> At daybreak they went. A strong wind started to blow. The sky became entirely dark. Waves began to rise, tall like a coconut tree. The one that had knocked over the container of oil came, asking: "Where do you think you are going?"
>
> "We have come so you will be punished. Why did you knock over my daughter's coconut oil?"

"I don't know, I don't know about that."

"You are lying!"

Then the North Wind said: "In that case, we will have to go to war." And he said: "Terngun, you try your weapons first!"

Terngun said: "No. You try your weapons first." High seas, dark, rocking, waves, oh! With that wind trees were creaking and falling. He took the sea urchin and put him down. Although the canoe was full of water it did not sink. And the canoe stayed in place in spite of the wind. Three times the enemy tried but he was not strong enough. The canoe did not sink and nothing came to it, it just stayed in place.

Thus the North Wind said: "Now it is your turn."

Thus he asked the three people: "Eagle, how about it?"

"Old Man, no problem. When we get to it they will be swimming, and I will go down and destroy them."

The sea urchin said: "We will go there and I will suck in all water in the sea, and it will surge and destroy the village."

The octopus said: "I will dig the seafloor and the soil under the village and it will fall onto the ground." Thus they fought and the old man was the winner.

When the fighting was over the North Wind said: "Terngun, stop! I give up! Anything you want I take and bring out for you! What do you want, Terngun? I have told you I surrender. The fight is over. All the people are dead. I'm alone here. What do you want?"

Terngun said: "I only want two things."

"What two things?"

"Saif Sarean and Seng Rer Bed Mar."

These things were brought. We kept them until the giant wave destroyed our village, and then my father buried them in the ground. In the ground in that village square. We looked for them but did not find them. But Saif Sarean was taken away by Bin Koi who married in Watlaar. It is in Watlaar now, Saif Sarean is in Watlaar.

Terngun's adventure is preceded by the elopement or rape of his daughter, signified by the knocked-over coconut oil she uses to tend her hair. Refusing to recognize his opponent as a person, Terngun says he is going to wage war against the northern wind. One should note that Terngun's village – the original settlement at the site of Tuburlai – is calm during the north-west monsoon, the period during which traders used to arrive in Kei. The appropriate place to confront the outsider is at the northern tip of the cigar-shaped island. The animals who join Terngun and help him are the totemic ancestors of his subordinate people. The narrative represents their different abilities as aspects of Terngun's own prowess. Terngun is a chiefly figure that represents society's ability to act together; his relationships to other people are only differentiated by action. The precious objects which Terngun acquires as booty make it possible to value these relationships in terms of social categories.

Significantly, the end of the myth and the following exegetic commentary stress the fate of two heirlooms. One was buried in the ground and lost from sight, and thus completely incorporated in the autochthonous society. The other, however, served as a marriage payment and signifies the relationship between the hero's successors and the ruler of Watlaar, the highest chief in northern Great Kei. Far from claiming Terngun as his ancestor, Johannes later explained that his line had become extinct: repeatedly the village had to call in outsiders to assume the chiefly function, and the fertility of the chiefly line was only secured by virtue of the heirloom given to its outside allies.

The gendered images of the alien other in the two myths correspond to the consequences and value of the hero's action for the continuous existence of society. The Bunga myth implies that if chiefs allow themselves to be encompassed by the autochthonous society, their distinction takes the form of chronological or historical succession, a transmission of distinctive names in the chiefly line. From this point of view, genealogical continuity is important because it signifies and depends on the vitality of society. According to Marilyn Strathern's (1988: 192) argument about same-sex relations in Melanesia, the key to such expansion is the replication of the self. By launching arrows the boys detach something of themselves without alienating it: the purpose of each encounter is to gain back the arrow. Failure and success in doing so defines the contrast between the elder and the younger brother as a differential value. If the arrow is a metonymic extension of the shooter's masculinity (1988: 213), the scene in which one brother makes the other emerge from the ogre's belly can be seen as an act of self-reproduction: by provoking the ogre he incites the birth of someone like himself. The name he receives from the princess recognizes his continuing status as outsider: his clan is called Belyanan, literally, 'children of friends,' from *bel* which refers to allies to whom one is not related through kinship ties, or indeed someone with whom one does not intermarry. Omaratan, the clan name of the elder brother (from *oma* 'village square' and *ratan* 'above', 'along'), suggests his continuing presence in society.

Instead of two brothers, the myth about Terngun ends by outlining the trajectory of two objects which derive from encounters with the foreign enemy. The manner in which one is incorporated in society and the other given away is parallel to the fate of the brothers in the Bunga myth. The object which is out at the ruler's house is subject to general discourse, and its existence can be affirmed with some authority; we might call it the "younger" object since it offers a possibility for the public comparison and evaluation of something which is still "here." Pairs of similar objects have indeed been displayed in dispute settlements, in order to demonstrate the existence of ancestral alliances between groups which do not continue their relationship by intermarrying or otherwise. But the risk of such displays lies in acknowledging a historical relationship without a public recognition of its mythical significance. Rather like Pacific societies in which the younger brother can take over the elder's position (Siikala 1991: 103), younger brothers and "younger" objects represent the point at which Kei society is open to transformation.

Horizons of being

In spite of the politically-charged context in which the two myths were told to me, a fruitful way to interpret them is not to suggest how they speak from different positions (those of chiefs and ordinary people, Christians and Muslims, or the different origin groups concerned) in the politically-interested discourse of the moment. I suggest instead that the narrators take seriously the predicament of different parties in a scene of (potential) elopement and construct ideas of a social "whole" as the grounds for what they see as appropriate action. While the "seven" and the "four" famous houses – the girl's and boy's side in the dispute – largely depend on each other for marriage partners, each group also thinks of itself as a cosmological entity with a "seaward" and "landward" side, implicit in the contrast between the two myths. In the absence of negotiated marriage payments, each new relationship between the two groups is potentially a source of antagonism which arises from the unresolved separation and differentiation of gendered elements. In Kei society it is the role of chiefs to mediate such antagonisms between equals. Appropriate action by chiefs thus depends on the way in which their person incorporates different elements of cosmology – a way which appears starkly different in the two myths discussed above.

The clearest contrast between the two stories lies with the horizon which provides the backdrop of heroic, male actions. The cape which separates the eastern coast of the island from the wider Indonesian society, and the mountain which marks the source of autochthonous life, are suggestive of the contrast, drawn in Patricia Spyer's ethnography of Aru, between two separate "elsewheres" represented by the national and the autochthonous pasts (Spyer 2000: 7–8). Spyer's account of them is focused on the seasonally changing conditions in which alternating presence and absence of trade and national modernity produces a space which is too unstable for either nationally or locally grounded identities. In the case described in this article, the failure to perform a dispute settlement could be read in comparable terms, as a symptom of the inability of political authority to objectify itself as custom or the inability of custom to express itself as political action. Instead of focusing on the question about the stability or instability of social order based on *habitus*, however, my analysis is based on the mytho-poetic possibilities of framing a response to specific events with the potential to transform the order. From this point of view, the horizon is not the limit of the "universe of discourse" (Bourdieu 1977: 168) but something more enabling: it makes it possible to invent culturally differentiated forms of experience and objectify them as aspects of collective existence (Wagner 1981: 44). By connecting a general, cosmological view of existence to a specific horizon, each myth thus expresses an ontological perspective. As Bruce Kapferer (1988: 79) argues, several different ontologies can be at play in a single cultural universe and their relative importance and effects on society are dependent on ideological processes.

According to Cécile Barraud, a distinctive feature of the Kei Islands ideology is that it implicitly acknowledges a universe wider than itself, but only as a dimension of its own order of hierarchic encompassment (Barraud *et al.* 1994: 118). Rituals addressed to *lor*, as this order is known in Kei, are aimed at controlling the excessive vitality and differentiation which accompany encounters with foreign outsiders. Through its symbolic reference to *lor*, Kei society acknowledges the potential of each human life to transcend its significance for reproductive relations within society, but normally this potential – represented as a number of soul-like beings called *inya* – can only be valued when it is visibly embodied by a living person, and realized when this person is incorporated in the society of ancestors. The so-called "disappeared" people who have died elsewhere, without a funeral which would permit their bodies to rejoin the earth and their souls to disperse, represent a threat for this value-producing cycle. Keiese rituals treat these people as a collective category, a spillover of society's life-giving powers as it were, which interacts with the collective category of dead ancestors on a higher level of exchange (Barraud *et al.* 1994: 81).

As the Keiese notion of "disappeared people" suggests, the foreign domain is marked by the invisibility of actors – a condition considered to be in deviance from normal sociality in some societies of Maluku (Platenkamp 2006). The invisibility of actors, which makes it impossible to maintain distinctions between self and other and so determine the value of actions, is perhaps most obvious in the second myth, Terngun's oracular battle against the wind. While the hero undertakes this battle as a revenge for the abduction of his daughter, his actions appear as the mirror-image of his opponent's actions. It is worth noting that he receives help from marine animals which represent the totemic ancestors of his subordinate clans. Human agency is thus fused with natural forces and animal capabilities, and the myth is as much about controlling these forces as confronting them. It is only by reference to the two objects gained in ransom that the hero is able to represent the dynamism of nature as social existence, both in the sense of locally anchored social being and relations of exchange.

The ontological importance of visibility in Kei is illuminated by the way in which names are handled in the rituals of this society. Barraud (1990: 221) points out that at one phase of the postpartum rituals the name of a newborn child is captured from the sea to be "eaten" by the ancestors. While the fact of having a name suggests responsivity to the regard of others, it appears that this responsive quality is from the start divested from the individual and assumed by society at large.[3] But in addition to the personal name, the Keiese construct of the person also includes beings called *inya*, described by Barraud (1990: 218) as soul-like entities which make it possible to acknowledge a person's value. In my understanding this refers to the person's capacity to be valued for various actions which extend beyond routine social interactions

---

3 This is reminiscent of Rutherford's argument, cited earlier, according to which the people of Biak incorporate rather than introject the evaluative point of view of foreign others, refusing a stable intersubjective relationship with them.

and reach the same level of general significance as the forces of the external universe. In this sense, *inya* seem to refer to different potentials of achieving fame. Fame is an important element of value, but in order to be realized as value it has to be embodied and manifested in a visible form.

This theme is present in the myth about the two brothers who make their conquering intentions known by shooting arrows, even as their fate is evident from the flowers they leave behind. The problem of visibility arises when the first Bunga is eaten by the ogre and loses the ability to signify his own fame, but his life is rescued by the actions of his younger brother through which society asserts its ability to produce life. It is worth noting that this younger brother exits in the end to found his own kingdom. The origin and actions of the two brothers are parallel to the extent that they can be considered as one person; all differentiations of action and awareness are suspended until the point at which the marriage of the first Bunga separates him from the second Bunga. Marriage thus emerges as the symbol that obviates their self-destructive mode of action.

Horizons of narration

The importance of visibility for Keiese constructs of value implies a culturally specific concern with horizons. In the Maussian argument followed by Barraud's ethnography, the cosmological perspectives of the external world are determined by the forms in which society represents itself and the practices that constitute it as social reality. From this point of view, the horizon is something determined by the physical, historical and social environment, such as the cape and mountain through which the myths discussed in this article anchor their plot to social experience.

I began this article by asking what organizes the different experiential perspectives of people living in the same place. One answer is that different ways of narrating myths are organized by the local cultural landscape in which the chronotopic positions of the myths can immediately be recognized (Siikala and Siikala 2005: 127–128). This does not mean that the meaning of myths derives from their social context. As Jukka Siikala points out, the nightly sessions of storytelling embrace Cook Islands people in another kind of universe (Siikala 1991: 1). Place names are altered to indicate a horizon towards the past. We may ask what defines the factuality of this horizon, in the same sense as mountains and capes are social facts. Citing Paul Ricoeur's argument in which a narrative sense of duration is a basic feature of human existence, Jukka Siikala points out that its effects on historical awareness rely on temporal continuity at different levels: the internal continuity of the narrative plot, the continuity of tradition in which the narratives belong, and finally, the continuity of external things that narratives tell about (1991: 4–5).

Tum, the generic name for Keiese origin myths, suggests an unfolding of a differentiated universe from a single source, often through the hero's movement through space which is differentiated into named places and their distinguishing features. The myths discussed in this article are emphatic on the names of ancestors, places and valuable objects. Circulating and passing on such names is an important part of the continuity of tradition. The sense in which society seeks to "eat" names and encompass the things signified by them produces a tension with the representation of history as interconnected events of larger scale. In an analysis of the socio-cosmic dualism of Central Maluku, another case in which society implicitly recognizes the outside world as an element of its own structure, Valerio Valeri (1989: 137) suggests that dual order of this particular type is often found in societies located at the periphery of centralized political systems. As Leonard Andaya (1993: 25) puts it, Maluku communities are "neither political states nor stateless societies:" instead of simply resisting integration into larger political frameworks they incorporate these orders in their own differentiating schemes.

Incorporating the outside world in society as an element of its hierarchical order makes it into a party of cosmological exchange. Kei society makes this possible by representing a diversity of cosmic and natural forces as one form of society itself in embodied, symbolic forms. This, however, presupposes differentiated knowledge of what exists in the outside world. One is reminded of Claude Lévi-Strauss's argument which questions such a totalizing view of knowledge. Without the ability to deal with the entire universe as signifying relations, human thought is forced to apprehend the external world through symbolism as a signifying totality (Lévi-Strauss 1987: 60). Lévi-Strauss's point of view seems to match particularly well with the worldview of Pacific societies in which the external world is a cosmological horizon, a source of the origins of society as well as new, potentially transforming events.

Lévi-Strauss questions the Durkheimian view in which the categories of apprehending nature derive from social forms. But my argument is not that the people of Kei only pay attention to those aspects of their environment onto which they are able to project their social categories. The concern with different types of animals and natural and historical forces in the myth about Terngun's voyage suggests systematic attention to natural phenomena which are "good to think," and through acknowledging the invisible humanity outside society, the Kei Islands ideology is open to historical events as well. The focus of my description of Keiese society in this article, however, has not been on systematic cosmological ideas but on mythical perspectives on the objectification and embodiment of value. The narrative chronotopes of the two myths discussed above bring attention to different aspects of this process. The mountain in the interior of the island is identified with the source of ancestral life, whereas the cape separates the local society from the larger world of trade and political centers. In mythical narratives these horizons also indicate the source of things which are vital for continued social existence: life itself and the signs for valuing it. By referring to different horizons, myths elaborate the ontological theme of visibility and social existence into several local views of this cosmological process and help explain why the people of Kei insist on framing external trade as a predatory relationship to the outside world.

REFERENCES

Andaya, Leonard 1993. Cultural state formation in Eastern Indonesia. In: Anthony Reid (ed.) *Southeast Asia in the Early Modern Era: Trade, Power, and Belief.* Cornell University Press. Pp. 23–41.

Barraud, Cécile 1990. Kei society and the person: an approach through childbirth and funerary rituals. *Ethnos* 55(3–4): 214–231.

Barraud, Cécile, Daniel de Coppet, André Iteanu and Raymond Jamous 1994. *Of Relations and the Dead. Four societies viewed through the angle of their exchanges.* Oxford: Berg Publishers.

Bourdieu, Pierre 1977. *Outline of a Theory of Practice.* Cambridge University Press.

Eijbergen, H.C. 1866. Verslag eener reis naar de Aroe- en Key- Eilanden in de maand Junij 1862. *Tijdschrift voor Taal-, Land- en Volkenkunde* 15: 220–272.

Geurtjens, Hein 1921. *Uit een vreemde wereld.* 's Hertogenbosch: Teulings' Uitgevers-Maatschappij.

Heeres, J. E. 1896. Dokumenten betreffende de ontdekkingstochten van Adriaan Doortsman 1645–1646. *Tijdschrift voor de Indische Taal-, Land- en Volkenkunde* VI(2): 246–279; 608–619; 635–662; 689–709.

Kamma, Freerk C. 1982. The incorporation of foreign culture elements and complexes by ritual enclosure among the Biak Numforese. In: P.E. de Josselin de Jong and Eric Schwimmer (eds.) *Symbolic Anthropology in the Netherlands.* The Hague: Martinus Nijhoff. Pp. 43–84.

Kapferer, Bruce 1988. *Legends of People, Myths of State.* Washington D.C.: Smithsonian Institution Press.

Lévi-Strauss, Claude 1987. *Introduction to the Work of Marcel Mauss.* London: Routledge and Kegan Paul.

McKinnon, Susan 1991. *From a Shattered Sun: Hierarchy, Gender and Alliance in the Tanimbar Islands.* Madison: University of Wisconsin Press.

Miller, W.G. 1980. An account of trade patterns in the Banda Sea in 1979, from an unpublished manuscript in the India Office library. *Indonesia Circle* 23: 41–57.

Munn, Nancy 1986. *The Fame of Gawa.* Cambridge University Press.

Platenkamp, Jos 2006. Visibility and objectification in Tobelo ritual. In: Peter Crawford and Metje Postma (eds.) *Reflecting Visual Ethnography – Using the Camera in Anthropological Fieldwork.* Aarhus: Intervention Press and Leiden: CNWS Press. Pp. 78–102.

Rutherford, Danilyn 2003. *Raiding the Land of the Foreigners: The Limits of the Nation.* Princeton University Press.

Sahlins, Marshall 1985. *Islands of History.* Chicago: University of Chicago Press.

Siikala, Jukka 1991. '*Akatokamanāva: Myth, History and Society in the Southern Cook Islands.* Auckland: The Polynesian Society and Finnish Anthropological Society.

Siikala, Anna-Leena and Jukka 2005. *Return to Culture. Oral Tradition and Society in the Southern Cook Islands.* Helsinki: Academia Scientarum Fennica.

Spyer, Patricia 2000. *The Memory of Trade. Modernity's Entanglements on an Eastern Indonesian Island.* Durham: Duke University Press.

Strathern, Marilyn 1988. *The Gender of the Gift.* Berkeley: University of California Press.

Valeri, Valerio 1989. Reciprocal centers: the Siwa-Lima system in the Central Moluccas. In: D. Maybury-Lewis and Uri Almagor (eds.) *The Attraction of Opposites: Thought and Society in the Dualistic Mode*. Ann Arbor: University of Michigan Press. Pp. 117–142.

Wagner, Roy 1977. Analogic kinship: a Daribi example. *American Ethnologist* 4(4): 623–642.

Wagner, Roy 1981. *The Invention of Culture*. Chicago: University of Chicago Press.

Afterword

Cosmological Journeys

Bruce Kapferer

A prolegomenon

Human process is conditioned if not necessarily determined cosmologically. Such cosmology is always in one way or another a human construction, the imaginal creation of human beings in terms of which they objectify and position themselves experientially within their worlds of existence. It is by means of such cosmologies that human beings define and grasp their existential progress, chart their life course. Within cosmology, human beings both comprehend the known and hitherto unknown, putting in place the phenomena of existential encounter. Cosmologies are totalizing, both explicitly and immanently. As in the world religions and in science, they set out the horizons and limits of existence, the space/time coordinates of such existence, and the relations among the phenomena included within the cosmological universe.

Anthropologists have long stressed the importance of their cultural approach, the relativity of action, meaning and understanding. In much anthropology, culture is sometimes used interchangeably with cosmology, recognizing that cosmology must always in some way or another be a cultural construction. But of course, cosmology is at once more and less than the notion of culture in most usages. The idea of cosmology is all-embracing, an implicate order, perhaps less a view (in a Geertzian sense) than an ontological scheme in terms of which human beings come not only to locate themselves in relation to all phenomena and the constantly changing circumstances of life, but also to generate and produce existential relations as well as to incorporate what they may conceive and engage as the new. Cosmologies do not represent the totality of existence so much as virtualize it, project the dimensions of existential realities in which the motion, orientations and process of human beings and other phenomena come to be interrelated and set.

Cosmologies do not merely arrange and order (the etymological connection between the concept of cosmology and cosmetic is often noted), they are also cosmogenic and intrinsically regenerative. They are powerfully so at their horizons, at their limits, or at the points where they, and human being, are most at risk. Cosmologies often most apparent at existential margins are constructions not just for the holding on to reality or steering through it, but establish the terms or orientational frame for the production of reality in its depth or what some anthropologists refer to as culture. The cosmological embraces the cultural and may overarch or contain and enable the integration of considerable cultural difference and variability.

Cosmologies often attain full potency at the conjunctures of ongoing existence, at cultural and existential breaks and interfaces, where perhaps meaning is not yet or is at risk or threat. For example, in a diversity of different historical realities, the edifices and structures of ritual and religion that embed and intensely express the cosmological are situated not only at centers but also frequently at the dimensional borders or margins of existence – at high, low and subterranean points, at sites of danger, confusion, crossover, indeterminacy. Here the cosmological and the mythological, the latter being one concrete if also imaginal manifestation of the former, have an identity, being projections for the (re)generation of meaning as well as expressing the breaks, challenges and risks of existence and facilitating passage across them.

The island worlds of the South Pacific are remarkable as spaces of conjuncture, realities indeed which give particular potency to social and political dynamics of linkage and separation and movement, and which, moreover, often extend conceptually and practically into more expansive fields of action. Malinowski, who arguably gave anthropology its defining fieldwork method, was quick to see this and to make the parallel with the worlds of the Mediterranean and its networks of trade and war and their articulations in grand cosmological mythologies. The anthropologists of Pacific regions have virtually made it a tradition. Sahlins is a contemporary exemplar who, while insisting on the cultural, effectively conceives of the greater import of the cosmological, particularly at the points where ongoing cultural and social realities are challenged and placed at risk. It is little surprise that the essays in this volume dedicated to Jukka Siikala, not only a scholar of the Pacific but also himself a seafarer of no mean skill and familiar with dangers and risks, should address cosmological issues.

Anthropology, cosmology and pacific ethnography

These issues have particular relevance at this particular historical moment not just for anthropology but for a general understanding of human potentials which is a major excitement of the discipline. This is especially so now at a general time of intellectual and scientific exuberance, indeed, a period of creation and shift of cosmological proportion. The certainties of the recent past, themselves embedded and driven in specific cosmological commitments (apparent both in science and religion and their conjunction in the course of western imperial expansion wherein an anthropology of the Pacific as elsewhere saw much of its impetus), are in some retreat, or at least are more aware of their own limits. I make this last statement somewhat hesitantly.

216

This is so, for an anthropology once very alive to difference appears to be on the wane. I refer to that anthropology that stressed exotic worlds at the edge of a cosmopolitan expansion largely driven from centers in Europe and North America. The argument in various quarters of anthropology is that there is no exotic reality that is completely outside the globalized spread of modernity, if this was ever so in the past. As an empirical statement this may well be the case, but in my opinion still requires further verification. It also misses a point that the very idea of the exotic (the strange, the outside) is formed within a particular kind of cosmological attitude as is also the statement that the exotic is no more. These kinds of notions are connected to a cosmological dynamic, one that could be said to describe that of a capitalism that saw its particular, if not unique, origin in European and North American history (see Said on Orientalism and, more recently, Gunder Frank). Such a capitalist cosmology involves the recognition of limits (the exotic) or horizons of expansion that are eventually to be overcome and incorporated. This totalizing process is probably diversely inherent in all cosmologies. Thus the globalization discourse in which a lot of anthropology is immersed these days and which often refuses an outside, or which denies the stress on difference of yesteryear, may be seen as the extension of a particular cosmology of capital. The denial of the exotic is a return from the limit to the center: an announcement of a totalization completed as well as, perhaps paradoxically, an implicit declaration of its particular truth.

I make this point of reservation, furthermore, in the context of a critical discourse in anthropology that seeks to distance itself from what might be phrased as an island anthropology. That is, an anthropology that wrote of discrete socio-cultural worlds and whose ideal sites were often seen to be those of the island worlds of the Pacific (see Metcalf's essay and his opening reference to Firth). But, as I have already intimated, it was many of those early anthropologists of the Pacific who from almost the very beginning – and Malinowski is only one instance – were concerned to demonstrate that the apparently small realities that they explored were enmeshed in wider complexes of socio-economic and mythic relations. Whatever their apparent discreteness or isolation they often were articulated and motivated in their practices within larger more encompassing projections that denied isolation. In fact, in many ways the anthropology of islands confounded an island anthropology that may have arisen in some quarters of the discipline and certainly became imbued as a stereotype of anthropological practice.

The essays here don't represent a return to the past, rather an extension from it and in many instances new directions through a concern with what I see to be largely cosmological issues. An attention to cosmology involves an entrance within the orientational parameters according to which not only social relations are articulated but specific kinds of knowledge are constructed. It is through cosmology that the factualities of existence are composed (as well as its practicalities achieved) and gain their truth value, which as Damon shows, may open up possibilities that other cosmologies, even the most scientific, may shut out.

217

Wagner develops an intriguing argument in which he wonderfully captures the mediating and conjunctural role of an anthropologist who is able to bring the different potentialities of understanding that may be located in particular cosmological orientations into mutually informing juxtaposition. He does so without subordinating the truth values of one to those of the other, but works an ingenious interplay of suggestion which releases the potentials of larger understanding in each. Rather than counter-positioning cosmological orientations, as if they were different ways of doing similar things, he places them in parallel although they occasionally touch or cross into each other through the mediating role of those positioned within them. Thus different cosmological attitudes maintain their particular authenticity and develop their particular potential. Wagner does not reduce the one to the terms of the other which is often unavoidably the approach of much anthropological comparison or relativizing. Wagner's characters – individual Daribi, the anthropologist, missionaries, colonial officers – interact but are not necessarily oriented along the same "lines of flight." There is no necessary transformation or transformational repetition, as might be pursued in an analysis of a Sahlins kind, but a mutual participation that elaborates its difference and achieves its specific enabling because of the difference.

Wagner's approach indicates a movement away from those approaches to cosmology (and culture) that are univocal and which stress an over-determining systemic coherency. The comparative sweep of Harri Siikala's argument (is there a kind of Polynesian continuity of the father through the son here?) avoids, it seems to me, the type of homogeneous comparison/ contrast common in some of the anthropological comparativist theorizing of yesteryear. The articles here allow for different effects of, and positionings within, particular cosmological/ontological orientations and, as in Kaartinen's discussion, an attention to what can be regarded as their situational invocation which selects for one kind of orientation within cosmology over another.

The emphasis is on the human constitution of reality within cosmology. No doubt cosmological orientations are influenced by factors that might be conceived as external to them – as in the forest worlds of Papua New Guinea, or the jungle dwellers of Borneo. But ecological or environmental contexts are sites of potential, rather than determination. Cosmologies realize certain of these potentials, create others, and also close off potentials. The Daribi living in dense forest contexts have cosmological orientations that do not extend towards the shifting limits of horizons. They do not constrain themselves within a cosmological order that is necessarily premised on the notion of horizon or its limit, nor do they operate necessarily a cosmological dynamic of exclusion or exoticization. It appears they are not so much oriented to the heavens as a means for structuring their life course, as Polynesians and many other human populations, whereby the motion or stasis of points in the heavens provide key time/space reference. The Daribi, like some other New Guinea peoples, are directed in their cosmological orientations towards inner, introspective or subterranean worlds – to spaces underneath rather than above.

Here I note that cosmologies are as much engaged in the charting of inner space as they are in that of external realities, which is the stress in much Pacific ethnography whose narratives are so much about travel and voyaging. Hegel's "night of the world" is a cosmological understanding of collapse. The dreadful shapes and nightmarish spectres of destruction, those demonic forms that crowd the imagination of human beings as they lose conscious grasp of their worlds, are the transmogrification of the cosmological points whereby human beings sustain and steer themselves through their shifting existential horizons. These are the kinds of intrapersonal realities that shamans enter, as Sather describes for the Iban, and who, as helmsmen of sorts, steer a course through. In such ritual work, shamans, and other kinds of ritualists, reestablish orientation in a restored cosmology that enable erstwhile victims of cosmological collapse to regain their course in their life-world. The adventures of Jason and his Argonauts or the cosmological spin of the Odyssey, key references at the start of the ethnography of the Pacific, are as much about interiority as they are about exteriority. The organization and selection of the essays in this volume realize this fact excellently.

* * *

I see this book as a major discourse in an anthropology directed to issues in cosmology. As I implied at the start, cosmology is not the same as culture, although cosmologies as human construction are inescapably cultural. But the idea of culture is relatively static, often indicating a symbolic order of codified value, a structure of representations. There is an essential, normative feel to the concept. Cosmology in the approach expressed here is a mode of articulation into ongoing, ever-changing realities, more a scheme for constructing in spaces that are as yet unfilled, still outside or at the edges of meaning. Cosmology in my usage here is something akin to the phenomenological concept of apperception or appresentation, a kind of framework which aids the filling out of information and understanding, that guides the filling out of form and assists the creative movement in worlds that otherwise defy certainties. Cosmology perhaps more than culture, at least in the usages of this concept by anthropologists, is a dynamic structure of articulation and construction.

The anthropology that developed in ethnographic contexts of the island Pacific already had immanent within it potentialities that defied many of the stereotypes of anthropology. The essays in this volume continue in the spirit of that anthropology that went before, but also often open out in radical new directions. Jukka Siikala has constantly championed the importance of an anthropology that cleaves to the depth of understanding achieved and the more general insights that can emerge from an attention to the authority of those in the ethnographic realities that anthropologists encounter on their voyages. This volume is indeed a tribute to Jukka and the significance of his work.

Jukka Siikala's Academic career

Most of us know Jukka Siikala for his ethnography of Pacific societies and his broad interest in diverse theoretical topics in anthropology. He played a central role in reviving the Finnish tradition of the discipline after its relative oblivion in the decades that followed World War II. The revival of anthropology in Finland began with the appointment of an associate professor in social anthropology at the University of Helsinki in 1971 and the founding of the Finnish Anthropological Society in 1975. In 1986 cultural anthropology became a separate discipline with a full professor in the faculty of humanities. During the years that followed, teachers and students grouped around the two chairs were placed in separate faculties and departments at the University of Helsinki. Jukka was instrumental in organizing the cooperation between these groups which developed into a joint teaching program and ultimately led into the combination of social and cultural anthropology under one department in the beginning of 2004.

The scholars who oversaw the rebirth of the discipline were necessarily trained in other, related fields. Jukka's undergraduate studies took place in three faculties, those of Theology, Arts and Social Sciences at the University of Helsinki. The theological background can still be detected by his ease with philosophical issues and concepts; in addition, it provided the first context for his ethnographic interest in Polynesia, evident in his 1976 M.A. thesis about the Mamaia cult of Polynesia. Two years later, the publication of Jukka's Licentiate thesis (in Finnish) on "Cultural Specificity as Metaphysics" marked his move towards a broader, anthropological agenda. In the spring of 1982 Jukka received his Ph.D. in Turku University, where he worked as a research fellow of the Finnish Academy. His closest teacher was Aarne Koskinen, an internationally known specialist on Polynesia who held a professorship of ethnology at Helsinki until his death in late 1982.

Jukka's scholarly and teaching careers are almost impossible to separate. In 1976 he was appointed lecturer of cultural anthropology at the University of Joensuu, an Eastern Finnish town. During his doctoral work he became involved in international discussions with scholars of the Pacific and visited the School of Oriental and Asian Studies in London. The Festschrift in honor of Aarne Koskinen, edited by Jukka and published in the same year as his dissertation, suggests the extent of his scholarly contacts which were later expanded by research visits to the centers of Pacific scholarship in Australia, New Zealand, and the U.S.A.

In 1982, the year Jukka received his doctorate, he began teaching at the University of Helsinki as junior lecturer of social anthropology. At this point, advanced sociology students were allowed to choose anthropology as their specialization. The tenured staff responsible for supervision and class offerings was limited to one associate professor and an assisting junior lecturer. Increasing numbers of students were attracted to anthropology by its international orientation, and Jukka's sustained interest and supervision encouraged several of the incoming group to continue their studies to the doctoral level. Students mentored by Jukka did not necessarily pursue ethnographic interests or theoretical agendas similar to his own. Jukka's influence on students was substantial, however, in encouraging and helping them to do fieldwork, attend conferences, and visit or study at anthropology departments abroad. Upon his appointment as associate professor in 1987 Jukka was well aware of Finnish anthropology's potential to expand. The interest in studying the problems of the Third World which animated much of the earlier interest in anthropology was transforming into an awareness about the global system and the need to understand its structuring cultural differences. This intellectual shift is evident in Jukka's own work (for instance, the research project called "Culture and the World System in the Third World") as well as in the range of dissertation topics he has advised and sponsored during his two decades as professor. They include historical and archival studies as well as fieldwork-based anthropology and focus on other continents as well as Europe and Finland. In addition to the personal choices of the students, this ethnographic coverage speaks about Jukka's holistic view of anthropology. The discipline in his view is neither about exotic area studies or cultural and ethnic minorities: it lives or dies with its comparative ethnographic agenda.

Jukka has been absent from Finland for several long periods – during his fieldwork in the Cooks in 1983–1984, and later in 1980s and 1990s. Furthermore, he was a research fellow in Australia and the United States but continued to supervise students from a distance. In 2001 his teaching and academic leadership earned him the Eino Kaila prize (named after a leading Finnish scholar in philosophy in the inter-war years) awarded by the University of Helsinki. In 2004, the year in which social and cultural anthropology at Helsinki were reorganized as one discipline, Jukka was promoted to a full professor.

Jukka's international orientation distinguishes the whole community of anthropologists he has helped build. One of his early initiatives was the series of Edvard Westermarck Memorial Lectures, hosted in turn by the Finnish Anthropological Society and the Edvard Westermarck Society every year since 1983. In 1990-1996 he was president of the Finnish Anthropological Society, and editor-in-chief of its journal *Suomen Antropologi* in 1997–1999.

In addition to the Finnish academic scene, Jukka has been involved in numerous research projects, publication activities and scientific societies abroad. He has taken part in cooperative research organized by the Association of Social Anthropology in Oceania and organized the conference of the European Society for Oceanists in 1996. He participated as a Polynesian specialist in the Comparative Austronesian Project organized by the Research School of Pacific Studies at the Australian National University which continued from 1989–1996. He has also worked at the University of Virginia as a visiting fellow in 1996–1997. He has belonged to the editorial board of several international journals, including *Ethnos*, *Anthropological Theory*, and *Local and Global*.

Jukka's own research has focused on the Pacific islands, but his ethnographic work has consistently engaged broader comparative and theoretical issues. His interest in structural history, which evolved from the focus of his early work on the effects of missionary and colonial contact on indigenous societies, led him to engage in debates on structural history in the 1980s. In early 1987 he arranged a conference, "Culture and History in the Pacific," which brought a number of foremost anthropologists of Oceania to Helsinki. The question of how politics and history are informed by mythology was also the focus of *'Akatokamanâva*, his first monograph based on his Cook Islands fieldwork.

Another theoretical argument in Jukka's work arose from his observations of the skewed demographic constitution of Polynesian island societies and from his fieldwork among Cook Island migrants in New Zealand. In the "Departures" project, Jukka developed these observations into the claim that, in spite of their physical separation in different locations, islanders still constitute a holistic society which "distributes its people" in characteristic ways. Jukka's refusal to treat migrations and diasporas as purely empirical phenomena is thus part of his defense of a holistic methodological approach – one that has also provided inspiration for this book.

One sustained theoretical theme in Jukka's writing has been a concern with culture and textuality. The hand-written family books he documented in the Southern Cooks are an obvious outcome of missionary influence, but they are also evidence of a people's interest in objectifying certain cultural discourses and representing them as tradition. Jukka's ethnographic attention to such practices – as, for example, narrating stories, reciting genealogical information, writing things down, and inscribing the past in architectural objects and the landscape – is motivated by his reading of Paul Ricoeur, particularly Ricoeur's view of texts as sites of "surplus" meaning. In his recent writings he also engages the perspectives offered by linguistic anthropology on the semiotic processes which enable culture to be instantiated and reproduced. These themes are most fully developed in *Return to Culture*, a monograph co-written with Anna-Leena Siikala, which draws upon their joint Cook Islands fieldwork.

In some of his latest publications Jukka is concerned with tensions and interactions between indigenous hierarchies, state institutions and the global system. In "Chiefs and Impossible States," an article published in 2001, he questions Western models of political development which characterize a large number of the world's polities as "failed states" and disregard significant forms of political agency which are enabled by hierarchical social settings.

While Jukka's work shows sustained commitment to the ethnographic and comparative interests that define the anthropological project, he has been able to draw from interactions with people working in a number of related fields – folklore studies, comparative religion, sociology, political science, to name but a few. Another characteristic, perhaps most dear to Jukka's fellow scholars, is his openness to serious debate with people of varied backgrounds and points of view. Jukka, happily, is still some years from retirement. He continues to write and lecture and with the hope, and, indeed, confidence, that such debates will continue, we dedicate this book to him.

Jukka Siikala's Publications

MONOGRAPHS

2005, with Anna Leena Siikala. *Return to Culture: Oral Tradition and Society in the Southern Cook Islands.* FF Communications 287. Helsinki: Finnish Academy of Sciences.

1991. *'Akatokamanâva: Myth, History and Society in the Southern Cook Islands.* Auckland: Polynesian Society, in association with the Finnish Anthropological Society.

1982. *Cult and Conflict in Tropical Polynesia: A Study of Traditional Religion, Christianity and Nativistic Movements.* FF Communications 233. Helsinki: Finnish Academy of Sciences. Doctoral dissertation, University of Turku.

1978. *Kulttuurispesifisyys metafysiikkana. Eräiden antropologisten teorioiden metafyysisyydestä ja sen perusteista* (Cultural Specificity as Metaphysics. About the Metaphysicality of Certain Anthropological Theories and its Foundations). Karelia Research Institute Publication 31. Joensuu: Joensuun korkeakoulu.

EDITED WORKS

2001 *Departures: How Societies Distribute their People.* TAFAS 46. Helsinki: Finnish Anthropological Society. Based on the papers given in the symposium on "Departures" at the University of Helsinki in June 1997.

1998, with Ulla Vuorela and Tapio Nisula. *Developing Anthropological Ideas: The Edvard Westermarck Memorial Lectures 1983–1997.* TAFAS 41. Helsinki: Finnish Anthropological Society.

1990 *Culture and History in the Pacific.* TAFAS 27. Helsinki: Finnish Anthropological Society. Based on the papers given in the symposium "Culture and History in the Pacific" in Helsinki, January 1987.

1982 *Oceanic Studies. Essays in Honor of Aarne A. Koskinen.* TAFAS 11. Helsinki: Finnish Anthropological Society.

ARTICLES

2007. Ethnography and the denial of difference. In: Minna Ruckenstein and Marie-Louise Karttunen (eds.) *On Foreign Ground. Moving between Countries and Categories*. Studia Fennica Anthropologica 1. Helsinki: Finnish Literature Society. Pp. 19–27.

2006. The ethnography of Finland. *Annual Review of Anthropology* 35: 153–170.

2006. Lahjan henki. *Duodecim* 122(23): 2825–2830.

2005. Theories and ideologies in anthropology. In: Bruce Kapferer (ed.) *The Retreat of the Social. The Rise and Fall of Reductionism*. New York: Berghahn Books. Pp. 79–88.

2005. Argumentteja auditoinnista (Arguments about auditing). *Tiede & Edistys* 30(1): 27–37.

2004. The politics of voice in the pacific. In: Michael E. Harkin (ed.) *Reassessing Revitalization Movements: Perspectives from North America and the Pacific Islands*. Lincoln: University of Nebraska Press. Pp. 88–103.

2004. Theories and ideologies in anthropology. *Social Analysis* 48(3): 199–204.

2003. "God spoke different things:" Oral tradition and the interpretive community. In: Lotte Tarkka (ed.) *Dynamics of Tradition: Perspectives on Oral Poetry and Folk Belief. Essays in Honor of Anna-Leena Siikala on her 60th birthday 1st January 2003*. Studia Fennica Folkloristica 13. Helsinki: Suomalaisen Kirjallisuuden Seura. Pp. 21–34.

2001. Chiefs and impossible states. *Communal/Plural: Journal of Transnational and Crosscultural Studies* 9(1): 81–94.

2001. Introduction: Where have all the people gone? In: Jukka Siikala (ed.) *Departures: How Societies Distribute their People*. TAFAS 46. Helsinki: Finnish Anthropological Society. Pp. 1–6.

2001. Tilling the soil and sailing the seas. Cadastral maps and anthropological interpretations. In: Jukka Siikala (ed.) Departures: How Societies Distribute their People. TAFAS 46. Helsinki: Finnish Anthropological Society. Pp. 22–45.

2000. This is my beautiful line of chiefs. Social life and how it is talked about. *Suomen Antropologi* (Journal of the Finnish Anthropological Society) 25(1): 15–28.

1999. Writings between cultures. In: Jopi Nyman and John A. Stotesbury (eds.) *Postcolonialism and Cultural Resistance*. Studia Carelica Humanistica 14. Joensuu: Humanistic Faculty of the Joensuu University. Pp. 48–57.

1997. Hierarkia, luokat ja moderni Cookin Saarten valtio (Hierarchy, classes and the modern Cook Islands state). *Suomen Antropologi* (Journal of the Finnish Anthropological Society) 22(3): 4–16.

1997. Kulttuurin käsite ja etnografian ongelma (The culture concept and the problem of ethnography). In: Anna-Maria Viljanen and Minna Lahti (eds.) *Kaukaa haettua: kirjoituksia antropologisesta kenttätyöstä*. A Festschrift for professor Matti Sarmela on his 60th birthday. Helsinki: Finnish Anthropological Society. Pp. 20–34.

1996. The elder and the younger: Foreign and autochthonous origin and hierarchy in the Cook Islands. In: James J. Fox and Clifford Sather (eds.) *Origins, Ancestry and Alliance: Explorations in Austronesian Ethnography*. Canberra: Australian National University. Pp. 41–54.

1996. A comment on Marshall Sahlins's article "The Sadness of Sweetness: The Native Anthropology of Western Cosmology." *Current Anthropology* 37(3): 420–421.

1994. Kulttuuri, emansipaatio, autonomia (Culture, emancipation, autonomy). *Synteesi* (a publication of the Society for Art Education Research and the Department of Art and Culture Studies, University of Jyväskylä) 13(4): 11–20, 71.

1991. Edvard Westermarck etnografina: vertailevan menetelmän traditio (Edvard Westermarck as ethnographer: The tradition of the comparative method). *Suomen Antropologi* (Journal of the Finnish Anthropological Society) 16(2): 25–31.

1991. Vanhempi ja nuorempi – vieras ja paikallinen. Alkuperä ja hierarkia Cookin saarilla (The elder and the younger – foreign and autochthonous. Origin and hierarchy in the Cook Islands). *Suomen Antropologi* (Journal of the Finnish Anthropological Society) 16(1): 34–44.

1990. Chiefs, gender and hierarchy in Ngâpūtoru. Jukka Siikala (ed.) *Culture and History in the Pacific*. Helsinki: Finnish Anthropological Society. Pp. 107–124.

1990. Introduction. Jukka Siikala (ed.) *Culture and History in the Pacific*. Helsinki: Finnish Anthropological Society. Pp. 5–8.

1989. Names, myths and society. In: Anna-Leena Siikala (ed.) *Studies in Oral Narrative*. Studia Fennica 33. Helsinki: Finnish Literature Society. Pp. 221–225.

1989. Aika, historia ja myytti antropologian näkökulmasta (Time, history and myth from the anthropological perspective). Pirkko Heiskanen (ed.) *Aika ja sen ankaruus*. Helsinki: Gaudeamus. Pp. 217–228.

1988. Riippumattomuus, dekolonialismi ja kulttuuri (Independence, decolonization and culture). In: Lassi Heininen and Jyrki Käkönen (eds.) *Tyynimeri – tyyntä vai myrskyä?* Helsinki: Suomen Rauhanpuolustajat. Pp. 18–36.

1987. Aika, kertomus, vaikutus: kerronnallistettu historia ja kertomuksen teho (Time, narrative, effect: narrativized history and the effect of narrative). *Sosiologia* (Journal of the Westermarck Society) 24(4): 273–281, 330–331.

1986. Linjasukukäsitteen ongelmallisuus (The problematic nature of the concept of direct kinship). *Suomen Antropologi* (Journal of the Finnish Anthropological Society) 11(2): 50–55.

1986. Mykkä ihminen ja karvaton majava: rakenteiden ja eletyn elämän suhteesta (Mute men and hairless beavers: on the relationship between structure and experience). *Sosiologia* (Journal of the Westermarck Society) 23(2): 127–133, 185–186.

1985. Nimet, myytit ja yhteiskunta (Names, myths and society). *Tiede & Edistys* 10(2): 132–136.

1983. Culture and nature. The social organisation of the mediation. In: Jukka Siikala (ed.) *Oceanic Studies. Essays in Honour of Aarne A. Koskinen.* Helsinki: Finnish Anthropological Society. Pp. 79–89.

1983. Luonto ja sen voimat varhaiskantaisissa kulttuureissa (Nature and its forces in early cultures). In: Auvo Kostiainen (ed.) *Ihminen ja luonto.* Historian perintö 9. Turku: Turun yliopiston historian laitos. Pp. 26–38.

1983. Ajan hukasta ajan tajuun. Antropologia ja historia kolonialismin tutkimuksessa (From the waste of time to awareness of time. Anthropology and history in the study of colonialism). In: Rauno Endén (ed.) *Historian päivät 6–7.11. 1982.* Helsinki: Finnish Historical Society. Pp. 119–132.

1982. Nainen, piano ja pöytähopeat: näkökulmia kolonialistisen yhteisön syntyyn Tyynellämerellä (Lady, piano and silverware: Perspectives on the emergence of a colonial community in the Pacific). *Suomen Antropologi* (Journal of the Finnish Anthropological Society) 7(2): 48–59.

1979. The Cargo Proper in Cargo Cults. *Temenos* 15: 68–80.

1979. Mitä rahdissa on palvomista (Why Cargo?) *Suomen Antropologi* (Journal of the Finnish Anthropological Society) 4(3): 124–134.

1978. Mamaia – uskonnollinen liike yhteiskunnallisten ristiriitojen kentässä (Mamaia – a religious movement in a field of social contradictions.) *Suomen Antropologi* (Journal of the Finnish Anthropological Society) 3(1): 23–33.

REVIEWS

2005. A review of Ron Crocombe and Marjorie Tua'inekore (eds.): Akono'anga Maori: Cook Islands Culture. *The Contemporary Pacific* 17(1): 248–250.

2005. Yliopistopolitiikasta yliopistojen hallintaan (From academic politics to the governance of universities). A review of Heikki Patomäki: Yliopisto Oyj. Tulosjohtamisen ongelmat – ja vaihtoehto. *Tiede & Edistys* 30(3): 262–264.

2001. A review of Geoffrey M. White and Lamont Lindstrom (eds.): Chiefs Today: Traditional Pacific Leadership and the Postcolonial State. *Journal of Intercultural Studies* 22(1): 100–101.

1999. A review of Anne Salmond: Between Worlds: Early Exchanges between Maori and Europeans 1773–1815. *The Australian Journal of Anthropology* 10(3): 393–395.

1998 Balanced insights into early exchanges. A review of Anne Salmond: Between Worlds. Early Exchanges between Maori and Europeans 1773–1815. *Suomen Antropologi* (Journal of the Finnish Anthropological Society) 23(2): 54–56.

1994. A review of Kirsten Hastrup (ed.) Other Histories. *Man, N.S.* 29(4): 1015–1016.

1994. Portugalilaiset laivoissaan (The Portuguese in their ships). A review of Ilkka Ruohonen: Purjeet kohti Guineaa: Lusitaaninen löytöretkikulttuuri. *Suomen Antropologi* (Journal of the Finnish Anthropological Society) 19(1): 62–64.

1994. Aika aikaa kutakin, sanoi pässi kun päätä leikattiin. Mihin korkeakoululaitoksen leikkaukset olisi kohdennettava? *Kanava* 21(3): 149–152.

1991. A review of Philip R. DeVita: The Humbled Anthropologist. Tales from the Pacific. *American Anthropologist* 93(1): 225.

1991. A review of Alan Howard and Robert Borofsky (eds.) Developments in Polynesian Ethnology. *Ethnos* 56(1–2): 117–118.

1986. Uskontoelämän alkeismuodot uudelleen (Rethinking the Elementary Forms Of Religious Life). A review of Valerio Valeri: Kingship and Sacrifice: Ritual and Society in Ancient Hawaii. *Sosiologia* (Journal of the Westermarck Society) 23(4): 353–354.

1985. A review of K. R. Howe: Where the Waves Fall. *Journal of the Polynesian Society* 94(3): 293–295.

1983. Kalendaaririiteistä keskikaljaan (From calendric rituals to medium strength beer). A review of Matti Virtanen: Änkyrä, tuiske, huppeli. *Sosiologia* (Journal of the Westermarck Society) 20(4): 340–341.

1982. Heerosten aika (The heroic age). A review of Anita Kelles-Viitanen (ed.) Suomalaisen antropologian uranuurtajia. *Sosiologia* (Journal of the Westermarck Society) 19(4): 304–305.

EDITORIALS, NEWS ARTICLES AND COMMENTARY

2007. Nomads and global governance: An editorial comment. *Suomen Antropologi* (Journal of the Finnish Anthropological Society) 32(3–4): 3–5.

2001. Yliopistoista on tulossa opintokerhoja (Universities are becoming study circles). Op-ed. in *Helsingin Sanomat*, 27th March 2001.

2000. Matti Sarmela retires. *Suomen Antropologi* (Journal of the Finnish Anthropological Society) 25(2): 89–90.

1999. Ajassa edestakaisin (Back and forth in time). *Yhdestoista hetki: ajasta kiinni.* Helsinki: Ulkomaisen taiteen museon julkaisuja 13. Helsinki: Sinebrychoff.

1998. Missä ollaan, mihin mennään: Amerikan antropologipäivät 1997 (A news article about the annual meeting of the American Anthropological Association 1997). *Suomen Antropologi* (Journal of the Finnish Anthropological Society) 23(1): 77–79.

1997. Antropologiat ja maailmat (Anthropologies and worlds). *Suomen Antropologi* (Journal of the Finnish Anthropological Society) 22(3): 3.

1993. Kulttuurien tutkimus suomalaisessa yliopistolaitoksessa (The study of cultures in the Finnish university system). *Tiede & Edistys* 18(2): 97–102, 193.

1992. Eurooppa maailmanyhteisössä (Europe in the global community). In: Mikko Telaranta (ed.) *Eurooppa edessämme.* Helsinki: Opintotoiminnan keskusliitto. Pp. 101–111.

1991. Kulttuuri ja talous: sisäistetty vastakkaisuus (Culture and economy: an internalized opposition). *Suomen Antropologi* (Journal of the Finnish Anthropological Society) 16(1): 3–4.

1984. Häpäisty heeros kadotetussa paratiisissa (Disgraced demigod in a lost paradise. A comment on the public reactions to the Mead/Freeman controversy in Finland). *Suomen Antropologi* (Journal of the Finnish Anthropological Society) 9(4): 178–179.

1983. Tui Finilani: Aarne A. Koskinen 7.4. 1915–2.12. 1982. Obituary. *Suomen Antropologi* (Journal of the Finnish Anthropological Society) 8(1): 39–41.

1983. Aarne A. Koskinen (1915–1982). Obituary. *Temenos* 19: 147–149.

1982. Tui Finilani, Aarne A. Koskinen. Introduction and selected bibliography. In: Jukka Siikala (ed.) *Oceanic Studies. Essays in Honour of Aarne A. Koskinen.* Helsinki: Finnish Anthropological Society. Pp. 5–11.

1982. Kansa ja herrat: välittymätön oppositio (People and gentlemen: an unmediated opposition). *Sosiologia* (Journal of the Westermarck Society) 19(1): 56–57.

Information about the Authors

Petra Autio is a Ph.D. candidate in social and cultural anthropology at the University of Helsinki, supervised by Jukka Siikala. She has worked with Siikala as a student since 1996 and done fieldwork for her Ph.D. in Kiribati, Central Pacific. Her forthcoming dissertation discusses forms of social differentiation and "undifferentiation" in the contexts of the meeting-house and dancing in a southern Kiribati community. Her previous study, which resulted in her master's and licentiate theses, was based on a shorter period of fieldwork among Palauan migrants on Guam, and focused on the migrants' conception and practices of "custom."

Frederick H. Damon (Princeton Ph.D, 1978) is Professor of Anthropology at the University of Virginia where he has been teaching and organizing research since 1976. Since 1973 he has conducted more than 40 months of research in the Kula Ring of Milne Bay Province, Papua New Guinea. Initial interests focused on exchange and production questions; since 1991 he has researched environmental issues in general and ethnobotany in particular. He is currently organizing research in East Asia at a point on the dividing line between the East Asian and Austronesian worlds, designed as a comparison with and contrast to his work in the Kula Ring.

James J. Fox was educated at Harvard (AB '62) and Oxford (B.Litt. '65, D.Phil. '68) and has been based at the Australian National University since 1975. He is a former Director of the Research School of Pacific and Asian Studies and currently an ANU Distinguished Professor. He has taught at various universities in the United States: Harvard, Cornell, Duke and Chicago and at various European Universities: Leiden, Bielefeld, Frankfurt and the École des Hautes Études en Sciences Sociales. His primary area of interest is Indonesia, with special attention to Java and eastern Indonesia, as well as East Timor. He began fieldwork on the island of Roti in eastern Indonesia in 1965 and has continued to visit the island since then, most recently in 2006.

Antony Hooper is Emeritus Professor of Social Anthropology at the University of Auckland. He has an M.A. from Auckland and a Ph.D. from Harvard, based on fieldwork in the Iles-sous-le-vent, French Polynesia.

230

After teaching at Brown University he moved back to Auckland for 24 years, specializing in research on Island Polynesia, and, more particularly, Tokelau. He then spent three years as a Research Fellow at the Pacific Islands Development Program at the East-West Center in Honolulu before becoming an independent consultant in Sydney, where he worked on development issues in Samoa and Tokelau for the World Bank, UNDP, ILO and UNESCO. He now lives in Wellington, New Zealand. Among his publications are *Why Tikopia has Four Clans* (RAI, 1981); *Tokelau: a Historical Ethnography* (Hawaii, 1986, jointly with J. Huntsman); and various edited or jointly edited volumes including *Transformations of Polynesian Culture* (Polynesian Society, 1985); and *Culture and Sustainable Development in the Pacific* (Canberra, 2000).

Judith Huntsman retired as Associate Professor of Social Anthropology at the University of Auckland in 2001 and thereafter has been an Honorary Professorial Research Fellow. Her 40 years of research among Tokelau people in their home atolls and in New Zealand has resulted in two major works: *Tokelau: A Historical Ethnography* (1996) co-authored with Antony Hooper, and *The Future of Tokelau: Decolonising Agendas 1975 to 2006* (2007), both published by Auckland University Press, as well as numerous contributions to journals and edited volumes. For many years, most recently from 1997 to the present, she has been the Polynesian Society's Honorary Editor, responsible for the quarterly *Journal of the Polynesian Society* as well as the Society's other publications, most recently *Kimihia te mea ngaro: Seek that which is lost* by the late Bruce Biggs and a new edition of the classic collection of Maori *waiata* in four volumes entitled *Nga Moteatea: The Songs*.

Timo Kaartinen is Lecturer of Cultural Anthropology at the University of Helsinki where he began his academic career as Jukka Siikala's student. His Ph.D. dissertation, accepted at the University of Chicago in 2001, was based on fieldwork in the Indonesian islands of Maluku and focused on different forms of ritual and narrative temporality. He has also published articles about sociolinguistics, state-society relations, nationalism and the theory of ritual, and his recent fieldwork is concerned with linguistic diversity and local responses to political transition in Kalimantan. From 2001 until 2007 he was president of the Finnish Anthropological Society. At present he edits the monograph series *Studia Anthropologica Fennica* published by the Finnish Literature Society.

Bruce Kapferer is Professor of Anthropology at the University of Bergen and honorary professor at the University College of London. His Ph.D. work at the University of Manchester was focused on social and political processes in Zambia, and his subsequent fieldwork has covered a number of sites in Southern Africa, South Asia, and Australia. In his more recent work he has studied nationalism from a comparative view and developed an argument about ritual and political practices as inherently connected by practices of power. His current research deals with the shifting structure and mythology of the state and the production of ethnic and political violence. Presently he is the general editor of *Critical Interventions*, a book series focusing on social analysis, and co-editor of the journal *Anthropological Theory*.

Peter Metcalf is Professor of Anthropology at the University of Virginia. He has conducted research in Sarawak, Malaysian Borneo, since the mid-1970s, and written three ethnographies and numerous articles about the region. His latest book is: *They Lie, We Lie: Getting on With Anthropology* (Routledge, 2003), a defense of ethnographic techniques against their post-modern critics.

Joel Robbins is Professor of Anthropology and Chair of the Anthropology Department at the University of California, San Diego. His research has been carried out primarily in Melanesia and has focused on issues of Christianity and cultural change. He is the author of *Becoming Sinners: Christianity and Moral Torment in a Papua New Guinea Society* (University of California Press) and is the co-editor of several volumes focused on cultural change in the Pacific, including *The Making of Global and Local Modernities in Melanesia: Humiliation, Transformation, and the Nature of Cultural Change* (Ashgate). He is also co-editor of the journal *Anthropological Theory*.

Clifford Sather received his Ph.D. in social anthropology from Harvard University in 1971. His principal publications include *The Bajau Laut: Adaptation, History, and Fate in a Maritime Fishing Society of Southeastern Sabah* (1997, Oxford UP) and *Seeds of Play, Words of Power: an ethnographic study of Iban shamanic chants* (2001, Tun Jugah Foundation & Borneo Research Council). He also co-edited (with James J. Fox) *Origins, Ancestors and Alliance: explorations in Austronesian ethnography* (1996, Australian National University). He taught and held research positions in Southeast Asia (Universiti Sains Malaysia, Universiti Malaysia Sarawak, and National University of Singapore), Australia (Research School of Pacific and Asian Studies, Australian National University), and the United States (Vassar, Reed College, and University of Oregon) and retired in 2005 as Professorial Fellow from the University of Helsinki. He is currently editor of the *Borneo Research Bulletin*, the annual journal of the Borneo Research Council.

Harri Siikala began his studies in anthropology at the University of Helsinki. In 2002 he received a master's degree from The Sainsbury Research Unit for the Arts of Africa, Oceania & the Americas at the University of East Anglia. Currently he is a Ph.D. candidate at the department of anthropology at the University of Virginia. His topics of interest include hierarchy, cosmology, art and material culture, house society theory, and metaphor theory. He was first exposed to anthropology at the age of six when he joined his parents, Jukka and Anna-Leena Siikala, on their first long field trip to the Cook Islands in 1983–1984.

Roy Wagner received his Ph.D. from the University of Chicago in 1966. In addition to extensive fieldwork and ethnography focused on New Guinea, he is known for several influential books and articles on symbolism, ritual, and social theory. These include *The Invention of Culture* (1981, Prentice Hall), *Symbols that Stand for Themselves* (1986, U. of Chicago Press) and *An Anthropology of the Subject* (2001, U. of California Press). At present Roy Wagner is Professor of Anthropology at the University of Virginia.

Acknowledgements

We thank Anna-Leena Siikala for initially broaching the idea of a Festscrift volume to mark Jukka Siikala's sixtieth birthday, Jukka's many friends and colleagues for their personal encouragement throughout its writing, and the contributing authors for their part in making the present volume a reality. We are grateful to Rupert Stasch and Bruce Kapferer for reviewing the entire manuscript and for their insightful and useful suggestions. Professor Kapferer has kindly contributed a concluding appreciation of Jukka's work in the Epilogue. We would also like to thank Päivi Vallisaari and Kati Lampela of the Finnish Literature Society for their advice at various stages of the editorial work. Our greatest debt is to Louise Klemperer Sather who has followed the progress of the book from the beginning and done an immense amount of work in carefully editing the introduction and each chapter for style and presentation, rereading them a number of times in the process. The book would not be the same without her dedication to clarity and her close attention to detail.

Subject Index

Agency 35; human 13, 16, 28–29, 52, 58, 198, 210, 223; ancestral or spiritual 12, 30, 33, 38, 46, 51–52, 55–65, 71–72, 86, 109, 148, 153, 179, 186–188, 200

augury, see divination

Austronesian languages 10, 42, 145, 181; societies 101, 111, 114, 115n, 145, 182, 222

Birth 30–31, 62, 84, 113, 149, 149n, 208

Boats 10, 14, 46, 61, 63, 69–70, 105, 123–126, 128–129, 131–134, 136–143, 138n, 199; canoes 13–14, 37–39, 41–44, 46, 49, 91–197, 101–119, 159, 161, 165, 171, 187–188, 194, 206–207

Borneo 11–12, 38–40, 42–44, 46, 48–49, 62n, 218

canoes, see boats

chaos 14, 106, 117, 126, 133, 143; chaos theory, 14, 131

Christianity 11, 24–28, 32–35, 37, 96, 98, 104, 158, 160, 170, 186n, 201, 209

colonialism 27–28, 32, 39, 78, 109, 113, 158–159, 172, 197, 199, 202, 218

Cook Islands 7, 11, 13, 23, 111–113, 117, 145, 157, 198, 211, 222–223

chiefs 61, 69, 101, 104–119, 166–167, 206; chiefly authority, 175, 182, 199, 207–209; descent 102, 111–113, 205, 208; status 105, 107, 114–115, 117, 151, 158, 201–202; titles 107–108, 110, 118, 199n; power 14, 118, 182

concepts 7–8, 10, 115, 119, 124, 126, 181, 216; conception 25–26, 35, 78, 145, 149, 153; conceptualization 11, 13, 15, 54, 58, 101, 111, 146, 200

conceptual world 7–9

contact 10, 12, 25, 27, 43–44, 73, 109, 198, 200, 222

convention 48, 51n, 54, 132n, 172, 179, 200, 203

cosmology 17, 145, 153, 209, 215; cosmological orientations 10–12, 24, 102, 218–219; origins 110, 114, 212; totality and differentiation 12–14, 26–27, 56, 71, 101, 107, 110–119, 197–198, 200, 205, 207, 209–213, 217

dancing 16, 24, 94, 97n, 151, 159, 177–186, 188–194

Daribi 13, 75–87, 218

death 45, 76, 83, 85, 96, 115, 117, 140; the dead 12, 38, 44–45, 52, 56–58, 76, 85–86, 109, 111, 115, 150, 210

directions, see space; spatial orientations

discourse 7–8, 16–17, 26n, 76–77, 125, 180, 198, 208–209, 222

distance 17, 45, 49, 52, 61; geographic 82, 109, 116, 118, 123–124, 199; social 75, 197; perceptual 9–10, 61, , 71–72; length 46, 131–133; difference 12, 77, 173

divination 41, 46, 69, 86; augury 12, 86; omens 12, 45–46, 84, 86

elders 14–16, 92–99, 159, 163–165, 167–170, 172, 182; matai 108

embodiment 70, 170, 212

environment 14, 63, 124–125, 130, 211–212, 218

events 7–10, 12, 14–16; historical and mythical 27, 31, 79–80, 83, 85, 99, 114, 117, 126, 134, 138–139, 142, 157, 160–162, 172–173, 186–187; 193–194, 198–199, 201, 203, 205, 212; ritual and performative 54, 56, 60–62, 64, 69, 71–73, 177, 179, 181, 183–185, 187, 193–194, 201

exchange 8, 13–16; material 30, 76–78, 82–84, 102, 106, 126, 138–139, 142, 150n, 199; cosmological 68, 145, 200,

202, 210, 212; marriage 97n, 102, 109; communication 180

experience 8–10; technical 14, 41, 95–97, 99, 125, 132; familiar 25, 52–53, 76, 82; historical 27, 34, 141, 183, 199; social and phenomenal 37, 52, 58, 60, 71–72, 140, 198, 200, 202, 209, 211

fishing 91–98, 203; nets 153, 159

food 29, 31, 51, 91, 94–96, 125, 132, 165n, 186, 199, 203–204; cooking 82, 142, 145, 159, 165–166, 205–206

future 8, 10–11, 17, 23–26, 33–35, 69; 85, 157, 160, 200

gender 107, 116, 145–146, 182, 186, 189, 202, 208–209; male 14–15, 91, 98–99, 209; female 128, 148–149, 184

guest 16, 61, 70–71, 182, 184–185; guesthouse 105–109, 114, 116, 118

hierarchy 11, 13–14, 16; spatial 26–27, 30–33, 107; social 27, 58, 99, 101, 104, 106, 108–112, 117–119, 126, 160, 182, 197, 202; cosmological 114–115, 210, 212

history 7, 10–13, 15–17, 23–24, 26, 34–35, 42, 98, 119, 125, 141, 161, 217; oral 16, 48–49, 169, 186–187; structural 35, 101, 109–110, 113–114, 202, 212, 222; chronology 157, 172

homeland 23, 42, 48–49, 101–102, 104, 111–112, 197, 202

horizon 7–19, 23–25, 35, 39, 51–52, 51n, 64, 75–83, 87, 101, 106, 123, 197–198, 200, 209, 211–212, 215, 217–219

houses 13, 28–31, 78, 81, 86, 91, 97, 101, 105–106, 113–115, 147, 149–150, 203; house societies 49, 102–104, 119, 201, 205, 209; longhouses 11–12, 38–73 (passim), 75; meeting houses 94, 97, 104, 107–116 (passim), 178, 182, 184, 192

Iban 12–13, 51–58, 61–66, 71–72, 219

imagery 13, 32, 39, 51–56, 58, 63–64, 67, 72–73, 79, 126, 142, 188, 200, 208; picture 45, 85, 139

imagination 9, 23, 25, 29n, 30, 32, 34, 77, 83, 86, 99, 142, 153, 175, 215–216, 219

interaction 7, 9–10, 15, 17, 37, 109–110, 162, 181, 186, 210

invention of culture 9, 20, 77, 82, 209, (142, 183)

Kei Islands (Indonesia) 197–203, 207–210, 212

kings 98, 169, 205, 211; ali'i 108; aliki, 98, 169–170; stranger–king 43, 112,

117–119, 182

Kiribati 16, 177–187, 189–190, 192–194

knowledge 27, 33, 58, 76, 81, 83, 153, 160–161, 173, 179, 183–184, 188, 212, 217; technical knowledge 14–15, 43, 72, 96–99, 125, 131, 141–142, 145, 159

Kula Ring 14, 123, 125–128, 132, 138–140, 142–143

landscape 27, 30, 48, 52, 83, 86, 111, 119, 211, 222; mountains 39, 41, 43, 46, 48–49, 60–61, 76, 83, 86, 127, 131, 140–141, 197–198, 201, 204–205, 209, 211; rainforests 11–12, 28–30, 37–41, 43, 45, 49, 63, 73, 82, 129; seascapes 11, 15, 37, 46, 48, 69–70, 92–97, 101, 105, 107, 111–113, 116–118, 138, 142, 145–148, 151–153, 182, 197, 199, 206–207, 210

magic 67, 75, 83, 87, 117, 179

manhood, see gender

maps 9, 27–30, 45, 47–49, 79, 81, 101–102, 107–108, 110, 124, 129n, 198

marriage 97n, 102, 112, 150, 158, 197, 202, 204–205, 208–209, 211

metaphor 9, 12, 14, 25, 34, 111, 113, 117–118, 126, 129, 177n, 178, 180–181, 186–188, 194

metonymy 9, 73, 113, 115, 188, 208

migrations, see travel

millennial movements 11, 24, 34, 77, 220

mobility, see travel

morality 10–11, 24, 34, 97, 131, 205

myth 7, 10, 13–17, 23, 28, 39, 56–57, 75, 102, 104–106, 108–117, 119, 128, 138, 142, 186, 194, 197–198, 200–203, 205, 207–212, 216–217, 222

names 44, 68, 85, 103, 107, 108, 109, 110, 112, 123, 127, 134, 164, 166, 168, 170, 186, 187, 203, 205, 208, 210, 211, 212; naming 39, 43, 45, 64, 72, 86, 84, 109, 111, 113–114, 124, 147, 180, 204

narrative 9–10, 15–16, 18, 63–65, 69, 102, 112, 119, 146, 152–153, 157, 172–173, 186–187, 203, 205, 207, 211–212, 219, 222

navigation 10, 12, 29, 39, 42, 81, 131–132

Papua New Guinea 11, 13, 17, 24–25, 26n, 29–31, 33, 75, 87, 81, 123, 139, 218

New Zealand 43, 91, 98–99, 104, 111, 113–116, 158, 161, 167n, 221–222

objectification 8, 15, 46, 58n, 101, 104, 107, 110, 114, 119, 198, 212, 215, 222

Name Index